WORDPERFECT® 5.1 MADE EASY

KATIE LAYMAN

Document
Page
Line

default mode always puts you into insert mode
up to 8 letters . + 3 more no spaces - name a document.

REGENTS/PRENTICE HALL
Englewood Cliffs, New Jersey 07632

Library of Congress Cataloging-in-Publication Data

Layman, Katie.
   WordPerfect 5.1 made easy / Katie Layman.
     p. cm.
   Includes index.
   ISBN 0-13-963125-9
   1. WordPerfect (Computer program) 2. Word processing—Computer
programs. I. Title.
   Z52.5.W65L38 1990
   652.5'536—dc20   90-23422
                                           CIP

This book is dedicated to my sister, Judith L. Nice, and my brothers,
Paul R. Layman and H. Michael Layman.

Editorial/production supervision and
  interior design: Tally Morgan, WordCrafters Editorial Services, Inc.
Cover design: Karen Stephens
Manufacturing buyers: Ilene Levy/Ed O'Dougherty
Acquisitions editor: Liz Kendall

 © 1991 by Prentice-Hall, Inc.
A Simon & Schuster Company
Englewood Cliffs, New Jersey 07632

Printed in the United States of America
10 9 8 7 6 5

ISBN 0-13-963125-9

Prentice-Hall International (UK) Limited, *London*
Prentice-Hall of Australia Pty. Limited, *Sydney*
Prentice-Hall Canada Inc., *Toronto*
Prentice-Hall Hispanoamericana, S.A., *Mexico*
Prentice-Hall of India Private Limited, *New Delhi*
Prentice-Hall of Japan, Inc., *Tokyo*
Simon & Schuster Asia Pte. Ltd., *Singapore*
Editora Prentice-Hall do Brasil, Ltda., *Rio de Janeiro*

CONTENTS

PREFACE

WordPerfect® 5.1 Made Easy is one in a series of "Word Processing Made Easy" textbooks. The series includes separate textbooks for WordPerfect, WordStar, and Microsoft Word word processing programs. Each book follows a comparable table of contents and includes specific function instructions, formatting directions, language arts reinforcement skills, and chapter exercises.

The purpose of these textbooks is to provide specific word processing function instructions, proper formatting techniques, and final document preparation practice. In addition, emphasis is placed on reinforcing language arts skills and providing all the word processing skills needed to produce a mailable document.

The book can be used for individualized instruction or teacher-directed instruction. The basic word processing program functions are generically explained. Specific step-by-step instructions are given for each program function such as centering, underlining, paginating, merging, spell checking, and so on.

Formatting procedures are illustrated for letters, memorandums, tables, and reports. The formatting explanations include margins, spacing, and style for the appropriate arrangement of a document on a page.

A practice exercise is presented in each chapter to explain specific function instructions and to demonstrate proper document format. Five exercises to reinforce the format and program instructions learned are provided at the end of each chapter. The fifth exercise in each chapter contains spelling and grammar errors that are to be corrected by the learner.

The exercises provided are authentic documents used in private businesses and public institutions. Edited documents are included to give the learner a realistic approach to creating and producing final copy documents.

Each chapter includes an "Enriching Language Arts Skills" section. The language arts reinforcement section provides three vocabulary words with definitions and a punctuation, capitalization, or typing rule. Italicized words and sentences in the exercises refer to the vocabulary words or punctuation/capitalization rule discussed.

Appendix 1 provides the procedures for controlling files. For example, a file from one disk can be easily copied to another disk. Also, a file can be deleted from the disk, renamed, or moved.

Appendix 2 explains how to use the pull-down menus. In addition, each pull-down menu is printed in Appendix 2.

An Instructor's Resource Manual is available which contains teaching suggestions and recommended time requirements for each chapter. The manual includes production tests and additional exercises. A set of 25 transparencies for WordPerfect menus is also available to adopters. In addition, a Data Disk with unformatted files for all exercises in the book will be provided free to instructors adopting this text. Please contact your local Prentice Hall representative to obtain a copy of the data disk, or write to:

> College Software Department
> Prentice Hall
> Route 9W
> Englewood Cliffs, NJ 07632

TO THE STUDENT

First, read the word processing function explanation; second, read and work through the step-by-step function and format instructions; and third, perform the instructions while creating a practice document.

Answer the Self-Check Questions and check your answers against the answer key provided in the back of the book. If desired, study the chapter vocabulary words and punctuation, capitalization, or typing rule provided. Each vocabulary word and an example of the grammar rule discussed are printed in italics in the chapter exercises. Last, you can reinforce your learning by completing the exercises provided at the end of each chapter.

ACKNOWLEDGMENTS

Many thanks to the various people who contributed to the development of this book. Special appreciation is due to the reviewers who provided practical suggestions and pertinent guidance. The manuscript was reviewed by Melba Jean Coles, Fullerton College; Linda Mallinson, Orlando Vocational Technical Center; Dolores Hoffman, Bryant & Stratton—Rochester Campus; Katherine Blair Hartman, Northern Virginia Community College—Loudoun Campus; Josephine Messina, Grossmont Collge; Marjorie Perren, Foothill College; Michael Davis, Delaware Technical and Community College; and Jane Schmid, Lakewood Community College.

A very special appreciation is due to my editor, Liz Kendall, for her creative ideas and constant enthusiasm and support for this project. Thank you for finding solutions to the many challenges of producing a book.

A hearty thanks to the students at the College of San Mateo who worked through the instructions and exercises in the manuscript. A special thank you to the College of San Mateo instructors who took time to share suggestions and specific corrections for the manuscript. Thank you, Marian Thomas and Betty Wittwer.

Thank you, Mary Jean Willis, College of San Mateo Emeritus student, for keystroke testing the initial chapters and providing specific suggestions for clarity of instructions.

Thank you to Lora Todesco, Director of the Business Division, College of San Mateo, who always provides encouragement and compliments for my professional work.

I especially thank Roberta Anderson, College of San Mateo, and Joe Lugo, San Jose City College, who worked through every instruction and exercise and provided specific details for accurate instructions.

Additionally, a heartfelt thanks to Roberta Anderson for her constant interest in contributing technical assistance and for her proofreading and editing expertise that was provided during the progress of the manuscript.

Sincere thanks are due to Doris Sadovy, San Jose City

College, for taking time from her busy schedule to write a comprehensive Instructor's Manual. Thank you, Doris, for your interest and thoroughness in providing teachers with an excellent resource for teaching WordPerfect 5.1.

A huge thank-you to the people at Prentice Hall, Inc. who provided support for the success of this textbook. Thank you Jane Baumann, Christine Culman, Debra Garvin, Michelle Jay, Liz Kendall, Sally McPhearson and Sheila Woods.

A genuine gratefulness is extended to Tally Morgan, Word-Crafters Editorial Services, Inc., for understanding the detailed design needs of the manuscript and for producing the book in a timely manner. Many thanks for your patience and support. Your sense of humor is truly appreciated.

Special thanks to Janet Grant, Skyline College, and Leslie Smith, Rappahannock Community College for keystroke testing the WordPerfect 5.1 supplement material. A heartfelt thank you for testing these instructions under a most compressed schedule.

A huge thanks also to Dr. Meredith Flynn, Bowling Green State University, for keystroke testing all the WordPerfect 5.1 exercises and procedures. Your suggestions and corrections are extremely helpful in revising the WordPerfect textbook.

Thank you, Dr. Aileen McClean, Sheridan Vocational Technical School, for sharing your original idea of providing language arts skills reinforcement in a word processing textbook. Your foresight to provide spelling and grammar reinforcement is most timely.

Introduction

THE MICROCOMPUTER SYSTEM

The microcomputer system consists of two basic elements: hardware and software. The physical components of the microcomputer system are called hardware; the programs that instruct the computer to perform functions are called software.

HARDWARE

The microcomputer hardware includes the monitor (TV-like screen), keyboard, mouse, computer unit, disk drives, and printer. The hardware can be seen, felt, and touched. The IBM PC and compatible computers enclose the disk drive(s) with the computer. The monitor, keyboard, mouse, and printer are attached to the computer via cables (see Exhibit I.1). The computer unit and the attached hardware make up a computer system.

The computer unit holds the electronic circuitry where the main memory and central processing unit (CPU) reside. The CPU processes and controls information by storing data, performing operations, and transferring information from one location to another. The CPU is often referred to as the "brains" of the computer.

SOFTWARE

The software programs are lists of instructions that tell the computer what to do. The master program is the disk operating system (DOS). DOS directs the basic operation of the computer system and carries out procedures within application programs. Application programs are more advanced software designed to perform specific tasks. Common application programs are word processors, spreadsheets, databases, communications, and desktop publishing.

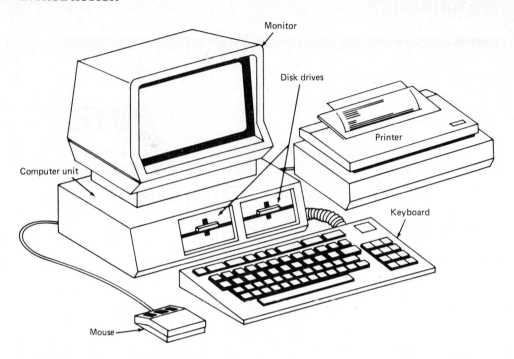

EXHIBIT I.1   The PC hardware

DOS and application programs are stored on master disks. A copy of DOS and of an application program can be transferred to the computer's memory when the computer is turned on. Transferring a copy of a program to the computer's memory is called "loading the program." The disk is being "read" when a copy of a program or other information is transferred from the disk into the computer's memory.

DISKS

Because the computer's memory is temporary, information that is processed and used by a computer must be stored on a computer disk. All programs and data are erased from memory when the computer is turned off. Computer disks are rigid or flexible. A rigid disk, referred to as a hard disk, resides inside the computer; it is not removed by the user. A flexible disk, referred to as a floppy disk or diskette, is usually enclosed in a protective vinyl jacket or plastic case and is handled by the user. Generally, a disk enclosed in vinyl is 5¼" and a disk enclosed in plastic is 3½" (see Exhibit I.2).

Information that has been created by the user is saved on a 3½" or 5¼" disk, known as a file disk or data disk. Information such as letters, memoranda, or statistical data must be saved. If the information is not saved on a disk, the information will be lost when the computer is turned off. When a copy of the

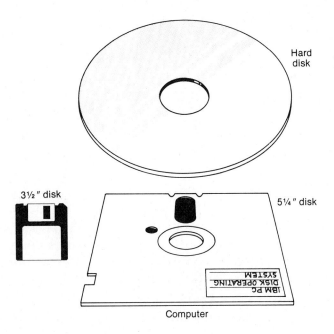

EXHIBIT I.2 Computer disks

information is transferred from the computer's memory to the data disk the process is called *saving*. Saving information on a data disk is called ''writing'' to a disk.

Care for Diskettes

Diskettes should be labeled using a felt tip pen. Store diskettes in a dry, protected location. Avoid dust, smoke, bending, and extreme temperatures; keep diskettes out of the sun and away from beverage containers! Any magnet or magnetized object can damage the data on a disk. Avoid using a paper clip on a diskette, especially a paper clip that has been stored in a holder with a magnetized ring at the top.

THE DISK OPERATING SYSTEM (DOS)

The disk operating system is a collection of related programs that control and manage computer operations. DOS is necessary to handle the temporary storage and processing of information and directs the orderly transfer or sharing of information between the computer unit and the disk, monitor, keyboard, printer, and so on. DOS can be stored on the hard disk or on a floppy diskette.

Use of DOS

With DOS the user can direct the computer to access a disk drive, format a diskette, list the file names on a disk, and perform many other operations. An application program utilizes DOS to perform many of the DOS operations within the application program.

BOOT THE COMPUTER

When the power switch is first turned on and DOS is loading, the computer is being "cold booted." Booting is the process of the computer's "waking up" and taking inventory of the connected hardware, making sure all hardware is working properly, looking at how much memory is available, and so on.

When the power is already on and the **Alt**, **Ctrl**, and **Del** keys are pressed simultaneously, the computer is being "warm booted." A warm boot briefly turns the computer system off and on again by using the keys on the keyboard. A warm boot reloads DOS into the computer's memory.

After a cold or warm boot the cursor will be located beside a DOS prompt **C:** or **A>**. On some computer systems a menu of choices is displayed on the screen.

FORMAT A DISKETTE

Before information can be saved on a disk, the disk must be formatted (prepared) with electronic instructions partitioning the disk into storage areas, creating a directory, checking for disk defects, and so on.

The formatting process is usually performed only once. If a disk is formatted a second time, all information previously saved on the diskette is erased.

Procedure to Format a File Disk Using a Floppy Diskette

1. With your thumb on the label, place a DOS disk in the A disk drive. Gently latch the door.

2. Turn on the computer.

3. A prompt requesting the date is displayed; press **Enter** to bypass the prompt. (If desired, type the current date using hyphens between the numbers—for example, type **6-25-91**.)

4. A prompt requesting the time is displayed; press **Enter** to bypass the prompt.

5. The cursor should be located beside the **A>** prompt. Type *format b:*. (This instructs the computer to format the diskette in disk drive B.)

6. Press **Enter**.

7. The message is displayed: **Insert new diskette for drive B and strike ENTER when ready**. Insert a new or used diskette in disk drive B.

Note: *If a used diskette is formatted, any information on the disk is erased.*

8. Press **Enter**.

9. The message is displayed: **Formatting . . .**; wait a few moments.

10. During the formatting process, watch the red disk drive lights illuminate while instructions are copied from one disk to another.

11. When the formatting is completed, the message **Format complete** is displayed . . . **Format another (Y / N)?**

12. Press **n** for no.

Procedure to Format a File Disk Using a Hard Disk

1. Turn on the computer.

2. A prompt requesting the date is displayed; press **Enter** to bypass the prompt. (If desired, type the current date using hyphens between the numbers—for example, type **6-25-91**.)

3. A prompt requesting the time is displayed; press **Enter** to bypass the prompt.

4. The **C:** prompt is displayed on the screen.

5. If the disk to be formatted is in drive A, type *format a:*; if the disk to be formatted is in drive B, type *format b:*.

6. Press **Enter**.

7. The message is displayed: **Insert new diskette for drive A (B) and strike ENTER when ready**. Insert a new or used diskette in disk drive A or B.

Note: *If a used diskette is formatted, any information on the disk is erased.*

8. Press **Enter**.

9. The message is displayed: **Formatting . . .;** wait a few moments.

10. During the formatting process, watch the red disk drive lights illuminate while instructions are copied from one disk to another.

11. When the formatting is completed, the message **Format complete** is displayed **. . . Format another (Y/N)?**

12. Press **n** for no.

CHANGE DISK DRIVES

The computer must be told which disk drive is to be used for reading from a disk or writing to a disk. If the **C:** prompt is on the screen, type **a:** and press **Enter** to access the A drive. If the **A:** prompt is on the screen, type **b:** and press **Enter** to access the B drive. In summary, to change disk drives type the disk drive letter followed by a colon and press **Enter**.

DISPLAY A DIRECTORY

A list of all file names saved on a disk can be displayed on the screen. Each file name is eight or fewer characters in length. Some file names have three-character filename extensions, for example, **jordan.ltr**.

Procedure to Display a Directory Using DOS

1. If the **A:** or **A>** prompt is displayed on the screen, type *dir* and press **Enter**. A list of filenames for the diskette in drive A is displayed on the screen.

2. If the **B:** or **B>** prompt is displayed on the screen, type *dir* and press **Enter**. A list of filenames for the disk in drive B is displayed on the screen.

3. If the **C:** prompt is displayed on the screen, type **a:** or **b:**; press **Enter**. **Note:** If the list of files displays on more than one screen, type **dir/p** (for pause); press **Enter**.

COPY A FILE TO ANOTHER DISK

In order to keep a second copy of a file on another disk, a file can be copied from one disk and placed on a second disk. Copying a file from one disk to another is often referred to as making a backup copy. When working with files of any type, the best policy is to *always* make a backup copy.

Procedure to Copy a File

From the DOS prompt, type the word copy, the file name, and the drive letter and colon where the file is to be copied. For example, from the **A:** prompt, type **copy jordan.ltr b:**.

*Note: This copy command tells the computer to copy the file named **jordan.ltr** from the A drive to the B drive.*

If the file is located on the C drive and is to be copied to a file disk in the A drive, type *copy jordan.ltr a:*. If the file is located on a disk in drive A and is to be copied to a file disk in drive B, type *copy jordan.ltr b:*.

All files from a disk in drive A can be copied to a second disk in drive B. From the **A:** prompt, type **copy *.* b:**.

DIRECTORIES AND PATHS

When using a hard disk, many application programs are stored on the hard disk. In addition to the word processing program, a spreadsheet program, database program, etc. can be stored on the hard disk. The files for each application program can be kept in one location.

Usually special directories are created to keep all the files for one application program in one area of the disk under a distinctive directory name. The directory name recommended for WordPerfect 5.1 is **wp51**.

A second directory can be created under the **wp51** directory. The second directory is a subdirectory. The WordPerfect graphic files can be located in a subdirectory named **wpg**. When a graphic file is to be retrieved from a subdirectory, the *path* must be typed in order to tell the computer exactly where to find the graphic file. For example, from the **C:** prompt, type the directory name **\wp51**, type the subdirectory name **\wpg**, and type the name of the specific graphic file to be retrieved: *c:\wp51\wpg\balloons.wpg*.

Chapter 1

CREATE A
MEMORANDUM

After successfully completing this chapter, you should be able to:

● Load the program and obtain a clear screen.

● Access a disk drive.

● Correct errors by backspacing.

● Move the cursor.

● Center word(s) horizontally.

● Understand word wrap.

● Format a memorandum in two different styles.

● Save a file and keep the document on the screen.

● Print a document using print screen and the print menu.

● Clear the screen.

A memorandum is informal written correspondence commonly used in offices. A memorandum is used to communicate information that is important to the employees within the same company. Therefore, the memorandum is often referred to as an interoffice memorandum. Instructions for typing and formatting a memo while using the WordPerfect 5.1 program follow.

▷ Use the following procedure to load the WordPerfect program and obtain a clear screen.

1

Procedure to Load the Program and Obtain a Clear Screen Using a Hard Disk

1. Turn on the computer and monitor.

2. When the **C:** prompt is displayed on the screen, type **cd**; press the space bar once; **wp51**, press **Enter**.

   *Note: By typing **cd**, this changes the directory to where the Word Perfect program is located. (If necessary, see your instructor for changing the directory or making a menu selection.)*

3. Type **wp**; press the **Enter** (⏎) key once.

4. The copyright screen and a **Please Wait** message are displayed briefly.

5. A partially clear screen is displayed with the cursor blinking in the top left corner and the status line displayed in the bottom right corner. *Note:* The status line shows the exact location of the cursor; this is explained in Chapter 4.

Procedure to Load the Program and Obtain a Clear Screen Using Floppy Diskettes

1. With your thumb on the label, place a DOS disk in disk drive A. (If DOS is on the WordPerfect 1 diskette, place the WordPerfect 1 diskette into disk drive A.) Gently latch the door.

2. Turn on the computer.

3. After a few messages and a short delay, a prompt requesting the date is displayed; press **Enter** to bypass the prompt. (If desired, type the current date using hyphens between the numbers—for example, type **6-25-91**.)

4. A prompt requesting the time is displayed; press **Enter** to bypass the prompt.

5. The cursor should be located beside the **A>** prompt. *If DOS is on a separate disk*, remove the DOS disk from the A drive and place the WordPerfect 1 diskette into disk drive A. Gently latch the door.

6. Place a formatted file disk in drive B. Gently latch the door.

7. Type b:; press **Enter**. The cursor is located beside the **B>** prompt.

8. Type a:wp; press **Enter**. The WordPerfect program will begin loading.

9. After a few seconds the **WordPerfect Copyright** information is displayed on the screen along with the message **Insert diskette labeled "WordPerfect 2" and press any key**.

10. Remove the WordPerfect 1 disk from disk drive A and place the disk labeled WordPerfect 2 into drive A; press **Enter**. A **Please wait** message is displayed on the screen briefly.

11. A partially clear screen is displayed with the cursor blinking in the top left corner and the status line displayed in the bottom right corner.

Note: The status line shows the exact location of the cursor. The status line is explained in Chapter 4.

Note: The WordPerfect 2 disk must remain in drive A. Your file disk must remain in disk drive B.

⇨ Use the Procedure to Access a Disk Drive where the file disk is located.

Procedure to Access a Disk Drive

1. Press the **F5** key (List Files) {*File, List Files*}. (The words in braces indicate the pull-down menu selections. See Appendix 2.)

2. A message is displayed: **Dir C:\wp51*.***.

3. Press the equals key (=).

4. The prompt **New directory = c:\wp51** . . . is displayed.

5. Type the letter of the disk where the disk is located followed by a colon. For example, type **a:** or **b:**. *Note:* When a character is typed, the drive letter displayed will be replaced by the character typed.

6. Press the **Enter** key.

7. A message is displayed: **Dir . . *.***.

8. Press **F1** to Cancel the prompt at the bottom of the screen and return the cursor to the clear screen.

Procedure to Correct Errors by Backspacing

If an error is made, press the **backspace** key to delete the error. Then type the correction. Deleting errors with the **Del** key is explained in Chapter 2.

Procedure to Move the Cursor

Use the arrow keys on the 10-key numeric key pad to move the cursor up, down, left, or right. On some keyboards the arrow keys are located on the 10-key numeric key pad and also on separate keys. *Note:* The cursor will move to characters and lines that have been typed. The cursor will not move into blank space unless the **Enter** key or **space bar** has been pressed.

Procedure to Center Horizontally

1. The cursor should be located on the left side of the screen.

2. Press and hold the **Shift** key while tapping the **F6** key (**Shift** and **F6**). *Note:* Pressing **Shift** and **F6** is the process of giving the center instruction.

3. The cursor moves to the center of the line.

4. Type the text to be centered.

5. Press the **Enter** key.

6. To view the center code, press and hold the **Alt** key while tapping the **F3** key {*Edit, Reveal Codes*} to display the reveal codes. (See Exhibit 1.1.) The center code **[center]** will display on the left side of the centered text. Press **Alt** and **F3** to exit Reveal Codes and return the cursor to the text on the screen.

   Note: To delete the center instruction, place the cursor on the [Center] code and press the Del key once.

Word Wrap

While typing a paragraph, the cursor will automatically return from the end of a line to the beginning of the next line. This automatic return feature is called word wrap. Lines are typed using word wrap. The **Enter** key is pressed only after a short line or at the end of a paragraph. When the **Enter** key is pressed, a hard return code [HRt] is placed in the reveal code screen (see Exhibit 1.1).

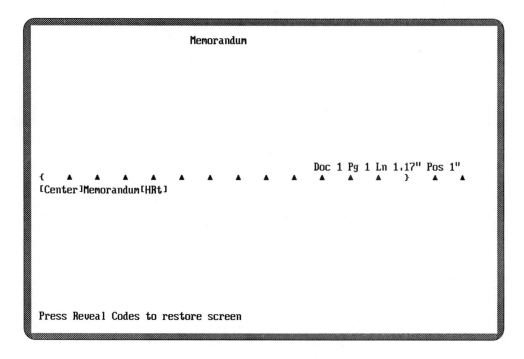

EXHIBIT 1.1 Reveal Codes display the center instruction code

Formatting

Formatting is the process of determining the style and arrangement of a document when printed on a page. Style includes the number of vertical and horizontal spaces used between words and lines, capitalization, and punctuation. The arrangement of a document includes the amount of space to be placed in the left, right, top, and bottom margins.

▷ Use the Procedure to Format a Memorandum: Style 1 and type the practice memorandum 1, shown in Exhibit 1.2. Type the paragraphs using word wrap.

▷ Backspace and correct errors while typing. For now, ignore any errors noticed after the memorandum is typed. *Note:* The paragraph lines may not end with the same words as shown in Exhibit 1.2.

Procedure to Format a Memorandum: Style 1

1. Press the center instruction (**Shift** and **F6**) and type the word *Memorandum* on the first line of the screen.

2. Press the **Enter** key 3 times.

```
                              ↓ 1"
                           Memorandum
                             ↓ 3
   To:         All Departments
                      ↓ 2
   From:       Anthony Mignetto
                      ↓ 2
   Date:       (Use current date)
                      ↓ 2
   Subject:   Employee Guidelines
                       ↓ 3

   Packages that are being delivered to the building are left in
   the reception area.  As packages arrive Terry will contact
   each department.  Pick up your packages promptly.
                        ↓ 2
   Smoking is accepted in designated smoking areas.  No smoking
   in the restrooms.
                      ↓ 2
   In order to provide a good working relationship with our
   customers, the phones should be answered after the first ring.
                    ↓ 2
   (your initials)
```

EXHIBIT 1.2   Memorandum style 1

3. Type the word *To* followed by a colon; press the **Tab** key twice; type the name of the person(s) to whom the memorandum is being written; press **Enter** twice. (See Exhibit 1.2.)

   *Note: The **Tab** key is pressed once or twice after the lead words in order to align the heading information.*

4. Type the word *From* followed by a colon; press the **Tab** key twice; type the name of the person writing the memorandum; press **Enter** twice.

5. Type the word *Date* followed by a colon; press the **Tab** key twice; type the current date; press **Enter** twice.

6. Type the word *Subject* followed by a colon; press the **Tab** key once; type the subject of the memorandum; press **Enter** three times.

7. Use word wrap and type the paragraphs single spaced.

8. Press the **Enter** key two times after each paragraph, including the last paragraph.

9. Type your initials in lowercase letters, for example, rte.

▷ Use the Procedure to Save a File and Keep the Document on the Screen.

Procedure to Save a File and Keep the Document on the Screen

1. A file disk should be in the disk drive that has been accessed. (To access a disk drive, press **F5**, **=**, type **a:** or **b:**, **Enter**, **F1**.)

2. Press the **F10** key once {*File, Save*}.

3. The prompt is displayed: **Document to be saved:**.

4. Type a filename **1pmemo1** (Chapter 1, practice memo 1). *Note:* The filename can be eight or less characters with no spaces and a filename extension of three or less characters that can be typed after the period. For example, **miller.mem**.

5. Press the **Enter** key.

6. If the file disk is in drive A, the message **Saving A:\ . . .** is displayed. (The filename is displayed.)

7. If the file disk is in drive B, the message **Saving B:\ . . .** is displayed. (The filename is displayed.)

8. The document is kept on the screen, and the document name is displayed on the bottom left corner of the screen. For example, **B:\1pmemo1.c1** is displayed.

PRINTING

Sending a document to print is accomplished by a direct print or by using one of WordPerfect's menus. Also, a sentence or paragraph can be printed by blocking text. (See Chapter 5.)

A direct print is called a print screen (**Shift** and **PrtSc**) and prints all characters and words displayed on the screen. The print menu (**Shift** and **F7**) is used to print one, several, or all pages of a document. Printing is also accomplished by using List Files (**F5**) (discussed in Chapter 4).

▷ Use Procedure 1: Using the Print Screen (**Shift** and **PrtSc**) to print one copy of the practice memorandum—style 1.

▷ Turn on the printer.

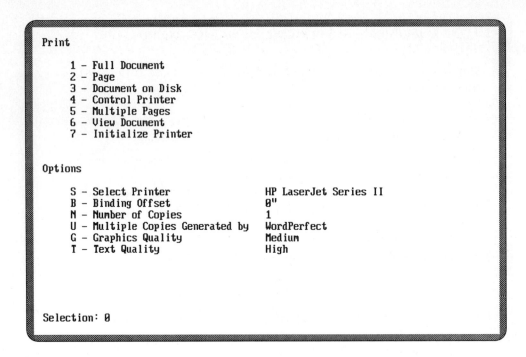

```
Print
        1 - Full Document
        2 - Page
        3 - Document on Disk
        4 - Control Printer
        5 - Multiple Pages
        6 - View Document
        7 - Initialize Printer


Options
        S - Select Printer                HP LaserJet Series II
        B - Binding Offset                0"
        N - Number of Copies              1
        U - Multiple Copies Generated by  WordPerfect
        G - Graphics Quality              Medium
        T - Text Quality                  High




Selection: 0
```

EXHIBIT 1.3   Print menu

Procedure to Format a Memorandum: Style 2

1. Press the **Caps Lock** key once. Type the words *INTER-OFFICE MEMO* in all capital letters.

2. Press **Alt** and **F6** to move the cursor to the right side of the screen. *Note:* The text will end at the right margin; this is called flush-right alignment.

3. Type the company name in all capital letters. *Note:* The company name should end almost even with the right margin.

4. Press the **Enter** key three times.

5. Type the word *DATE* in all capital letters followed by a colon; press the **Tab** key twice; type the current date in upper- and lowercase letters; press **Enter** twice. (See Exhibit 1.4.)

6. Type the abbreviation *RE* in all capital letters followed by a colon; press the **Tab** key twice; type the subject of the memorandum in upper- and lowercase letters; press **Enter** twice.

7. Type the word *FROM* in all capital letters followed by a colon; press the **Tab** key once; type the name of the person writing the memorandum in upper- and lowercase letters; press **Enter** twice.

8. Type the word *TO* in all capital letters followed by a colon; press the **Tab** key twice; type the name of the person(s) to whom the memorandum is being written in upper- and lowercase letters; press **Enter** three times.

9. Use word wrap and type the paragraphs single spaced.

10. Press the **Enter** key two times after each paragraph including the last paragraph.

⟡ Use the filename **1pmemo2** (chapter 1, practice memo 2). Save the document and keep the document on the screen. (**F10**, type **a:** or **b:** followed by the filename, press **Enter**.) *Note:* It's unnecessary to type the disk drive letter, if the disk drive where the file disk is located has been accessed.

⟡ Use the print procedure 1 (**Shift** and **PrtSc**) to print one copy. *Note:* If desired, press the FF (form feed) on the printer after printing the memo.

⟡ Clear the screen (**F7**, **n**, **n**).

Procedure 1: Using the Print Screen

Note: The document must be displayed on the screen.

1. Press and hold the **Shift** key while tapping the **PrtSc** key once.

2. All information on the screen will print. *Note:* The status line and filename will also be printed. The memorandum will not print centered on the paper.

Procedure 2: Using the Print Menu

1. The document must be displayed on the screen.

2. Press and hold the **Shift** key while tapping the **F7** key {*File, Print*} to display the Print menu. See Exhibit 1.3.

3. Press **t** for Text Quality.

```
                ↓ 1"

INTEROFFICE MEMO                            SIMPSON, INC.
                ↓ 3
DATE:      (Use current date)
                ↓ 2
RE:        FAX Machine Rental
                ↓ 2
FROM:      Sangho Lee
                ↓ 2
TO:        Tyrone Smith

                ↓ 3
You suggested that I send a request for the Ricoh Fax machine
that is to be rented for the Midewest Sales Office.
                ↓ 2
The Fax rents for approximately $85 a month, including service
charges.    ↓ 2

This request has been approved by the Executive Director,
Barbara Tyler.  If you have any questions, please call me at
extension 4455.
                ↓ 2
(your initials)
```

EXHIBIT 1.4   Memorandum style 2

4. Press **2** for Draft Quality.

5. Press **1** for Full Document.

6. The message ***Please Wait*** is displayed briefly at the bottom of the screen.

7. The document prints and the cursor returns to the document screen.

▷ Use the Procedure to Clear the Screen.

Procedure to Clear the Screen

*Note: The file should be saved (press **F10**; type the filename; press **Enter**) before clearing the screen.*

1. Press the **F7** key to exit {*File, Exit*}.

2. The prompt **Save document? Yes(No)** is displayed.

3. Press **n** for no.

4. The prompt **Exit WP? No(Yes)** is displayed.

5. Press **n** for no.

6. The document is erased and a partially blank screen is displayed.

⇨ Use the Procedure to Format a Memorandum: Style 2.

⇨ Type practice memorandum 2 shown in Exhibit 1.4.

⇨ Type the paragraphs using word wrap. Backspace and correct errors made while typing. Ignore any errors noticed after the memo is typed.

SUMMARY

● A memorandum is written correspondence used to communicate between individuals within the same company. Generally, a memorandum is an informal message.

● Program loading is the process of transferring a copy of the WordPerfect program from the disk to the computer's memory. (Turn on the computer; if using a hard disk, at the **C:** prompt, type **cd wp51**, press Enter, **wp**; if using floppy diskettes, at the **A:>** prompt, type **wp**.)

● Accessing a disk drive is the process of directing the computer to enter the disk drive where the film disk is located. A computer with a hard disk drive automatically accesses the C:\ drive when the computer is turned on. A computer without a hard disk automatically accesses the A drive when the computer is turned on. Since the file disk is usually placed in drive B, it is necessary to tell the computer to change to drive B (**F5**, press **=**, type disk drive letter followed by a colon, for example, **B:**, press **Enter**, press **F1**).

● Pressing the backspace key will delete the letter or the character located to the left of the cursor.

● The keys that move the cursor up, down, left, and right are located on the 10-key pad and on some keyboards are also located on separate keys.

● Centering text is the process of placing text horizontally on a page so that the amount of space on the left side of the text is approximately equal to the amount of space on the right side of the text (**Shift** and **F6**).

● Word wrap is the automatic movement of the cursor from one line to the next. While typing a paragraph, the cursor will automatically move from the end of a line to the beginning of the next line.

● Formatting is the process of arranging text on a page. Formatting includes making decisions for line spacing, margins, tabs, etc.

● Formatting a memorandum includes centering the word *Memorandum*; typing the words *To, From, Date,* and *Subject*; pressing the **Tab** key to align words that follow the lead words; and using word wrap.

● Saving the memorandum is the process of transferring a copy of the memorandum from the computer's memory to the file disk (**F10**, type **a:** or **b:** followed by a filename of 8 or fewer characters, **Enter**).

● Printing the screen is the process of sending all text and symbols on the screen to the printer, including screen information such as **Doc 1 Pg 1.** . . . (**Shift** and **PrtSc**).

● Printing from the menu will print only the text that has been typed (**Shift** and **F7, t, 2, 1**).

● Clearing the screen is the process of removing a document from the screen in order to begin a new document. The document should be saved before clearing the screen (**F7, n, n**).

SELF-CHECK QUESTIONS

(True / False—Circle One)

T,F   1. An interoffice memorandum is a document used to communicate between individuals within the same company.

T,F   2. Loading is the process of transferring the WordPerfect program to the file disk.

T,F   3. A disk drive can be assessed by pressing the **F6** key.

T,F   4. When the backspace key is pressed, the character to the right of the cursor is erased.

T,F   5. The cursor can be moved up one line by pressing the up arrow key once.

T,F   6.   To center, press the **Shift** and **F6** keys, then type the text to be centered.

T,F   7.   After the leading word **From** is typed in the Style 1 memorandum, the tab key is pressed twice before typing the name of the person who wrote the memorandum.

T,F   8.   The paragraphs of a memorandum are typed in single spacing and the **Enter** key is pressed two times between paragraphs.

T,F   9.   All text on a screen can be printed by pressing the **Shift** and **P** keys.

T,F 10.   Clear the screen by pressing **Shift** and **F7** and then pressing the **n** key twice.

ENRICHING LANGUAGE ARTS SKILLS

Each chapter contains vocabulary and spelling words and selected rules for punctuation, capitalization, or grammar. The vocabulary words are italicized and illustrated in the following chapter exercises. The word(s) and sentence(s) that illustrate rules for punctuation, capitalization, and grammar are also italicized in the exercises.

Exercise 5 in each chapter has mistakes in spelling, punctuation, capitalization, and/or grammar that are to be corrected. After a spelling word or grammar rule has been presented in one chapter, it could be an error to be corrected in exercises of the following chapters. The exercise should be proofread and corrected in order to produce a document that is perfect (mailable) and ready for distribution.

Spelling/Vocabulary Words

expedite   help along, quicken, facilitate.
podium   a stand used by a lecturer or choir conductor that serves as a support for books or notes.
utilizing   using for a certain purpose; using.

Capitalization Rule

Generally a person's title is not capitalized if the title replaces an individual's name.

Example   A decision was made today by the *manager* to schedule the annual company picnic for the third Saturday in July.

EXERCISES

Exercise 1.1

1. Load the WordPerfect program and obtain a clear screen.

2. If necessary, access the disk drive where the file disk is located (**F5**, = type the disk drive letter where the file disk is located followed by a colon, **Enter**, **F1**).

3. If errors are made while typing, use the **backspace** key to delete. For this chapter ignore any errors noticed after the memo is typed.

4. Use memorandum style 1 (refer to Exhibit 1.2) and type the following memorandum.

```
                        Memorandum

To:         Gentek Managers

From:       Carol Ivanicki

Date:       (Use current date)

Subject:    Controller's Organization Changes


In the past several months, the controller's
organization has undergone certain personnel
changes.

A new functional organization chart will be
provided next week to expedite your service
requirements by identifying key management
personnel by department, responsibilities,
location, and telephone extensions.

Utilizing the chart will ensure that your inquiries
and information requests are addressed in a
controlled and expeditious manner.

(your initials)
```

---

5. Use the filename **1memo1** (chapter 1, memo 1). Save the file (**F10**, type file name, press **Enter**) and keep the document on the screen).

6. Use Procedure 2: Using the Print Menu (**Shift** and **F7**, **t**, **2**, **1**) and print one copy.

7. Clear the screen (**F7**, **n**, **n**).

Exercise 1.2

1. If necessary, load the WordPerfect program.

2. The screen should be clear (**F7, n, n**).

3. The disk drive should be accessed where the file disk is located (**F5, =**, type the disk drive letter where the disk is located followed by a colon, **Enter, F1**).

4. If errors are made while typing, use the **backspace** key to delete. For this chapter ignore any errors noticed after the memo is typed.

5. Use memorandum style 1 (refer to Exhibit 1.2) and type the following memorandum.

```
                         Memorandum

To:          All Employees

From:        Donald Silva

Date:        (Use current date)

Subject:     New Conference Rooms


Our new facility across the street has three
conference rooms available for meetings. The Main
Conference Room is the large one located next to
the photocopy room. The Network Conference Room is
located by the breakroom, and the Executive
Conference Room is located next to my new office.

Both the Main and Executive Conference Rooms have
very nice wooden tables. Coasters will be purchased
for each conference room. In the meantime, use a
paper towel or napkin under a cup or mug.

After using the conference room, clean up at the
end of your meeting. Place chairs under the table
and return the podium to the front table.

(your initials)
```

---

6. Use the filename **1memo2** (chapter 1, memo 2). Save the file and keep the document on the screen.

7. Use Procedure 2: Using the Print Menu (**Shift** and **F7, t, 2, 1**) and print one copy.

8. Clear the screen (**F7, n, n**).

Exercise 1.3

1. If necessary, load the WordPerfect program.

2. The screen should be clear.

3. The disk drive should be accessed where the file disk is located.

4. If errors are made while typing, use the **backspace** key to delete. For this chapter ignore any errors noticed after the memo is typed.

5. Use memorandum style 2 (refer to Exhibit 1.4) and type the following memorandum.

```
INTEROFFICE MEMO                        OAKVIEW PLACE


DATE:    (Use current date)

RE:      Tennis Court Rules

FROM:    Sawyer Martin, Resident Manager

TO:      Oakview Homeowners


Oakview residents have first priority on the tennis
courts. Guests of a resident may utilize the
courts; however, the resident is responsible for
accompanying the guests while they are on the
courts. The homeowner dues allow each resident the
use of the tennis courts, but the resident does not
have the authority to transfer his/her privilege to
someone else.

The tennis courts are for tennis only. No skates,
bikes, animals, baseballs, etc. are allowed on the
courts. Wear only nonmarking tennis shoes. Use a
metal racquet carefully—metal can damage the
expensive court surface.

(your initials)
```

---

6. Use the filename **1memo3** (chapter 1, memo 3). Save the file and keep the document on the screen.

7. Use Procedure 2: Using the Print Menu (**Shift** and **F7, t, 2, 1**) and print one copy.

8. Clear the screen (**F7, n, n**).

Exercise 1.4

1. If necessary, load the WordPerfect program.

2. The screen should be clear.

3. The disk drive should be accessed where the file disk is located.

4. If errors are made while typing, use the **backspace** key to delete. For this chapter ignore any errors noticed after the memo is typed.

5. Use memorandum style 2 (refer to Exhibit 1.4) and type the following memorandum.

```
INTEROFFICE MEMO        CALIFORNIA OFFICE ACADEMY

DATE:    (Use current date)

RE:      New Seminars—The Effective Office Manager

FROM:    Georgia Jimenez, Instructional Dean

TO:      Office Managers


The Effective Office Manager seminars will be held
in Chicago, New York, and San Francisco on the last
Monday of each month for the next three months.

These new seminars have been designed with the
specific needs of an office manager in mind. The
seminars will cover topics such as purchasing tips,
producing quality documents, building staff morale,
and much, much more.

Sign up for the seminars today! Call (800) 456-2288
to enroll. A major credit card can be used for the
registration fee.

(your initials)
```

---

6. Use the filename **1memo4** (chapter 1, memo 4). Save the file and keep the document on the screen.

7. Use Procedure 2: Using the Print Menu (**Shift** and **F7, t, 2, 1**) and print one copy.

8. Clear the screen (**F7, n, n**).

Exercise 1.5

1. If necessary, load the WordPerfect program.

2. The screen should be clear (**F7, n, n**).

3. The disk drive should be accessed where the file disk is located (**F5, =**, type the disk drive letter where the file disk is located followed by a colon, **Enter, F1**).

4. Proofread the memorandum and correct two spelling errors and one capitalization error.

5. If errors are made while typing, use the **backspace** key to delete. For this chapter ignore any errors noticed after the memo is typed.

6. Use memorandum style 1 and type the following memorandum.

```
                        Memorandum


To:          Howard Yamamoto

From:        Dr. Judy Mason

Date:        (Use current date)

Subject:     Fee Increase for Credential Applicants


Effective at the beginning of next month, the
Department of Justice is raising its fingerprint
card fee by $10 and is requiring that there be no
abbreviations on eye and hair color.

By having applicants utelize the standard
credential application form and mailing a check for
a total of $105, our administrative Assistant can
expidite the application process.

(your initials)
```

---

7. Use the filename **1memo5**. Save the file and keep the document on the screen.

8. Use Procedure 2: Using the Print Menu (**Shift** and **F7, t, 2, 1**) and print one copy.

9. Clear the screen (**F7, n, n**).

Chapter 2

EDIT A
MEMORANDUM

OBJECTIVES

After successfully completing this chapter, you should be able to:

- Retrieve a file using list files and the F10 key.

- Delete a character, word, space, return, and block of text.

- Use shortcuts for deleting text.

- Insert text.

- Replace text.

- Recapture deleted text.

- Save a file and clear the screen.

- Display and print the directory.

Once a memorandum has been created, the author can make revisions to the document. Revisions can include information to be deleted, inserted, or replaced.

When replacing text, new characters will delete the original characters by replacing them with new ones. For example, if the cursor is located under the character *b* in the word *band* and the character *s* is typed, the *b* is deleted and the character *s* displays on the screen, changing the word to *sand*. Replacing text is called typeover.

Text that has been deleted can be undeleted or put back into the document. When text is undeleted, the deleted text is retrieved to the screen. The last three deletions are remembered and can be undeleted. Undeleting text is also referred to as restoring text.

Procedure to Retrieve a File Using List Files: Method 1

Note: The screen should be clear (**F7**, **n**, **n**) *before retrieving a file.*

| 1. | Press **F5** {*File, List Files*} for List Files. *Note:* The disk drive

where the file disk is located should be accessed (**F5**, **=**, type disk drive letter followed by a colon, press **Enter** once.

2. If the file disk is in drive A, a prompt displays **Dir A:\ *.***.

3. If the file disk is in drive B, a prompt displays **Dir B:\ *.***.

4. Press the **Enter** key.

5. A list of filenames is displayed.

6. Press the **down** and/or **right** arrow keys to highlight the filename to be retrieved.

7. Press the **1** (one) key to retrieve the file. The file is displayed on the screen. (To exit without retrieving, press **F1**.)

Procedure to Retrieve a File Using the F10 Key: Method 2

Note: *The screen should be clear before retrieving a file to avoid combining two files.*

1. Press and hold the **Shift** key while tapping the **F10** key once (**Shift** and **F10**) {*File, Retrieve*}.

2. A prompt displays **Document to be retrieved:**.

3. Type the name of the file to be retrieved. *Note:* If the disk drive where the file is located has not been accessed, precede the filename with the drive letter followed by a colon. For example, type **b:1pmemo1**.

4. Press the **Enter** key.

5. The file is displayed on the screen.

6. The disk drive letter and the filename are displayed at the bottom left of the screen. For example, **B:\1pmemo1** is displayed.

▷ Obtain a clear screen (**F7**, **n**, **n**).

▷ Retrieve the file named **1pmemo1** that was typed in Chapter 1, page 6.

Procedure to Delete a Character or Space

1. Place the cursor under the character or space that is to be deleted.

2. Press the **Del** key once. *Note:* The **Del** key deletes the character where the cursor is located.

Procedure to Delete a Tab or Return

1. Press and hold the **Alt** key while tapping the **F3** key once to display the Reveal Codes (**Alt** and **F3**).

2. **a.** *To delete a return:* Place the cursor (large highlighted block) on the code **[HRt]**. *Note:* **[HRt]** represents a hard return. A hard return is placed in a document when the **Enter** key is pressed.
    b. *To delete a tab:* Press the cursor on the code **[Tab]**.

3. Press the **Del** key once to delete the return or tab.

4. Press and hold the **Alt** key while tapping the **F3** key once (**Alt** and **F3**) to return the cursor to the document screen.

Procedure to Delete Text by Blocking

1. Place the cursor under the first character of the word, sentence, or paragraph to be deleted.

2. Press and hold the **Alt** key while tapping the **F4** key once to block (**Alt** and **F4**)—or tap the **F12** key to block {*Edit, Block*}. The message **Block on** blinks continuously at the bottom left of the screen.

3. **a.** *To delete a word:* Press the character at the end of the word or press the space bar once to highlight the entire word.
    b. *To delete a sentence:* Press the period or punctuation mark that ends the sentence to highlight the entire sentence.
    c. *To delete a paragraph:* Press the **Enter** key once to highlight the entire paragraph. *Note:* If the paragraph to be deleted is the last paragraph in the document, the **Enter** key must have been pressed after the paragraph.

4. Press the **Del** key.

5. A message is displayed **Delete Block? No(Yes)**.

6. Press **y** for yes.

Note: Also delete any extra spaces that may be on the screen.

Shortcuts for Deleting

Place the cursor on the first character of the word or text to be deleted:

1. Press **Ctrl** and the **backspace** key to delete a word.

2. Press **Ctrl** and **End** to delete to the end of a line.

3. Press **Ctrl** and **PgDn** to delete to the end of a page; press **y** for yes.

Procedure to Insert Text or Spaces

1. Place the cursor under the character or space that will follow the text to be inserted.

2. Type the character, word, sentence, or paragraph that is to be inserted. *Note:* The words that follow automatically move to the right. Use the **up, down, left,** and **right** arrow keys to move through the text. *Note:* If the word "typeover" displays at the bottom right corner of the screen, press **Ins** to turn typeover off.

Procedure to Replace Text

1. Place the cursor under the first character of the text to be replaced.

2. Press the **Ins** key. The word **Typeover** is displayed in the bottom left corner of the screen. *Note:* If the word **Typeover** is not displaying on the screen, press the **Ins** key again.

3. Type the new characters.

4. Press the **Ins** key again to turn off **Typeover**.

⇨ Make the corrections shown for the file named **1pmemo1** (typed from page 6).

⇨ Print one copy using the print menu (**Shift** and **F7; t** for text; **2** for draft and **1** for full document). See Chapter 1, page 9.

⇨ Save the file and keep the document on the screen (**F10,** type **2pmemo1, Enter**).

Procedure to Recapture Deleted Text

Note: Place the cursor at the location where the text is to be recaptured.

1. After text has been deleted with the **Del** or **backspace** key, press the **F1** key to Cancel {*Edit, Undelete*}.

2. The deleted text is displayed and is highlighted.

3. The message **Undelete: 1 Restore; 2 Previous Deletion: 0** is displayed.

   a. Press **1** to restore the deleted text to the screen. The highlighting will disappear, indicating that the deletion has been returned to the document screen.

   b. The last three deletions are remembered and can be undeleted. Press **2** to display the last text that was deleted; press **1** to restore the text that is highlighted *or* press the **up** arrow key to display the next-to-the-last deleted text. Press the **up** arrow key again to display the first text that was deleted. If the displayed text is not wanted, press the **F1** key to Cancel.

```
                    Memorandum


To:          All Departments


From:        Anthony Mignetto


Date:        (Use current date)


Subject:     Employee Guidelines


Packages that are being delivered to the building

are left in the reception area. As packages arrive
       Kathy                   your
Terry will contact each department. Pick up your

packages promptly.
We would like to have an uncluttered reception area
to portray a better image to our "walk-in" clients.
Smoking is accepted in designated smoking areas. No

smoking in the restrooms. Outside in the patio is
another area where smoking is permitted.

In order to provide a good working relationship
```

```
with our customers, the phones should be answered
```
immediately
```
after the first ring.
```
^

```
(your initials)
```

⇨   Use the block delete method to delete the first sentence of the first paragraph in **2pmemo1**.

⇨   Restore the sentence.

⇨   Practice deleting and restoring several words. Restore the deleted words.

⇨   Print one copy using the print menu (**Shift** and **F7**, **t**, for text; **2** for draft and **1** for full document).

⇨   Use the Procedure to Save a File and Clear the Screen.

Procedure to Save a File and Clear the Screen

1. Press the **F7** key to exit the document {*File, Exit*}.

2. The message **Save document: Yes(No)** is displayed.

3. Press **y** for yes.

4. The prompt displays **Document to be saved:**.

5. The file named **2pmemo1** (chapter 2, practice memo 1) is displayed. *Note:* A new filename can be typed if desired.

6. Press the **Enter** key; press **y** to replace.

7. If the file disk is in drive A, the message **Saving A:\ . . .** is displayed. (The filename is displayed.)

8. If the file disk is in drive B, the message **Saving B:\ . . .** is displayed. (The filename is displayed.)

9. A prompt is displayed: **Exit WP? No(Yes)**.

10. Press **n** for no. *Note*: If desired, press **F1** to cancel and keep the document on the screen.

11. The screen is cleared, and the cursor is blinking in the top left corner of the screen.

Procedure to Display and Print the Directory

1. Press the **F5** key {*File, List Files*}.

2. If the file disk is in drive A and drive A is accessed, the prompt displays **Dir A:\ * . *** .

3. If the file disk is in drive B and drive B is accessed, the prompt displays **Dir B:\ * . *** .

4. Press the **Enter** key.

5. A list of the file names on the disk is displayed.

6. Press and hold the **Shift** key while tapping the **F7** key once to print the directory.

7. Press the **F1** key to Cancel the directory and return the cursor to the document screen.

⇨ Display the directory.

⇨ Print a copy of the directory (optional). Use print screen (**Shift** and **PrtSc**) or print function (**Shift** and **F7**).

SUMMARY

- A memorandum is revised by changing information. Information can be changed by inserting, deleting, or replacing.

- Text is inserted by placing the cursor on the character that will follow the new character(s) and typing the new text.

- Text is deleted by one of three methods, i.e., pressing the **backspace** key, pressing the **Del** key, or by blocking (**Alt** and **F4**) and then deleting (**Del**) text.

- Replacing text is the process of erasing the original characters by substituting new characters. (Press **Ins**; the message **Typeover** is displayed in the bottom left corner of the screen. Type the new character(s).)

- Retrieving a document is the process of transferring a copy of the file from the file disk to the computer's memory. A file can be retrieved using List Files (**F5**, **Enter**, place the cursor on the filename to be retrieved, press **1**) or by using the **F10** key (**Shift** and **F10**, type the filename, **Enter**).

- Text can be recaptured or undeleted (**F1**, press **1** to Restore, or press **2** for Previous Deletion).

- A document can be saved and the screen can be cleared by using the **F7** (Exit) key (**F7**, **y**, type the document name, **Enter**, **n**).

- Displaying the directory is the process of listing the names of all the files saved on a disk (**F5**, **Enter**).

- After the directory is displayed, a copy of the directory can be printed by using Print Screen (**Shift** and **PrtSc**) or **Shift** and **F7**.

SELF-CHECK QUESTIONS

(True / False—Circle One)

T,F 1. Revisions to a document can be accomplished by inserting, deleting, or replacing text.

T,F 2. A file can be retrieved by pressing **F5**, **Enter**, place cursor on document name, **F3**. *just enter*

T,F 3. A file can also be retrieved by pressing the **Shift** and **F9** keys and typing the name of the document. *Shift F10*

T,F 4. The **Del** key can be used to delete one character or space.

T,F 5. After placing the cursor at the beginning of a block to be deleted, press the **Alt** and **F4** keys to turn block on. *or F12*

T,F 6. To delete a hard return, Reveal Codes, place the cursor on the **[HRt]** code, press **Del**.

T,F 7. A word can be deleted by placing the cursor on the first character of the word and pressing **Alt** and the **backspace** keys. *control . backspace on any charac*

T,F 8. Before inserting text, press the **Ins** key and display the word *typeover* in the bottom left corner of the document screen.

T,F 9. Recapture deleted text by pressing the **F7** key. *F1*

T,F 10. Display a list of file names by pressing **F5** and **Enter**.

Spelling / Vocabulary Words

keypads   a structure on which a set of keys is located. The keys
    are identified by letters, symbols, or numbers.
facility   the method used to create a convenience.
monochrome   having one color or having shades of one color.

Introductory Clause

A comma should follow a dependent clause. (A dependent
clause has both a subject and verb but cannot stand alone as a
sentence.) An introductory clause often begins with an *if, when,*
since or *as.*

Example   If you have any questions, please contact me at extension 335.

EXERCISES

Exercise 2.1

1.   If necessary, load the WordPerfect program and obtain a
     clear screen. The disk drive where the file disk is located
     should be accessed (**F5**, **=**, type disk drive letter where the
     file disk is located followed by a colon, **Enter**, **F1**).

2.   Retrieve the file named **1memo1** that was typed in Chapter
     1, page 14.

3.   Make the revisions as shown.

4.   Proofread and correct any errors.

5.   Save the revised memo without clearing the screen. Name
     the revised memo **2memo1r**.

6.   Use print procedure 2 (**Shift** and **F7**; **t** for text; **2** for draft and
     1 for full document) and print one copy of the revised
     memo.

Memorandum

To: Gentek Managers

From: Carol Ivanicki

Date: (Use current date)

Subject: Controller's Organization ~~Changes~~ *Revised* *Chart*

In the past several months, the controller's
organization has undergone certain *organizational consolidations and* personnel
changes.

A ~~new~~ *revised* functional organization chart will be
provided next week to *expedite* your service
requirements by identifying key management
personnel~~, by department, responsibilities, location, and telephone extensions.~~ *The individuals as primary contacts on this*
Utilizing ~~the~~ chart will ensure that your inquiries
and information requests are addressed in a
controlled and expeditious manner. *Please replace last year's controller's organization chart with this revised chart.*

(your initials)

Exercise 2.2

1. Obtain a clear screen (**F7, n, n**).

2. Retrieve the file named **1memo2** that was typed in Chapter 1, page 15.

3. Make the revisions as shown.

4. Proofread and correct any errors.

5. Save the revised memo without clearing the screen. Name the revised memo **2memo2r**.

6. Use print procedure 2 (**Shift** and **F7, t** for text; **2** for draft and **1** for full document) and print one copy of the revised memo.

Memorandum

To: All Employees

From: Donald Silva

Date: (Use current date)

Subject: New Conference Rooms

Our new *facility* across the street has three
conference rooms available for meetings. The Main
Conference Room is the large ~~one~~ *room* located next to
the photocopy room. The Network Conference Room is
located ~~by~~ *to the right of* the breakroom *,* ~~and~~ *T*he Executive
Conference Room is located next to my ~~new~~ office.

Both the Main and Executive Conference Rooms have
very nice wooden tables. Coasters *have been ordered* ~~will be purchased~~
for each conference room. In the meantime, use a
paper towel or napkin under *any beverage container* ~~a cup or mug~~.

~~After using the conference room~~ *C*lean up at the
end of your meeting *s in the conference rooms*. Place chairs under the table
and return the podium to the front table. *Thank
you for your cooperation.*
(your initials)

Exercise 2.3

1.   Obtain a clear screen.

2.   Type the following memorandum. Use memorandum style
     1; see Chapter 1, page 5.

Memorandum

To: B. Bair

From: T. Loy

Date: (Use current date)

Subject: Requests for Title History

Please supply us with a brief memo when requesting
title history information. Specify the information
required, i.e., printing quantity, total plant
costs, unit costs, etc.

Please allow three days after receipt of memo for
title research. If you have any questions, please
contact me at extension 335.

(your initials)

---

3.   Use the filename **2memo3**. Save the memo without clearing
     the screen.

4.   Press and hold the **Shift** key while tapping the **PrtSc** key
     once to print one copy.

5.   Make the revisions shown. (Do not change the spacing.)

Memorandum

To: B. Bair

From: T. Loy

Date: (Use current date)

Subject: Requests for Title History

Please supply us with a brief memo when requesting

title history information. Specify the information

required, i.e., printing quantity, total plant

costs, unit costs, etc.

9 The memo must contain title, title code, and author's name. Send requests to the attention of Brandon in cost accounting.

~~Please~~ *^A* allow three days after receipt of memo for
The
^ title research. If you have any questions, please

contact me at extension ~~335~~ *366* .

(your initials)

---

6. Proofread and correct any errors.

7. Use the filename **2memo3r**. Save the memo without clearing the screen.

8. Use print procedure 2 (**Shift** and **F7; t** for text; **2** for draft and **1** for full document) and print one copy of the revised memo.

Exercise 2.4

1. Obtain a clear screen.

2. Type the following memorandum. Use memorandum style 2, see Chapter 1, page 10.

INTEROFFICE MEMO   SANDOVAL CONVENTIONS

DATE: (Use current date)

RE: Computers for Conventions

FROM: Linda J. Pavlakis

TO: Frank Caruthers

Presently we are working on the conventions being
held for the next two quarters. Please supply the
following information for each computer needed:
name of convention, type of computer, monochrome or
color monitor, and printer.

If you are in need of a computer, don't wait until
the last minute to order one. Remember time is

```
needed to order extra furniture and electricity,
and the Purchasing Department needs a signed
purchase order before the computer can be ordered.

(your initials)
```

---

3.   Use the filename **2memo4**. Save the memo without clearing the screen.

4.   Press and hold the **Shift** key while tapping the **PrtSc** key once to print one copy.

5.   Make the revisions shown. (Do not change the spacing.)

```
INTEROFFICE MEMO                 SANDOVAL CONVENTIONS

DATE:    (Use current date)

RE:      Computers for Conventions

FROM:    Linda J. Pavlakis

TO:      Frank Caruthers
```

Presently we are working on the conventions, ~~being~~ *that will be*

held ~~for~~ *during* the next two quarters. ~~Please~~ *S*upply the

following information for each computer needed:

name of convention, type of computer, monochrome or

color monitor, and printer.

If you *will* ~~are in~~ need ~~of~~ a computer, don't wait until

the last minute to order one. Remember time is

needed to order extra *equipment* ~~furniture and electricity~~,

and the Purchasing Department needs a signed

purchase order before the computer can be ordered.

Your help in this matter will be very much appreciated.

```
(your initials)
```

---

6.   Proofread and correct any errors.

7.   Use the filename **2memo4r**. Save the file without clearing the screen.

8.   Use print procedure 2 (**Shift** and **F7, t** for text; **2** for draft and **1** for full document) and print one copy of the revised memo.

Exercise 2.5

1.   If necessary, load the WordPerfect program.

2.   The screen should be clear (**F7, n, n**).

3.   Proofread the memorandum and correct three spelling errors and two punctuation errors.

4.   Use memorandum style 1 and type the following memorandum.

```
                    Memorandum


To:        Pauline Powers

From:      Lisa Noller

Date:      (Use current date)

Subject:   Request for Computer Components


As the end of the fiscal year is nearing we have
extra monies which can be used to purchase
additional computer components such as special
keeypads, monachrome or color monitors, and 3 1/2
inch disk drives.

Your request for additional components should be
received by the end of this week.

To exppedite your request, use the request form
provided in your department's office. If you need
assistance call extension 688.

(your initials)
```

---

5.   Use the filename **2memo5**. Save the file and keep the document on the screen.

6.   Use print procedure 2 (**Shift** and **F7, t, 2, 1**) and print one copy.

7.   Clear the screen.

Chapter 3

CREATE A
DRAFT LETTER

After successfully completing this chapter, you should be able to:

● Enter a draft letter using the block letter style.

● Enter a draft letter using the AMS Simplified letter style.

● Change the vertical line spacing.

A letter is formal written correspondence used to communicate information from one business to another. A draft is the initial writing of a letter that will be revised at a later time.

The draft letter will be typed in single spacing (see Exhibit 3.1) and printed after the vertical line spacing has been changed to double spacing (see Exhibit 3.4). When the letter is printed, the double spacing provides extra space between lines for hand-written revisions to be noted on the printout. The double-spaced printed copy will print on two pages.

Reference initials and document identification are typed at the end of the letter. The reference initials include the initials of both the author and typist of the letter. The author's initials can be typed in uppercase letters and the typist's initials are often typed in lowercase letters—for example, CU/rts. The author's initials are optional, but the typist's initials should always be typed on every letter. The reference initials are typed two returns after the author's typed name and/or title.

The document identification includes the document name and the disk name or number—for example, weston.ltr/diskA. The document identification can be typed a single space below the reference initials.

AMS.

(Use current date) *shift F5, 1*

↓ 5

Curtis and Sheila Weston   *Put their address*
590 Willow Avenue   *Inside address*
Hayward, CA 94541
↓ 2
Dear Curtis and Sheila: *salutation or greeting.*
↓ 2
This letter is the first in a series that will be sent to you in
the next few years discussing some of the real estate issues in
our neighborhood.
↓ 2
My name is Carolyn Upshaw. I have been a Hayward resident for
25 years where my two children have attended the local schools.
My membership in the Alameda County Board of Realtors for five
years and my experience selling homes for the past 10 years gives
me practical information about the housing sales in our area.
↓ 2
Enclosed is information concerning homes for sale, homes that
have just sold, and any termite problems, roof inspection issues,
etc. in our neighborhood.
↓ 2
I look forward to working with you to serve all your real estate
needs.
↓ 2
Sincerely,   *closing*

↓ 4   *signature*

Carolyn Upshaw
Purcell Real Estate Co.
↓ 2
CU/xxx *typist initials*
weston.ltr/diskA *coding the letter*
↓ 2
Enc.

EXHIBIT 3.1   Draft letter block style typed with single spacing

4″   *6 tabs*

When additional papers are enclosed with the letter, the enclosure notation is typed a double space below the document identification. The enclosure notation can be abbreviated (Enc.) or can be typed in full (Enclosure).

⇨ Use the Procedure to Enter a Practice Draft Letter: Block Style.

⇨ Type the draft letter shown in Exhibit 3.1.

Procedure to Enter a Practice Draft Letter: Block Style

1. Type the current date on the first line of the screen. *Shortcut:* Press **Shift** and **F5** for Date; press **1** for Date Text {*Tools, Date Text*}.

2. Press the **Enter** key five times.

3. Type the name of the recipient, followed by one return (**Enter**); for example, type **Curtis and Sheila Weston**. See Exhibit 3.1.

4. If given, type the recipient's title and/or company name, followed by one return.

5. Type the street address followed by one return; for example, type **590 Willow Avenue**.

6. Type the city, state, and zip code followed by two returns; for example, type **Hayward, CA 94541**.

7. Type "Dear" followed by a title, surname, or first names and colon. For example, type **Dear Curtis and Sheila:**.

8. Press the **Enter** key two times.

9. Use word wrap and type the paragraphs single spaced.

10. Press the **Enter** key two times after each paragraph including the last paragraph.

11. Type the complimentary closing followed by a comma. For example, type **Sincerely,**.

12. Press the **Enter** key four times.

13. Type the author's name and title followed by two returns.

14. Type the author's initials in capital letters and your initials in lowercase letters (reference initials) followed by a document identification notation. For example, type

CU/nkl
weston.ltr/diskA

15. Press the **Enter** key two times.

16. If appropriate, type an enclosure notation two returns below the document identification notation. For example, type **Enc**.

Note: Draft letter style 1 is a standard block style letter.

▷ Use the filename **weston.tr**. Save the file and keep the document on the screen.

▷ Use the procedure to change the vertical line spacing; change to line spacing of 2. Save and replace the file named **weston.ltr**.

▷ Print one copy using draft print quality; clear the screen (optional).

Procedure to Change the Vertical Line Spacing

1. Place the cursor at the beginning of the text where the vertical line spacing is to be changed (press **Home** twice, **up** arrow key once).

2. Press and hold the **Shift** key while tapping the **F8** key (**Shift** and **F8**) to display the Format menu. See Exhibit 3.2.

3. Press **1** for Line {*Layout, Line*}. See Exhibit 3.3.

4. Press **6** for Line Spacing.

5. The cursor moves to the column beside the Line Spacing menu choice.

6. Type the number desired. For example, type **2** (for double spacing); press the **Enter** key once.

7. Press **F7** once to exit the menu and return the cursor to the screen. Your letter should look similar to Exhibit 3.4.

▷ Use the Procedure to Enter a Practice Draft Letter: AMS Simplified Style.

```
Format

    1 - Line
            Hyphenation                      Line Spacing
            Justification                    Margins Left/Right
            Line Height                      Tab Set
            Line Numbering                   Widow/Orphan Protection

    2 - Page
            Center Page (top to bottom)      Page Numbering
            Force Odd/Even Page              Paper Size/Type
            Headers and Footers              Suppress
            Margins Top/Bottom

    3 - Document
            Display Pitch                    Redline Method
            Initial Codes/Font               Summary

    4 - Other
            Advance                          Overstrike
            Conditional End of Page          Printer Functions
            Decimal Characters               Underline Spaces/Tabs
            Language                         Border Options

Selection: 0
```

EXHIBIT 3.2 Format menu

```
Format: Line

    1 - Hyphenation                      No

    2 - Hyphenation Zone - Left          10%
                          Right          4%

    3 - Justification                    Full

    4 - Line Height                      Auto

    5 - Line Numbering                   No

    6 - Line Spacing                     1

    7 - Margins - Left                   1"
                  Right                  1"

    8 - Tab Set                          Rel; -1", every 0.5"

    9 - Widow/Orphan Protection          No


Selection: 0
```

EXHIBIT 3.3 Format: Line menu

(Use current date)

Curtis and Sheila Weston

590 Willow Avenue

Hayward, CA 94541

Dear Curtis and Sheila:

This letter is the first in a series that will be sent to you in the next few years discussing some of the real estate issues in our neighborhood.

My name is Carolyn Upshaw. I have been a Hayward resident for 25 years where my two children have attended the local schools. My membership in the Alameda County Board of Realtors for five years and my experience selling homes for the past 10 years gives me practical information about the housing sales in our area.

EXHIBIT 3.4 Draft letter block style with vertical line spacing of 2

Enclosed is information concerning homes for sale, homes that
have just sold, and any termite problems, roof inspection issues,
etc. in our neighborhood.

I look forward to working with you to serve all your real estate
needs.

Sincerely,

Carolyn Upshaw

Purcell Real Estate Co.

CU/xxx

weston.ltr/diskA

Enc.

EXHIBIT 3.4 *(Continued)*

⇨ Type the draft letter shown in Exhibit 3.5.

Procedure to Enter a Practice Draft Letter: AMS Simplified Style

Note: *Draft letter AMS simplified style is the Administrative Management Society simplified style letter.*

1. Type the current date on the first line of the screen followed by five returns.

(Use current date)

↓ 5

Ms. Constance Estrada
Turner's Auto Craft
199 Redwood Street
San Rafael, CA 94901
↓ 3

YOUR CHECK NO. 2344

↓ 3

You are a valued customer of Enterprise Portable phones. Thank
you for selecting Enterprise as your cellular service provider.
↓ 2
Recently a batch of our customer checks were stolen from the
Post Office. Your check No. 2344 for $350 was in this batch.
Fortunately, these checks have been retrieved and the F.B.I.
will investigate and prosecute all persons involved.
↓ 2
My purpose in writing is to assure you that we have processed
your check No. 2344. Please accept my apologies if you have
received a notice of late payment.
↓ 2
Our objective is to provide you with the highest quality
service possible.

↓ 4

JAMES F. DAVENPORT, MARKETING DIRECTOR
↓ 2
JFD/xxx
davenp.ltr/diskA

EXHIBIT 3.5 AMS simplified letter style typed in single spacing

2. Type the name and address of recipient. Follow steps 3–6 in the Procedure to Enter a Practice Draft Letter: Block Style.

3. After typing the city, state, and zip code, press the **Enter** key three times.

4. Type the subject line in all capital letters. For example, type **YOUR CHECK NO. 2344**. See Exhibit 3.5.

5. Press the **Enter** key three times.

6. Use word wrap while typing the paragraphs.

7. Press the **Enter** key two times after each paragraph (except the last paragraph).

8. After the last paragraph, press the **Enter** key four times.

9. Type the author's name and title in all capital letters followed by two returns.

10. Type the reference initials and document identification notation. See step 14, p. 38.

⇨ Set the vertical line spacing to 2.

⇨ Use the filename **davenp.ltr**. Save the file without clearing the screen.

⇨ Print one copy using draft text quality (optional).

SUMMARY

- A letter is a formal communication used to send messages from one business to another.

- A draft letter is printed in double spacing (line spacing of 2) in order to provide space between lines for the author to make handwritten changes.

- Type a draft letter with the spacing that will be used when the document is printed in final form. Before printing the draft letter, place the cursor at the beginning of the letter (**Home** twice, press the **up** arrow key once), select vertical spacing of 2 (**Shift** and **F8**, **1**, **6**, **2**, **Enter**, **F7**).

- Two styles of business letters include a block style and a simplified (AMS) style. The simplified style omits the salutation and the complimentary closing. A subject line is used in the simplified style letter.

- Reference initials are the initials of the author and the typist, e.g., **TRS/wab**. Reference initials are typed two returns after the author's typewritten signature and title.

- A document identification notation includes the filename and disk description, e.g., **smith.ltr/disk1**. The document identification notation is typed on the line below the reference initials.

- If an additional paper is enclosed with the letter, press the **Enter** key twice after the document identification and type the abbreviation "Enc." for enclosure.

SELF-CHECK QUESTIONS

(True / False—Circle One)

T,F 1. A draft letter is used by an author to make handwritten revisions on the printed draft copy.

T,F 2. In a block style letter, the date is followed by 5 returns.

T,F 3. The draft letter is typed in single spacing and the line spacing is changed to 2 before printing.

T,F 4. After typing the city, state, and zip code for an AMS simplified style letter, press the **Enter** key twice.

T,F 5. Lowercase letters are used to type the author's initials.

T,F 6. To change the vertical line spacing to 2, press **Shift** and **F8**, press **1**, **6**, **2**, **Enter**, and **F7**.

T,F 7. In the simplified style letter, the subject line and type-written signature are typed in uppercase letters.

T,F 8. Press the **Enter** key 4 times after typing the last paragraph in a simplified style letter.

T,F 9. Press the **Enter** key 3 times after typing the salutation in a blocked style letter.

T,F 10. If an item is enclosed with a letter, type the abbreviation "Enc." and press two **Enters** below the document identification information.

ENRICHING LANGUAGE ARTS SKILLS

Spelling / Vocabulary Words

charter member   originating or founding participant.
pension   a regular payment made to a person after retirement.
complimentary   commending someone by giving something free as a courtesy.

Appositive

Appositives are words that immediately follow a noun and further identify the noun. Appositives are set off by commas.

Example   Our president, Verna Barrett, was recognized recently for her article concerning company marketing strategies.

Exercise 3.1

1. If necessary, load the WordPerfect program. Access the disk drive where the file disk is located (**F5**, **=**, type the disk drive letter followed by a colon, **Enter**, **F1**).

2. The screen should be clear (**F7**, **n**, **n**).

3. Type the following letter using draft letter block style.

(Use current date)

Ms. Paula Gabriel
R. A. Circuits
6005 N. Forest Park Drive
Peoria, IL 61656-9975

Dear Ms. Gabriel:

If you have concerns about the quality of our work force, this letter is for you.

Based on our belief that an educated work force is necessary for a thriving business economy, the Chamber of Commerce has formed a scholarship foundation to enhance educational opportunities for employees of Peoria businesses and for Peoria residents.

You are invited to become a *charter member* of the Peoria Chamber of Commerce Scholarship Foundation. We hope to raise a minimum of $6,000 this first year.

A well-educated work force will ensure the successes of our businesses and the quality of life in Peoria.

Sincerely,

Rodney Suter, President
Peoria Chamber of Commerce

RS/xxx
gabriel.ltr/disk4

---

4.   Locate the cursor at the beginning of the document (press **Home** twice; press the **up** arrow key once) and set the vertical line spacing for 2.

5.   Use the filename **gabriel.ltr**. Save the file and keep the document on the screen.

6.   Print one copy in draft form using draft text quality.

Exercise 3.2

1.   If necessary, load the WordPerfect program. Access the disk drive where the file disk is located.

2.   The screen should be clear.

3.   Type the following letter using draft letter block style.

━━

```
(Use current date)



Jeremy Ahmadi
3788 Miller Avenue
San Diego, CA 92127

Dear Jeremy:

In view of the recent trend, Enterprise Portable
Phones thought it might be prudent to protect our
employees' and retirees' earned benefits from
possible reductions.

Recently we adopted a pension protection plan. The
plan cannot be amended to adversely affect your
earned benefits. In the unlikely event that the
plan is terminated, provisions have been made for
the payment of your earned pension benefits, and
for remaining pension assets to be transferred to
the Enterprise Benefits Protection Trust.

We here at Enterprise value our employees. Our
interest for your continued benefits demonstrates
our commitment to you.

Sincerely,



Terry Bryant, President

TB/xxx
ahmadi.ltr/disk2/91
```

━━

4.   Locate the cursor at the beginning of the document (press

Home twice; press the **up** arrow key once) and set the vertical line spacing for 2.

5. Use the filename **ahmadi.ltr**. Save the file and keep the document on the screen.

6. Print one copy in draft form using draft text quality.

Exercise 3.3

1. If necessary, load the WordPerfect program. Access the disk drive where the file disk is located.

2. The screen should be clear.

3. Type the following letter using the draft AMS simplified style letter.

```
(Use current date)


Ms. Elizabeth Gordon
45 Cherry Road
Vancouver, WA 98668

NORTHWEST COMPUTER SHOW


Our company, Northwest Shows, Inc., produces
one-day computer shows throughout the Northwest. We
would like to give you an opportunity to attend one
of our shows.

The Northwest Shows, Inc. provides end users a
chance to purchase new and used computer
merchandise at low discount prices. The shows offer
big savings, especially useful for consumers on low
budgets. The show includes hardware, software,
supplies, and services available for personal
computers.

Enclosed are two complimentary tickets ($6.50
value) along with a brochure that describes the
various companies and suppliers who will be
exhibiting at the show.

I hope to see you at the show next week.


KATHY A. IRVINE, MARKETING DIRECTOR

KAI/xxx
gordon.ltr/d#5

Encs.
```

---

4. Locate the cursor at the beginning of the document (press **Home** twice; press the **up** arrow key once) and set the vertical line spacing for 2.

5. Use the filename **gordon.ltr**. Save the file and keep the document on the screen.

6. Print one copy in draft using draft text quality.

Exercise 3.4

1. If necessary, load the WordPerfect program. Access the disk drive where the file disk is located.

2. The screen should be clear.

3. Type the following letter using the draft AMS simplified style letter.

```
(Use current date)


Mr. Jake Becker, Editor
Spacefaring Gazette
4009 Everett Ave.
Oakland, CA 94602


THE GAZETTE NEWSLETTER


Congratulations on a newsletter that provides
pertinent and timely information for persons who
are interested in being actively involved in the
space program.

Last week I picked up a Gazette at my local
library. I read with curiosity the article
concerning the next shuttle launches. It is
exciting to know that engineers and technicians
have been busy improving the shuttle for meeting
safety regulations as well as keeping up with
demanding schedules.

I especially enjoyed reading the article on space
program benefits. The weather satellites that
provide current data on weather changes can save
many lives if people will evacuate when warned of a
severe storm.

Thank you for a very informative newsletter. I
eagerly look forward to next month's issue.


LOREN FRANKLIN, SPACEMOD, INC.

LF/xxx
becker.ltr/d#6
```

---

4.   Locate the cursor at the beginning of the document (press **Home** twice, press the **up** arrow key once) and set the vertical line spacing for 2.

5.   Use the filename **becker.ltr**. Save the file and keep the document on the screen.

6.   Print one copy in draft form using draft text quality.

Exercise 3.5

1.   If necessary, load the Wordperfect program.

2.   The screen should be clear (**F7**, **n**, **n**).

3.   Proofread the letter and correct two spelling errors, and three punctuation errors.

4.   Type the following letter using the block style.

```
(Use current date)



Mr. and Mrs. Michael Packard
489 Terrace Place
Lambertville, NJ 08530

Dear Mr. and Mrs. Packard:

Greetings to all our Mayfield Inn friends.

If you would like a relaxing experience during the
week visit us for three nights and the fourth night
is free! Also, if you stay with us any Sunday or
Monday, we will pack you a complemintary gourmet
lunch.

Our resident hair dresser Jerry Cole is available
for appointments any Monday through Saturday.

We have a new facillity with five rooms all with
private baths and air conditioners. All rooms
include a small living room with a library and
current magazines.

When you make plans for your next holiday remember
that our current special gives you one free night
after staying five nights with us.

Sincerely,



Valerie Oda

VO/xxx
packard.ltr/disk3
```

5. Use the filename **packard.ltr**. Save the file and keep the document on the screen.

6. Print one copy using draft or high text quality.

7. Clear the screen.

Chapter 4

REFINE A LETTER AND PRINT FINAL COPY

After successfully completing this chapter, you should be able to:

- Change left and right margins. ✓
- Change top and bottom margins. ✓
- Change justification. ✓
- Delete the vertical line space code. ✓ *spaces between lines*
- Print a letter in final form.
- Use WordPerfect's speller.
- Display and cancel a file from the print queue.

[handwritten margin note: 1.5 for all letter margins left & rt.]

[handwritten note: default margins are 1" on side & 1" on top. change. How do I format the document?]

REFINE A LETTER

After the content of a draft letter is reviewed and revised, decisions can then be made for the final document printing. Decisions need to be made to determine the final placement of the letter on a page, proofreading for any spelling or typographical errors, and the vertical spacing must be deleted to change the spacing to one.

When the document is ready for final printing, one of three printing selections for text quality are available—draft, medium, and high. The quality of the print will depend on the type of printer. A dot matrix and letter quality printer will print draft, medium, or high text quality. A laser printer will print high quality regardless of the text quality selection.

51

CHANGE MARGINS

Generally, the margins that have been preset (defaulted) on the WordPerfect program should be used. The top, bottom, left, and right margins are preset for one inch each. If a letter is unusually short or long, however, it may be desirable to change the margins.

The top margin of a letter can vary between 2 and 2½ inches depending on the information prepared in the letterhead. See Exhibit 4.1. The bottom margin of an average length letter generally remains unchanged.

▷ Retrieve the file named **weston.ltr** typed in Chapter 3 or type the letter in Exhibit 4.1.

▷ Use the Procedure to Change the Left and Right Margins and the Procedure to Change Top and Bottom Margins. Change the left and right margins to 1.5 inches. Change the top and bottom margins to 1.5 inches.

▷ Use the filename **weston.c4**. Save the file and keep the document on the screen.

▷ Print one copy using the print menu and draft text quality (**Shift** and **F7**; **t, 2, 1**).

Procedure to Change Left and Right Margins

1. Place the cursor at the beginning of the text where the margins are to be changed. *Note:* The cursor can be at the beginning of a clear screen.

2. Press and hold the **Shift** key while tapping the **F8** key once (**Shift** and **F8**).

3. Press **1** for Line {*Layout, Line*}. The Format Line menu is displayed.

4. Press **7** for Margins. The cursor moves to the right column beside the word *Left*.

5. Type the number (in inches) desired for the left margin. For example, type 1.5 for a 1½-inch left margin.

6. Press the **Enter** key once to move the cursor to the column beside the word *Right*.

7. Type the number (in inches) desired for the right margin.

Ctrl. F8 FONT

PURCELL REAL ESTATE COMPANY

89 Alta Street, Ste. 5   *Tel (415) 528-9988*
Castro Valley, CA 94546   *Fax (415) 538-7890*

(Use current date)

Curtis and Sheila Weston
590 Willow Avenue
Hayward, CA 94541

Dear Curtis and Sheila:

This letter is the first in a series that will be sent to you
in the next few years discussing some of the real estate issues
in our neighborhood.

My name is Carolyn Upshaw. I have been a Hayward resident for
25 years where my two children have attended the local schools.
My membership in the Alameda County Board of Realtors for five
years and my experience selling homes for the past 10 years
gives me practical information about the housing sales in our
area.

Enclosed is information concerning homes for sale, homes that
have just sold, and any termite problems, roof inspection
issues, etc. in our neighborhood.

I look forward to working with you to serve all your real
estate needs.

Sincerely,

Carolyn Upshaw
Purcell Real Estate Co.

CU/xxx
weston.ltr/diskA

Enc.

EXHIBIT 4.1   Letter block style in final print format

For example, type 1.5 for a 1½-inch right margin; press
Enter once.

8. Press the **F7** key once to exit and return the cursor to the
document screen.

Procedure to Change Top and Bottom Margins

Note: Generally the defaulted (preset) margins can be used.

1. Place the cursor at the beginning of the text where the margins are to be changed. *Note:* Since the top and bottom margins affect the entire page, it is desirable to change the margins at the beginning of the document.

2. Press and hold the **Shift** key while tapping the **F8** key once (**Shift** and **F8**).

3. Press **2** for Page {*Layout, Page*}. The Format Page menu is displayed.

4. Press **5** for Margins. The cursor moves to the right column beside the word *Top*.

5. Type the number (in inches) desired for the top margin. For example, type 1.5 for 1½ inches.

6. Press the **Enter** key once to move the cursor to the column beside the word *Bottom*.

7. Type the number (in inches) desired for the bottom margin. For example, type 1.5; press **Enter** once.

8. Press the **F7** key once to exit and return the cursor to the document screen.

JUSTIFICATION

Justification aligns characters at the same space on the left margin, right margin, or both. WordPerfect provides four choices for justification, i.e., left, center, right, and full.

Left justification begins all lines at the same space on the left margin and does not justify the right margin. Center justification centers text between the left and right margins. Right justification ends all lines at the same space on the right margin and does not justify the left margin.

Full justification is the default and justifies both the left and right margins by placing extra spaces between words. Full justification does not display on the editing screen but can be displayed by using the print menu (**Shift** and **F7**) and pressing **v** for view.

☞ Use the file named **weston.c4** that was previously edited.

☞ Use the Procedure to Change Justification (left justification) and the Procedure to Delete the Vertical Line Space Code.

☞ Use the filename **weston.c4r**. Save the file and keep the document on the screen.

☞ Print one copy using the print menu and draft text quality (**Shift** and **F7**; **t, 2, 1**).

Procedure to Change Justification

1. Press and hold the **Shift** key while tapping the **F8** key (**Shift** and **F8**) to display the Format menu.

2. Press **1** for Line.

3. Press **3** for Justification {*Layout, Justify*}.

4. Press **l** for left justification; **c** for center, **r** for right, or **f** for full.

5. The cursor returns to the Selection prompt at the bottom of the screen.

6. Press **F7** to exit and return the cursor to the document screen. Display the Reveal Codes (**Alt** and **F3**) {*Edit, Reveal Codes*}; the left justification code **[Just:Left]** is displayed. Press **Alt** and **F3** to exit Reveal Codes.

Procedure to Delete the Vertical Line Space Code

1. Press and hold the **Alt** key while tapping the **F3** key once (**Alt** and **F3**) {*Edit, Reveal Codes*}.

2. Place the cursor on the line space code **[Ln Spacing:2]**. *Note:* The line space code should be at the beginning of the document. Use the arrow keys to move the cursor.

3. Press **Del** once.

4. Press and hold the **Alt** key while tapping the **F3** key once (**Alt** and **F3**) to return the cursor to the document screen. Notice the letter is single spaced.

⇨   Use the file named **weston.c4r** that was previously edited.

⇨   Use the following Procedure to Print a Final Letter.

⇨   Print one copy using medium text quality on a dot matrix printer or high text quality on a laser or letter quality printer.

⇨   Use the filename **finlet.c4**. Save the file and keep the document on the screen.

Procedure to Print a Final Letter

1. Press **Shift** and **F7** to print {*File, Print*}.

2. Press **t** for Text Quality.
   a.   If using a dot matrix printer, press **3** for medium text quality or 4 for high quality.
   b.   If using a laser or letter quality printer, press **4** for high text quality. *Note:* Any of the selections for text quality, however, will print the same high-quality text.

3. Press **1** for Full Document. The document will print and the cursor will return to the document screen.

SPELLER

Speller is a WordPerfect feature that will check the spelling of each word in a document. (Another term used for speller is dictionary.) When an incorrectly spelled word is identified, a list of words similar to the unrecognized word is displayed on the screen. If the correctly spelled word is displaying in the list of words, the correct word can be selected, skipped, added to the dictionary, or edited.

⇨   Use the following Procedure to Use Speller.

⇨   Use the speller to check the spelling in the file named **finlet.c4** previously printed.

⇨   Use the filename **spellchk.c4**. Save the file and keep the document on the screen.

⇨   Print one copy (optional).

Procedure to Use Speller

1. The document to be checked for spelling should be displayed on the screen. If necessary, retrieve the document. *Note:* The cursor can be located anywhere in the document.

2. Press and hold the **Ctrl** key while tapping the **F2** key (**Ctrl** and **F2**) {*Tools, Spell*}.

3. Press **3** for Document.

4. A message ***Please Wait*** is displayed briefly.

5. An unrecognized word is highlighted.

6. The prompt displays **Not Found: 1 Skip Once; 2 Skip; 3 Add; 4 Edit; 5 Look Up; 6 Ignore numbers: 0.**

7. If the correctly spelled word is on the list, press the letter beside the desired word. The highlighted word will be corrected on the screen and the speller will continue.

8. If the correct spelling of a word is not on the list, other options can be selected:
   a. Press **1** to skip the word once.
   b. Press **2** to skip all occurrences of the word.
   c. Press **3** to add—save the word in the dictionary.
   d. Press **4** to edit. The cursor returns to the document screen and characters can be inserted or deleted. Press the **F7** key to exit and continue speller.
   e. Press **5** to look up. Type the first couple of letters of the word to be correctly spelled followed by an asterisk: for example, type **occ*** to obtain a list of words that begin with *occ* (you may be looking for the word occasion). Press the **Enter** key to return the cursor to the document screen.
   f. Press **6** to ignore numbers. Any words that contain numbers will be ignored by the speller.

9. When the entire document has been checked, a message is displayed at the bottom of the screen: **Word count:00**. Press any key to continue.

10. Press any key to return the cursor to the document screen.

THE PRINT QUEUE

When more than one document has been sent to be printed, a list of the filenames can be displayed. The print queue is the list of filenames in the order the files are lined up to print.

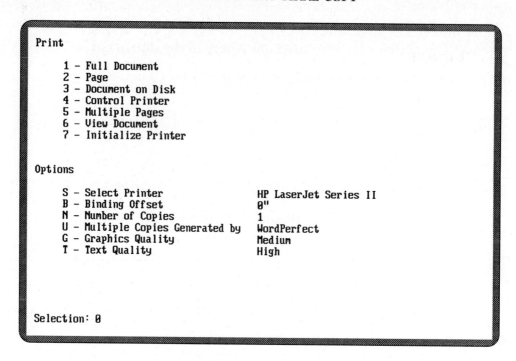

```
Print

     1 - Full Document
     2 - Page
     3 - Document on Disk
     4 - Control Printer
     5 - Multiple Pages
     6 - View Document
     7 - Initialize Printer


Options

     S - Select Printer              HP LaserJet Series II
     B - Binding Offset              0"
     N - Number of Copies            1
     U - Multiple Copies Generated by   WordPerfect
     G - Graphics Quality            Medium
     T - Text Quality                High




Selection: 0
```

EXHIBIT 4.2 Select printer menu

Procedure to Display and Cancel a File from the Print Queue

1. Press and hold the **Shift** key while tapping the **F7** key once (**Shift** and **F7**) {*File, Print*}.

2. Press **4** for Control Printer.

3. Documents that have been sent to print are displayed under the Job List. The program automatically numbers each document waiting to be printed.

4. Press **1** to Cancel Job(s).

5. A prompt is displayed: **Cancel which job? (** ∗ **= All Jobs)** _.

6. Type the asterisk and then press **y** to cancel all jobs. Press **Enter** to cancel the job number listed beside the prompt.

7. Press **F7** to return the cursor to the document screen.

Procedure to Print Using List Files

Note: *Before using list files to print, check that the correct printer is selected (**Shift** and **F7**, check printer name). See Exhibit 4.2. If necessary, press **s** to display printer name(s), highlight printer desired, press 1, press F7.*

1. Press **F5** to List Files; type the letter of the disk drive where the file disk is located followed by a colon; press **Enter**. If the disk drive letter where the file disk is located is already displayed, just press **Enter**.

2. Place the cursor on the name of the document to be printed.

3. Press **4** to Print.

4. Press **Enter** for All to print every page of the document.

5. Press **F7** to return the cursor to the document screen.

SUMMARY

- A final copy of a letter is printed after using the speller, deleting the vertical line spacing code, and deciding on the placement of the letter on the page.

- WordPerfect has three types of print quality, i.e., draft, medium, and high text quality. Dot matrix printers generally can print all three print qualities. Laser printers will print high quality only.

- The top, bottom, left, and right margins are defaulted (pre-set) by WordPerfect at one inch. In most cases, the defaulted left and right margins will be used for the final printing of a letter. The top margin of a letter will vary from 2 to 2½ inches depending on the amount of space used for the letterhead.

- Margins can be changed by using the Format function key, **Shift** and **F8**.

- To change the left and right margins, press **Shift** and **F8**, **1**, **7**, type desired left margin, **Enter**, type desired right margin, **Enter**, **F7** once.

- To change the top and bottom margins, press **Shift** and **F8**, **2**, **5**, type desired top margin, **Enter**, type desired bottom margin, **Enter**, **F7** once.

- Justification aligns left, right, or both margins. WordPerfect has four justification choices, i.e., left, right, center, or full. Full justification aligns characters at both the left and right margins. Justification can be changed by using the Format function key (**Shift** and **F8**, **1**, **3**, make desired selection, **F7**).

- The vertical line space code can be deleted by revealing codes (**Alt** and **F3**), placing the cursor on the line space code (**[Ln Spacing:2]**), and pressing the **Del** key once.

- Speller is used to verify the correct spelling of each word in a document. WordPerfect has a dictionary that checks each word for correct spelling. If a word is found in the dictionary, a correctly spelled word(s) is displayed on the screen. The user can select a displayed word, edit the word, add the word to the dictionary, look up another word, ignore words with numbers, or skip the word (**Ctrl** and **F2**).

- The print queue is a list of filenames that have been sent to be printed. To display the list of filenames, press **Shift** and **F7**, **4**. To remove a filename from the print queue, press **Shift** and **F7**, **4**, **1**, **Enter**.

- Printing can also be accomplished from the List Files menu (**F5**, type disk drive letter followed by a colon, **Enter**, place cursor on filename to be printed, **4**, **Enter**).

SELF-CHECK QUESTIONS

(True/False—Circle One)

T,F 1. A right margin is changed by pressing **Shift** and **F8**, **1**, **5**, typing the desired margin, and pressing **F7** twice.

T,F 2. The preset top margin is one inch.

T,F 3. The bottom margin of a letter usually remains unchanged.

T,F 4. Justification can be selected for full, center, left, or right by using the **Shift** and **F8** Format menu.

T,F 5. A line space code can be deleted by using the **Ctrl** and **F3** keys.

T,F 6. A document can be printed by using the List Files menu.

T,F 7. To add a word to the dictionary, press **Ctrl** and **F2**, press **3** for document, press **3** to add word.

T,F 8. When using the speller, a word can be edited to correct the spelling.

T,F 9. The left margin can be changed by pressing **Ctrl** and **F8**, **1**, **5**, typing the desired margin, and pressing **F7**.

T,F 10. Use the **Shift** and **F7** keys to select the print menu and press "**t**" to change the printing quality.

ENRICHING LANGUAGE ARTS SKILLS

Spelling / Vocabulary Words

remittance   sending money as a payment to someone.
waived   to postpone or eliminate.
roaming   to rove or wander over a wide area.

Numbers with Dollar Amounts

Dollar amounts are written in figures. Omit the decimal and zeros for whole dollar amounts.

Example   The $200 deposit was sent yesterday to reserve the banquet room.

EXERCISES

Exercise 4.1

1. The screen should be clear, and the disk drive should be accessed where the file disk is located.

2. Retrieve the draft letter **gabriel.ltr** that was typed in Chapter 3.

3. Delete the vertical line space code.

4. Set the left and right margins to 1.5 inches.

5. Use the speller to find and correct any incorrect words.

6. Select draft or high text quality (**Shift** and **F7**); press **F7** to exit the print menu.

7. Use the filename **4exer1**. Save the file and clear the screen.

8. Use the Procedure to Print Using List Files; print one final copy.

Exercise 4.2

1. The screen should be clear, and the disk drive should be accessed where the file disk is located.

2. Retrieve the draft letter **gordon.ltr** that was typed in Chapter 3.

3. Delete the vertical line space code.

4. Set the left and right margins to 1.5 inches.

5. Set the top margin to 2 inches.

6. Use the speller to find and correct any incorrect words.

7. Use the filename **4exer2**. Save the file and keep the file on the screen.

8. Print one final copy using draft or high text quality.

Exercise 4.3

1. The screen should be clear, and the disk drive should be accessed where the file disk is located.

2. Use letter block style, page 36, and type the following letter.

September 25, 1989

Ms. Candace Boardman
Newcastle, Inc.
6300 Marina Ave. Ste. 40
Emeryville, CA 94608

Dear Ms. Boardman:

Per our conversation of last Tuesday, enclosed is a remittance check for $300 on the disputed amount owed on my bill.

It is understood that my line of service will be reestablished. In the spirit of cooperation, $75 shall be waived by Newcastle as agreed by your collection manager, Samuel Alexander.

Sincerely,

Fred Thompson

JJ/btk
bdman.ltr/disk #4

Enc.

---

3. Set the left and right margins to 1.75 inches and set the top margin to 2½ inches.

4. Use left justification.

5. Use the speller to find and correct any incorrect words.

6. Use the filename **4bdman.ltr**. Save the file and keep the file on the screen.

7. Print one final copy using draft or high text quality.

Exercise 4.4

1. The screen should be clear, and the disk drive should be accessed where the file disk is located.

2. Use AMS simplified letter style, page 42, and type the following letter.

3. Set the left and right margins to 1.5 inches and set the top margin to 2 inches.

4. Use left justification.

5. Use the speller to find and correct any incorrect words.

6. Use the filename **4fms.ltr**. Save the file and keep the file on the screen.

7. Print one final copy using medium text quality.

```
(Use current date)



Forsythe Mobile Service
P. O. Box 680
Sherwood, OR 97140


INVOICE NO. 4599


After my car was stolen last month, my mobile car
phone bill increased from $600 to $1200. I am
responsible for the bill and the additional roaming
charges that obviously were incurred from outside
the 408 area code.

I would like to pay approximately $150 per month
until my mobile car phone bill is paid. Please
advise me if this arrangement is acceptable. The
```

first payment could be made at the beginning of the
month.

Your consideration in this matter will be very much
appreciated.

SANDRA BOSTON, CORNERSTONE PRODUCTS

SB/xxx
fms.ltr/disk#5

Exercise 4.5

1. If necessary, load the WordPerfect program.

2. The screen should be clear (**F7**, **n**, **n**).

3. Type the following letter using the block style.

4. Use the speller to find and correct three spelling errors. Also
    correct two punctuation errors.

(Use current date)

Mr. and Mrs. John Villefort
489 Terrace Place
Lambertville, NJ 08530

Dear Mr. and Mrs. Villefort:

Prices of utility stocks have come under pressure
recently due to expectations of rising interest
rates, slowing of growth rates, and the potential
liability of some of the companies with uncompleted
nuclear power plants.

Our Research Department has issued an overview of
four selected companies believed to be attractive
at the current time based on total potential
return. Call our research director Marylee Perkins
to receive a complimentery copy of this report.

Remitance of the full purchase price will ensure
that the broker's fee will be waved! If you would
like additional information concerning timely

```
investment ideas please let me know.

Sincerely,



Erika Baldwin
Vice President, Investments

EB/xxx
villefrt.ltr/disk?
```

---

5. Use the filename **villefrt.ltr**. Save the file and keep the document on the screen.

6. Print one final copy using draft or high text quality.

7. Clear the screen.

Chapter 5

USE AUTOMATIC WORDPERFECT FUNCTIONS

OBJECTIVES

After successfully completing this chapter, you should be able to:

● Move text.

● Copy text.

● Search and replace text.

● Use hyphenation.

● Use a temporary left margin.

● Print a block of text.

Automatic functions are special WordPerfect features designed to efficiently replace text and/or rearrange text. Text can be moved, copied, hyphenated, and searched automatically. Automatic functions can include rearranging text by indenting all lines of a paragraph. Also, once a letter has been arranged, a portion of the document can be printed.

MOVE TEXT

Moving text is the process of relocating text. For example, a paragraph in the middle of the letter can be moved to the end of the letter. The paragraph is deleted in the middle of the letter and is relocated as the last paragraph. Paragraphs, sentences, and lines can be moved. Generally, once text has been typed, retyping the text should be unnecessary.

Procedure to Move Text

1. Place the cursor on the first character or code of the text to be moved. *Note:* The character can be a code such as a tab or return code. Reveal Codes (**Alt** and **F3**) to locate the cursor on the desired code.

2. Press and hold the **Alt** key while tapping the **F4** key (**Alt** and **F4**) {*Edit, Block*} to block.

3. Move the cursor to the end of the text to be moved, including an **Enter** or space(s). The text is highlighted. If a mistake is made, press **F1** to Cancel.

4. Press and hold the **Ctrl** key while tapping the **F4** key (**Ctrl** and **F4**) {*Edit, Move*} to Move. *Note:* If using the pull-down menus, skip to step 7.

5. Press **1** to Move Block.

6. Press **1** again to Move. *Note:* The text disappears from the screen and is remembered in the computer's memory.

7. A message is displayed: **Move cursor; press Enter to retrieve.**

8. Move the cursor to the location where the text is to be moved.

9. Press **Enter**. *Note:* The moved text is deleted from the original location and displayed in the new location.

Shortcut: *A sentence, paragraph, or page can be moved by using the* ***Ctrl*** *and* ***F4*** *keys:*

a.   *Place the cursor anywhere in the sentence, paragraph, or page to be moved.*
b.   *Press and hold the* ***Ctrl*** *key while tapping the* ***F4*** *key once.*
c.   *Press* ***s*** *for sentence,* ***p*** *for paragraph, or* ***a*** *for page.*
d.   *The sentence, paragraph, or page will display highlighted on the document screen.*
e.   *Press* ***1*** *to Move.*
f.   *Move the cursor to the location where the text is to be moved; press* ***Enter****.*

⇨ Retrieve the file named **4bdman.ltr** typed in Chapter 4, page 62. Move the second paragraph to become the first paragraph.

▷ Place the cursor on the first character of the second paragraph.

▷ Press **Alt** and **F4** to block.

▷ Press the **Enter** key *twice* to highlight the paragraph and the returns following the paragraph.

▷ Press **Ctrl** and **F4** to Move.

▷ Press **1** *twice*.

▷ Move the cursor to the first character of the first paragraph.

▷ Press the **Enter** key. The second paragraph is now the first paragraph.

▷ Use the filename **5move**. Save the file and keep the document on the screen.

▷ Print one final copy using medium text quality.

▷ Clear the screen (**F7, n, n**).

(Use current date)

Ms. Candace Boardman
Newcastle, Inc.
6300 Marina Ave. Ste. 40
Emeryville, CA 94608

Dear Ms. Boardman:

Per our conversation of last Tuesday, enclosed is a
remittance check for $300 on the disputed amount
owed on my bill.

It is understood that my line of service will be
reestablished. In the spirit of cooperation, $75
shall be waived by Newcastle as agreed by your
collection manager, Samuel Alexander.

Sincerely,

Fred Thompson

FT/xxx
bdman.ltr/disk#4

Enc.

COPY TEXT

Copying text is the process of duplicating text. For example, a document, sentence, name, or paragraph may need to be typed again on the page or in another part of the document. The text is copied from the original location and repeated in a second location.

Procedure to Copy Text

1. Place the cursor on the first character or code of the text to be copied. *Note:* The character can be a code such as a tab or return code. Reveal Codes (**Alt** and **F3**) to locate the cursor on the desired code.

2. Press and hold the **Alt** key while tapping the **F4** key (**Alt** and **F4**) to Block {*Edit, Block*}.

3. Move the cursor to the end of the text to be copied. The text is highlighted. If a mistake is made, press **F1** to Cancel.

4. Press and hold the **Ctrl** key while tapping the **F4** key (**Ctrl** and **F4**) to Move {*Edit, Copy*}. *Note:* If using the pull-down menus, skip to step 7.

5. Press **1** to Move Block.

6. Press **2** to Copy.

7. A message is displayed: **Move cursor; press Enter to retrieve**.

8. Move the cursor to the location where the text is to be copied.

9. Press **Enter**. *Note:* The copied text is displayed in the original location and in the new location.

*Shortcut: A sentence, paragraph, or page can be copied by using the **Ctrl** and **F4** keys:*

   a.   *Place the cursor anywhere in the sentence, paragraph, or page to be copied.*

   b.   *Press and hold the **Ctrl** key while tapping the **F4** key once.*

   c.   *Press **s** for sentence, **p** for paragraph, or **a** for page.*

   d.   *The sentence, paragraph, or page will display highlighted on the document screen.*

   e.   *Press **2** to copy.*

   f.   *Move the cursor to the location where the text is to be copied; press **Enter**.*

➯ Retrieve the memorandum file named **2memo4** typed in Chapter 2, page 31.

➯ Move the cursor to the end of the last paragraph. There should be three returns after your initials. If necessary, press the **Enter** key.

➯ Move the cursor to the top left corner of the memorandum.

➯ Copy the entire memorandum. (See Procedure to Copy Text, steps 1–7.)

➯ Press the **down** arrow key until the cursor will not move down any further.

➯ Press the **Enter** key to retrieve a second copy of the memo.

➯ Use the filename **5memo4r**. Save the file and keep the document on the screen.

➯ Print one copy using medium text quality.

➯ Clear the screen.

SEARCH AND REPLACE TEXT

When every occurrence of a word or group of words is to be changed, the search and replace function is used. Search and replace is the process of locating and deleting specific text and inserting new text. The text is searched for a specific word or group of words. Each occurrence of the word(s) is replaced automatically.

Procedure to Search and Replace Text

1. Place the cursor at the beginning of the text to be searched.

2. Press and hold the **Alt** key while tapping the **F2** key (**Alt** and **F2**) {*Search, Replace*}.

3. A prompt is displayed: **w/Confirm? No(Yes)**.

4. Press **n** for no.

5. A prompt is displayed: →**Srch:**.

6. Type the word or words to be searched. For example, type *GHL*.

7. Press **F2**.

| 8. | The prompt is displayed: **Replace with:**. |

| 9. | Type the word or words to replace the searched word(s). For example, type *Guaranteed Home Loans*. |

| 10. | Press **F2**. |

| 11. | The prompt is displayed briefly: **Please Wait**. |

| 12. | All occurrences of the word(s) will be changed automatically. |

| 13. | The cursor will move to the last word(s) that has been replaced. |

➪ Type the following paragraphs.

➪ Set vertical spacing to 2. (Optional)

```
        Today you can borrow on the equity in your
home. GHL makes it simple to receive extra money
for home improvements, a vacation, or a new car!
GHL can quickly process a home loan because:

    The application form is short
    Employment is verified by a paycheck stub
    Tax returns are not required
    No charge for appraisals

        GHL has been in business for over 30 years.
Qualifying for one of our home loans can take less
than 7 working days. The emphasis for qualifying is
placed on the property, not on your past credit
history. Contact our office today and let GHL
design an equity loan to meet your needs. GHL will
process your application immediately.
```

➪ Use the filename **5ghl**. Save the file and keep the paragraphs on the screen.

➪ Print one copy using draft text quality.

➪ Search for *GHL* and replace with *Guaranteed Home Loans*.

➪ Use the filename **5ghlsrch**. Save the file and keep the paragraphs on the screen.

➪ Print one copy using draft text quality.

After text has been typed, edited, and proofread, a decision can be made to make the lines at the right margin end more evenly. Hyphenation is the process of dividing a word between two lines in order to make the line endings more uniform.

Hyphenation can be turned on before typing text, or can be accomplished after a document is edited and printed once. Hyphenating after a document is typed and is being prepared for final form is recommended. However, automatic hyphenation can be used if desired. Automatic hyphenation is turned on before typing a document by using the format menu (**Shift** and **F8**). In addition, the selection "Never Prompt for Hyphenation" is chosen in the setup menu (see steps 1–5 in the Procedure to Hyphenate After Typing a Document).

Compound words, such as *brother-in-law*, use hard hyphens. A hard hyphen is a hyphen that tells WordPerfect to treat the compound word as one word and to hyphenate at the hyphen only if necessary. To place a hard hyphen in a compound word, press the **Home** key then press the **hyphen** key. Reveal Codes (**Alt** and **F3**) to view a hard hyphen code (-).

A soft hyphen is a code placed in a document by the keyboardist (typist) [press **Ctrl** and **hyphen** (-) keys for a soft hyphen code] or by WordPerfect. A soft hyphen code tells WordPerfect where to hyphenate a word if the word falls at the end of a line and requires hyphenation.

If the keyboardist does not agree with the location of a WordPerfect-placed hyphen, the soft hyphen is used. A soft hyphen code remains in a document even if the word does not need hyphenation. A soft hyphen does not display on the screen but is displayed when codes are revealed (**Alt** and **F3**). In reveal codes, a soft hyphen code is a highlighted hyphen and a hard hyphen is not a highlighted hyphen.

If WordPerfect places a hyphen in a word that you choose not to hyphenate, the hyphen can be canceled. A hyphen is canceled by placing the cursor on the first character of the hyphenated word, pressing the **Home** key, and then pressing the **slash** (/) key.

The hyphen character typed from the keyboard tells WordPerfect where you want a word hyphenated, if needed, even if Hyphenation is turned off. A typed hyphen character displays on the screen and prints in a word exactly where it is typed. If WordPerfect hyphenates a word at a hyphen character that you type, it does not use a soft hyphen code.

⇨ Type the following paragraphs.

⇨ Use the Procedure to Hyphenate After Typing a Document. Also, use the following guidelines to make accurate hyphenation decisions:

1. Hyphenate only between syllables—use a dictionary, if necessary.

2. Avoid hyphenating words of five characters or less.

3. Avoid hyphenating a word where only two characters are left on a line.

4. Place a hyphen after a vowel.

5. Place a hyphen between two of the same consonants.

6. Do not hyphenate the last word in a paragraph.

Note: Once a document has been checked for words that could be hyphenated, there may not be any words that actually were hyphenated.

```
            FEES FOR SERVICES RENDERED

The fee for services rendered is based on a
contractual relationship between the doctor and
patient and is not contingent upon the allowance an
insurance carrier provides for any such services.
However, in a case where a financial burden has
occurred, arrangements can be made to work out a
payment schedule which will be reasonable and fair
without creating hardships on patients.

Our policy is to collect full payment for surgery
one week before the operation. This policy is in
accordance with the recommendations of the
Association of American Surgeons. Failure to
receive the fee within one week of the scheduled
operation will automatically cancel the operation.

Patients are encouraged to inquire about costs.
Where possible, an estimate of the operative fee
will be given prior to scheduling the operation.

Many times a medical assistant in the doctor's
office will provide information regarding surgical
costs and explain the fee requirements. In
addition, a brochure published by the Association
of American Surgeons is available upon request.
```

Procedure to Hyphenate After Typing a Document

1. Place the cursor at the beginning of the document (press the **Home** key twice and press the **up** arrow key once).
   a. Press **Shift** and **F1** for setup.
   b. Press **3** for environment.
   c. Press **7** for Prompt for Hyphenation.
   d. Press **3** for "always." *Note:* Press **1** for "never" when using automatic hyphenation.
   e. Press **F7** to exit and return the cursor to the document screen.

2. Turn on hyphenation; press and hold the **Shift** key while tapping the **F8** key once (**Shift** and **F8**).

3. Press **1** for Line {*Layout, Line*}.

4. Press **1** for Hyphenation.

5. Press **y** for yes.

6. Press **F7** to exit and return the cursor to the document screen.

7. Suggested hyphenations may be displayed at the end of some lines.

8. Press the **down** arrow key until a beep is heard and/or a prompt is displayed at the bottom left of the screen. Any word that needs a hyphenation decision is displayed at the bottom of the screen.

9. Move the cursor to locate the hyphen at the desired position. Press **Esc**. For example, if the cursor is located under the hyphen between the "n" and "s" in "relation-ship," press **Esc** to accept the hyphen position. If the hyphen is not desired, press **F1** (to Cancel). When the codes are revealed (**Alt** and **F3**) a [/] code is displayed before the word that was chosen for no hyphenation.

10. Once the **Esc** or **F1** is pressed, the next word that needs a hyphenation decision is displayed.

11. Repeat step 9 until no hyphenation prompt displays at the bottom of the screen.

▷ Use the filename **5fees**. Save the file and keep the document on the screen.

▷ Print one copy using draft text quality.

```
                        Swimming Pool Rules


     1.    Swimmers should familiarize  themselves with the depths
           of the water.

     2.    Remove barrettes, metal clips, and bobby pins from hair
           before swimming.

     3.    No running, pushing, or shoving is permitted inside the
           fenced pool area.

     4.    Guests  at the  pool must  be limited to  house guests.
           Residents  must  accompany  guests  to  the  pool.   On
           holidays residents may bring a limit of 2 guests to the
           pool.

     5.    Residents can  receive one  key per  home for use  when
           entering the  fenced pool area.  The  key shall be used
           only by residents and their house guests.

     6.    All refuse must be deposited in  the containers located
           on the  left  side  of the  clubhouse.   Non-breakable
           containers only can be used at the pool side.
```

EXHIBIT 5.1   Temporary indent

TEMPORARY LEFT MARGIN

Text can be arranged by indenting all lines of a paragraph automatically from the left margin. Also, text that follows an enumerated item can be indented to align the following lines with the text of the enumerated items. See Exhibit 5.1. The temporary left margin (also called temporary indent) indents all paragraph lines at the same tab. Generally, when all lines are indented from the left margin, the first tab is used. The temporary indent remains in effect until the **Enter** key is pressed.

Procedure to Use a Temporary Left Margin

1. Use the preset tab for the temporary left margin.

2. Press the **F4** key to begin the temporary margin (indent) {*Layout, Align, Indent*}.

3. Type the text to be indented.

4. Once the **Enter** key is pressed, the cursor will return to the original left margin.

⇨ Type the enumerated items in Exhibit 5.1.

⇨ Press the **F4** (indent) key after typing the period following the number.

⇨ Use the filename **5indent**. Save the file and keep the document on the screen.

⇨ Print one copy using draft text quality.

PRINT A BLOCK OF TEXT

Once a document has been typed, a portion of the text can be printed. The text to be printed is blocked, highlighted, and given an instruction to print.

Procedure to Print a Block of Text

Note: The printer should be ready for printing.

1. Place the cursor on the first character or code of the text to be block printed. *Note:* The character can be a code such as a tab or return code. Reveal Codes (**Alt** and **F3**) to locate the cursor on the desired code.

2. Press and hold the **Alt** key while tapping the **F4** key once (**Alt** and **F4**) {*Edit, Block*}.

3. Move the cursor to the end of the text to be printed. As the cursor is moved, the text is highlighted.

4. Press and hold the **Shift** key while tapping the **F7** key once (**Shift** and **F7**) {*File, Print*}.

5. A prompt is displayed: **Print block? No(Yes)**.

6. Press **y** for yes.

7. A **Please Wait** message is briefly displayed.

8. The partial text will print. *Note:* If the paragraph is in the middle of the page, the block will print in the middle of the paper.

⇨ Clear the screen (**Shift** and **F7**, **n**, **n**).

⇨ Retrieve the file named **5ghl**.

⇨ Block print the last paragraph.

SUMMARY

- Moving text is the process of repositioning text. Text is deleted in one location and moved to another location in the document (Block the text to be moved, **Ctrl** and **F4**, **1**, **1**).

- Copying text is the process of duplicating text. Text is copied from one location and is reproduced in another location in the document (Block the text to be moved, **Ctrl** and **F4**, **1**, **2**).

- Searching and replacing text is the process of finding word(s) and substituting different word(s) (**Alt** and **F2**, **n**, type word(s) to be found, **F2**, type new word(s) to be used, **F2**).

- Hyphenation is the process of dividing a word between two lines. Use the hyphenation procedure after typing a document if the lines at the right margin appear quite uneven (**Home** twice, **up** arrow key once, **Shift** and **F1**, **3**, **7**, **3**, **F7**, **Shift** and **F8**, **1**, **1**, **y**, **F7**).

- The temporary left margin is a tab used as a margin. All lines will indent at the tab location until the **Enter** key is pressed (**F4**).

- Printing a block of text is the process of printing a portion of a document (**Alt** and **F4**, move cursor to end of text to be printed, **Shift** and **F7**, **y**).

SELF-CHECK QUESTIONS

(True / False—Circle One)

T,F   1. Hyphenation is an example of an automatic function.

T,F   2. Moving text is the process of duplicating text.

T,F   3. Once text has been copied, the copied information is located in two locations.

T,F   4. The **F2** key is used to move and/or copy text.

T,F   5. Before text is copied or moved, the text is blocked and highlighted.

T,F   6. To begin the search and replace function, press **Alt** and **F4**.

T,F   7. A temporary indent refers to a temporary margin.

T,F 8. Hyphenation can be turned on before or after typing a document.

T,F 9. One paragraph from a document can be blocked and printed.

T,F 10. The **Shift** and **F8** keys are used to display the Format menu in order to turn hyphenation on; press **2** to select page; press **1** for hyphenation.

ENRICHING LANGUAGE ARTS SKILLS

Spelling / Vocabulary Words

template a plate designed to be used as a guide; in computers, a template overlays portions of the keyboard and gives names for the functions assigned to the various keys.
humidity damp and muggy air.
magnetic having magnetic properties; can be attracted by a magnet.

Compound Adjectives

Hyphenate two words that precede and describe a noun and function as a single adjective.

Example The designer sent a well-defined sample of the proposed meeting area.

EXERCISES

Exercise 5.1

1. The screen should be clear, and the disk drive should be accessed where the file disk is located.

2. Retrieve the file named **5fees**.

3. Search for the word fee and replace with CHARGE.

4. Use the filename **5exer1**. Save the file and keep the document on the screen.

5. Print one copy of all paragraphs using draft and high text quality.

6. Block and print one copy of the last paragraph.

Exercise 5.2

1. The screen should be clear, and the disk drive should be accessed where the file disk is located.

2. Use block letter style, page 36, and type the following letter.

3. Use the defaulted margins.

4. Use the temporary indent and indent the paragraphs as shown.

5. After the letter is typed, turn on the automatic hyphenation. *Note:* No hyphens may be needed.

6. Use the filename **5banks.ltr**. Save the file and keep the document on the screen.

7. Print one copy using draft high text quality.

```
(Use current date)



Ms. Elizabeth Banks
Optical Systems
808 E. Capital Blvd.
Rocklin, CA 95678

Dear Ms. Banks:

After speaking with Don Lyon yesterday, he
suggested that I write to you concerning the
low-cost personal computer templates available for
the PC keyboard.

Personal computer templates make a user comfortable
and confident when using a keyboard. Templates are
a tool that make software simple to operate.

    Enclosed are sample templates for your review.
    The plastic template has been popular with many
    personal computer users.

    The template is inexpensive and easy to use.

    With eight years of experience and over 70
    software publishers as clients, we are the
    experts for quality-keyboard template products.

After you have reviewed the sample templates,
please feel free to contact me. I will call you at
```

the beginning of next week to discuss your
questions or comments.

Sincerely,

Jean Crim
Director of Marketing

JC/xxx
banks.ltr/d8

Encs.

Exercise 5.3

1. Retrieve the file named **5indent** (Swimming Pool Rules).

2. Block and copy the entire file. Place the copied file approximately three lines below the original document. (Two copies of the file will be placed on one page.)

3. Use the filename **5copy3**. Save the file and keep the document on the screen.

4. Print one copy using draft or high text quality.

Exercise 5.4

1. The screen should be clear, and the disk drive should be accessed where the file disk is located.

2. Type the following paragraphs.

3. Use the defaulted margins.

4. Use the temporary indent to indent the enumerated items.

5. Use the filename **5disk4**. Save the file and keep the document on the screen.

6. Print one copy using draft or high text quality.

                    Diskette Care and Handling

1. Carefully insert the diskette into the disk
   drive. Avoid forcing the diskette into the

```
   drive.

2. Write on the label with a felt tip pen. A ball
   point pen can be used to write on a label before
   placing the label on the diskette.

3. Keep the diskette from extreme temperatures and
   humidity and shade the diskette from direct
   sunlight.

4. A magnetic field will erase the information
   stored on a diskette.

5. When storing the diskette, use the protection
   cover. Keep diskettes in an upright position
   inside a storage container.

6. Touch the diskette protection cover only. Do not
   touch the exposed portions of the diskette.
```

7. The file named **5disk4** should be displaying on the screen.

8. Move the items as shown. *Note:* Do not renumber the items now.

9. Use the filename **5disk4r**. Save the file and keep the file on the screen.

10. Print one copy using draft text quality.

```
              Diskette Care and Handling

1. Carefully insert the diskette into the disk
   drive. Avoid forcing the diskette into the
   drive.

2. Write on the label with a felt tip pen. A ball
   point pen can be used to write on a label before
   placing the label on the diskette.

3. Keep the diskette from extreme temperatures and
   humidity and shade diskette from direct
   sunlight.

4. A magnetic field will erase the information
   stored on a diskette.

5. When storing the diskette, use the protection
   cover. Keep diskettes in an upright position
   inside a storage container.

6. Touch the protection cover only. Do not touch
   the exposed portions of the diskette.
```

11. Renumber the items.

12. Print one copy using draft or high text quality.

Exercise 5.5

1. The screen should be clear, and the disk drive should be accessed where the file disk is located.

2. Type the following paragraphs as shown.

3. Correct one spelling error and four grammatical errors.

```
            WORDPERFECT 5.0 TO 5.1 UPDATE

Many features for WordPerfect's word processing
program have been upgraded and enhanced with the
version 5.1. Following are items that are available
with the 5.1 program.

1. A mouse can be used to display pull-down menus,
   make selections for menu items, position the
   cursor in text, scroll through documents, and
   block text.

2. Pull down menus can be accessed by pressing the
   Alt and equals (=) keys.

3. Fractions can be entered for measurements. For
   example, when entering a left margin of .5
   inches, the fraction 1/2 can be typed. When the
   Enter key is pressed the fraction is
   automatically changed to the decimal form.

4. The reveal code screen can be set to display
   more or fewer lines on the screen by uttilizing
   the set up menu (Shift and F1).

5. Tabs are relative, i.e., tabs "float" in relation
   to the left margin. If tabs are set every fourth
   space from the left margin and the left margin
   is changed, the tabs will remain set every
   fourth space from the left margin.

6. Selected pages can be chosen to print from
   within the print menu (Shift and F7).

7. Tables can be created with rows and columns
   similar to a spreadsheet. A table can be
   centered horizontally and vertically. (See
   Chapters 7 and 8.)

8. Labels can be prepared easily by selecting from
   preset Avery size labels for the label "Paper/size
   type." (See Chapter 11.)
```

---

4. Use the filename **5exer5**. Save the file and keep the document on the screen.

5. Use print procedure **2** and print one copy using draft or high text quality.

6. Clear the screen.

Chapter 6

CREATE A RÉSUMÉ

OBJECTIVES

After successfully completing this chapter, you should be able to:

- Boldface text.
- Underline text.
- Understand relative and absolute tabs.
- Clear all tabs and set tabs.
- Control horizontal spaces (hard spaces).
- Change text from upper- to lowercase letters.
- Create special characters (compose).

A résumé is a document that summarizes a person's education, work experience, and work skills. A résumé is submitted to a prospective employer when applying for a job. WordPerfect features such as boldfacing and underlining are used to emphasize a heading, date, or work experience information. See Exhibit 6.1.

BOLDFACE

Boldface prints the words darker on the page as compared to other printed words. (See Exhibit 6.1.) The boldface instruction is placed in the document before and after the text to be printed in bold. Text that is to be printed in bold will be displayed highlighted or in a color on the screen. When the document is printed, the designated text will print in boldface.

Résumé
Randy Benham
1505 Clayton Road
San Jose, CA 95127
Telephone: (408) 275-1022

↓ 3

EDUCATIONAL BACKGROUND

↓ 2

San Jose City College
    Studied air conditioning and refrigeration, air distribution,
    controls, solar energy, chemistry, and algebra.

↓ 2

Completed the Carrier Operating and Maintenance Training Course
Received certificates for the following seminars:
    Reciprocating Compressors
    Centrifugal Compressors
    Hydronics

↓ 3

WORK EXPERIENCE

↓ 2

City of San Jose, San Jose, California--October 1986-Present
    Air Conditioning Department--Tony Preston, Supervisor
        Install, operate, adjust, troubleshoot, and maintain heat-
        ing, ventilation, refrigeration, and cooling systems.

↓ 2

G. J. Yamas Company, South San Francisco, California--
October 1984-October 1986
    Service Department--Barry Simpson, Supervisor
        Diagnose, modify, install, and repair all types of HVAC con-
        trols systems.

↓ 2

Marriott's Great America, February 1983-October 1984
    Plumbing Department--Gary Potter, Supervisor
        Troubleshoot, repair, and maintain HVAC systems.

↓ 3

REFERENCES

↓ 2

Mr. Terry Rainer, Supervisor
Air Conditioning Department
San Jose Airport, San Jose, California
(408) 288-0044

↓ 2

Mr. Marcus Scott, Owner
Clarin Mechanic, Co.
Santa Clara, California
(408) 255-7600

EXHIBIT 6.1 Résumé

Procedure to Boldface Before Typing Text

1. Press the **F6** key to turn on boldface.

2. Type the text to be printed in boldface. On some monitors the text is displayed brighter on the screen; on a color monitor the text is displayed in a color.

3. Press the **F6** key again to turn off boldface.

4. To view the boldface codes, press **Alt** and **F3** to display the Reveal Codes. The word **[BOLD]** is displayed in all capital letters on the left side of the text and the word **[bold]** is displayed in lowercase letters on the right side of the text to be printed in boldface. (To delete a pair of codes, place the cursor on either code and press **DEL**.)

Procedure to Boldface After Typing Text

1. Place the cursor on the first character of the text to be printed in boldface.

2. Press **Alt** and **F4** to block {*Edit, Block*}.

3. Move the cursor to the end of the text to be printed in bold. *Note:* The text will be highlighted.

4. Press **F6** to boldface the highlighted text.

Note: On some monitors the text to be printed in bold is displayed brighter on the screen. On a color monitor the text to be printed in bold is displayed in a color.

UNDERLINE

Words are underlined in printed text to show emphasis. In a résumé, side headings, titles, or dates can be underlined. The underline instruction is given before and after text to be underlined. The text displays underlined on the screen or in a different color.

The underline instruction can be given before text is typed or after text is typed. Press **F8** to turn underline on and off.

Procedure to Underline Before Typing Text

1. Press the **F8** key before the text to be underlined.

2. Type the text to be underlined.

3. Press the **F8** key after the text to be underlined.

4. To view the underline codes, press **Alt** and **F3** to display the Reveal Codes. The abbreviation **[UND]** is displayed in all capital letters on the left side of the text and the abbreviation **[und]** is displayed in lowercase letters on the right side of the text to be underlined.

Procedure to Underline After Typing Text

1. Place the cursor on the first character of the text to be underlined.

2. Press **Alt** and **F4** to Block {*Edit, Block*}.

3. Move the cursor to the end of the text to be underlined. *Note:* The text will be highlighted.

4. Press **F8**.

5. Text is displayed underlined or in a color.

Note: Text to be printed in bold and underlined is displayed in a color that is different from the colors used to display the text to be printed in bold or underlined.

TABS

Tabs are preset (defaulted) every one-half inch. If desired, tabs can be changed to indent information at a position other than the position preset by the WordPerfect program. The defaulted tabs can be cleared and new tabs set. When using the indent feature, the lines of the paragraph are indented automatically from the left margin until the **Enter** key is pressed.

There are two types of tabs: relative and absolute. The default is for relative tabs that are measured from the left margin. If the left margin is changed, *the distance between the left margin and set tabs will always remain the same.* For example, the left margin begins at zero and a tab is set at 1.5 inches from the left margin. The distance between the left margin zero (0) and tab is 1.5 inches. If the left margin is changed to .8 inch, the tab will be set at 2.3 inches (.8 + 1.5 = 2.3). The distance between the left margin and tab remains at 1.5 (2.3 − .8 = 1.5).

An absolute tab is measured from the left edge of the page. If the left margin is changed, *the distance between the left margin and set tabs will change.* For example, the left margin begins at zero and a tab is set at 1.5 inches from the left edge of the paper. The

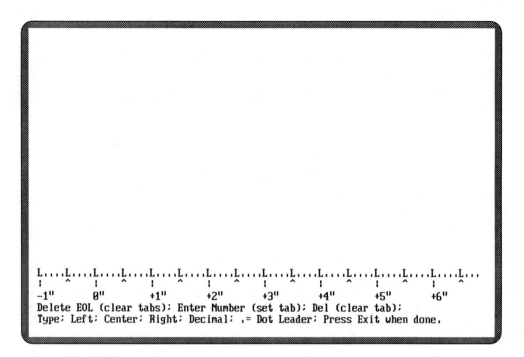

L....L....L....L....L....L....L....L....L....L....L....L....L....L....L...
!   ^   !   ^   !   ^   !   ^   !   ^   !   ^   !   ^   !   ^
-1"   0"   +1"   +2"   +3"   +4"   +5"   +6"
Delete EOL (clear tabs); Enter Number (set tab); Del (clear tab);
Type; Left; Center; Right; Decimal; .= Dot Leader; Press Exit when done.

EXHIBIT 6.2   Tab menu

distance between the left margin and set tab is 1.5 (1.5 − .0 = 1.5). If the left margin is changed to .8 inches, the tab setting remains at 1.5 inches. Note that the distance between the new left margin (.8 inches) and the tab set at 1.5 inches has changed to .7 (1.5 − .8 = .7).

In the Tab set menu, the selection called "Type" sets tabs as absolute or relative. The type of tab is changed by pressing **t** for type, **1** for absolute or **2** for relative to margin.

Tabs are set in a document where the cursor is located. If tabs are changed, the new tabs are in effect from the location of the cursor to the remainder of the document or until the tabs are changed again. For example, if the cursor is located at the beginning of the fourth paragraph in a document and tabs are changed, the tabs are effective for the fourth and following paragraphs and are not effective for the first three paragraphs.

Procedure to Clear All Tabs and Set Tabs

1. Press and hold the **Shift** key while tapping the **F8** key once (**Shift** and **F8**).

2. Press **1** for Line {*Layout, Line*}.

3. Press **8** for Tab set. The tab menu is displayed on the screen. (See Exhibit 6.2.)

4. Press the **Home** key twice; press the **left** arrow key once to move the cursor to the left side of the tab line. Notice that tabs are set beginning at minus 1 inch (−1″) every ½ inch (0.5″).

5. Press and hold the **Ctrl** key while tapping the **End** key once to clear all tabs (**Ctrl** and **End**). *Note:* The tab menu displays "Delete **EOL**" (clear tabs). This refers to pressing **Ctrl** and **End** (**EOL**—end of line).

6. All **L**'s will clear from the Tab menu.

7. There are four types of tabs: left, center, right, and decimal; only the left and decimal tabs will be used in this book.
   a. To set a left tab, type the position number desired; press **Enter**. For example, type 0.5; press **Enter**. Repeat for setting additional left tabs. *Note:* If a mistake is made, place the cursor on the **L** and press the **Del** key.
   b. To set a decimal tab, type the position number desired; press **Enter**. Then press **d** to convert the "L" to a decimal tab. Repeat for setting additional decimal tabs.

8. Press the **F7** key twice to exit the tab line and return the cursor to the document screen.

   *Note: Reveal Codes (**Alt** and **F3**) to check the tab settings. For example, the code [**Tab Set: Rel: + 0.5″, + 1″**] is displayed on the screen.*

HARD SPACES

Sometimes two words or numbers are dependent on each other for a complete thought and should be printed on the same line. The horizontal space that binds the words together can be required. A required space is called a hard space. An additional keystroke is pressed to instruct the program to keep the words on the same line.

Procedure to Control Horizontal Spaces

1. While typing, the cursor is on the space to be required.

2. Press the **Home** key once; then press the **Space bar** once.

3. Reveal Codes (**Alt** and **F3**) {*Edit, Reveal Codes*}; the [ ] symbol is displayed to indicate that the space is a hard space.

Note: If the words and space have already been typed: place the cursor on the space; press the **Ins** key to turn on typeover; follow step 2.

UPPER-/LOWERCASE CHANGE

After text has been typed in all capital letters (uppercase), the WordPerfect program can automatically change the text to lowercase characters. Also, text that has been typed in all lowercase characters can automatically be changed to uppercase characters.

Procedure to Change Characters from Upper- to Lowercase and Lower- to Uppercase

1. Place the cursor on the first character of the text to be changed.

2. Press and hold the **Alt** and **F4** keys {*Edit, Block*}.

3. Move the cursor to the end of the text to be printed in uppercase.

4. Press and hold the **Shift** key while tapping the **F3** key once.

5. The prompt is displayed: **1 Uppercase; 2 Lowercase: 0**.

6. Press **1** to change the text to uppercase; press **2** to change the text to lowercase; press **F1** to cancel. If **F1** is pressed, press **Alt** and **F4** to turn off block.

SPECIAL CHARACTERS

The diacritical mark that is printed above the letter *e* in the word *résumé* can be created by the WordPerfect program. Once the instructions for the diacritical mark have been given, most printers will automatically print the appropriate mark. WordPerfect refers to the special character's feature as *compose.*

Procedure to Create Special Characters

1. Press and hold the **Ctrl** key while tapping the **2** key once (**Ctrl** and **2**). Nothing is displayed on the screen.

2. Type the first character; type the second character. For example, type *e*, then type the apostrophe. *Note:* Some monitors do not display the diacritical mark on the screen. Also, some printers will not print the diacritical mark.

➩ Type the résumé shown in Exhibit 6.1.

➩ Clear all tabs. Set tabs at 0.5 and 1.0. Use the temporary indent feature for indenting paragraphs, as shown.

➩ Use the defaulted margins.

➩ Use left justification.

➩ Use bold, underline, all capital letters, and special characters as shown.

➩ Use the filename **6presume**. Save the file without clearing the screen.

➩ Print one copy using draft or high text quality.

SUMMARY

- A résumé is a summary of an individual's employment and educational background. A résumé is submitted to a prospective employer.

- Boldface prints characters or words darker on the paper as compared to other printed words. Generally, a dot matrix printing element will move twice over the characters to be made bold (**F6**).

- The underline instruction can be turned on before typing text or can be accomplished after the text is typed. All words and spaces are underlined until the underline instruction is turned off (**F8** to turn on and off).

- Tabs are defaulted every one-half inch. Tabs are changed where the cursor is located in the document when new tabs are set. The changed tabs are in effect throughout the remainder of the document, unless the tabs are changed again (**Shift** and **F8**, **1**, **8**, type position number, **F7** twice). One of two tab types can be selected: absolute or relative. A relative tab (the default) measures a tab from the left margin. If the left margin is changed, the distance between the left margin and tabs will remain the same. An absolute tab measures a tab from the left edge of the paper. If the left margin is changed, the distance between the left margin and set tabs will change.

- Hard spaces are required spaces used to bind words together so the words will print on the same line (**Home, space bar**).

- Changing from one case to another can be accomplished automatically. First the text is blocked, then the command is given to change the letter case (**Shift** and **F3**, **1** for uppercase or **2** for lowercase).

- Special characters such as diacritical marks use special instructions because the letter and diacritical mark are printed on the same vertical line space (**Ctrl** and **2**, type the letter, type the diacritical mark).

SELF-CHECK QUESTIONS

(True / False—Circle One)

T,F 1. A résumé is a summary of an individual's prior employment experience and educational background.

T,F 2. Boldface can be turned on before or after text is typed.

T,F 3. Press **F5** to turn on boldface.

T,F 4. To underline text that has already been typed, first block and highlight the text, then press **F8**.

T,F 5. Tabs are defaulted every inch.

T,F 6. Once the tab menu is displayed on the screen, all tabs can be cleared by pressing the **Home** key twice, pressing the **left** arrow key once, and pressing the **Ctrl** and **End** keys.

T,F 7. A hard space is used to bind words together.

T,F 8. Changing from uppercase to lowercase letters or vice versa is accomplished by using the **Ctrl** and **F3** keys.

T,F 9. A special character such as a diacritical mark is created by pressing **Ctrl** and **2** before typing the characters to be used.

T,F 10. All monitors will display the diacritical mark on the screen.

ENRICHING LANGUAGE ARTS SKILLS

Spelling / Vocabulary Words

computer programming   writing a list of instructions that tell the computer what to do.

microcomputer application a program written for the computer that performs specific functions such as word processing.

oscilloscope a device that displays electron motion on a screen.

Commas Used in a Series

Words and/or ideas listed in a series are separated by commas.

Example The mailing list was sent to Karen Smith, Georgia Cain, and Perry Arnston.

EXERCISES

Exercise 6.1

1. The screen should be clear, and the disk drive should be accessed where the file disk is located.

2. Type the following résumé.

3. Clear all tabs. Set a tab at 0.5 inches. Use the temporary indent feature for indenting paragraphs after each side heading as shown.

4. Use the 1-inch defaulted margins.

5. Use left justification.

6. Use bold, underline, all capital letters, and special characters as shown.

7. Use the filename **6resume1**. Save the file without clearing the screen.

8. Print one copy using draft or high text quality.

Résumé
Michelle Seals
125 Rose Park Rd.
Santa Rosa, CA 95401
Telephone: (415) 899-8055

EDUCATIONAL BACKGROUND

Santa Rosa Junior College
Studied *computer programming* courses;
microcomputer application courses; and business
administration courses.

Computer Learning Center
Obtained a certificate in computer programming.

WORK EXPERIENCE

Santa Rosa College, Santa Rosa, California--
October 1986-1988
Teacher's aide--duties included assisting in the
teaching of business application programs, *such
as WordStar, Lotus 1-2-3, and dBase III.*

College of San Mateo, San Mateo, California--
June 1985-June 1986
Lab assistant--Computer Science Lab.

Peninsula Oil Co., San Francisco, California--
May 1984-May 1985
Inventory control manager--duties included
opening office, balancing daily receipts, and
correcting all invoices. Handled sales and
customer services and controlled all incoming
inventory and restocking.

REFERENCES

Mr. Terry Martin, Instructor
Santa Rosa College, Microcomputer Lab
Santa Rosa, CA 95401
(415) 355-1002

Ms. Mary Scott, Supervisor
Peninsula Oil Co.
San Francisco, CA 95132
(415) 555-7400

Exercise 6.2

1.   If necessary, retrieve **6resume1**.

2.   Make the corrections as shown.

3.   Use the filename **6resume1.rev**. Save the file without clearing the screen.

4.   Print one copy using draft or high text quality.

```
                        Résumé
                    Michelle Seals
                    125 Rose Park Rd.
                    Santa Rosa, CA 95401
                 Telephone: (415) 899-8055  9866
```

EDUCATIONAL BACKGROUND

Santa Rosa Junior College, -- *September 1986 - June 1988*
    Studied *computer Programming* courses;
    microcomputer application courses; and business
    administration courses.

Computer Learning Center, -- *July 1984-May 1985*
    Obtained a certificate in computer programming/
    with an emphasis in COBOL and BASIC.

WORK EXPERIENCE

Santa Rosa College, Santa Rosa, California--October
1986-1988
    Teacher's aide--duties included assisting in the
    teaching of business application programs, such
    as WordStar, Lotus 1-2-3, and dBase III/, and
    SmartCom.
College of San Mateo, San Mateo, California--June
1985-June 1986
    Lab assistant--Computer Science Lab.

Peninsula Oil Co., San Francisco, California--May
1984-May 1985
    Inventory control manager--duties included
    opening office, balancing daily receipts, and
    correcting all invoices. Handled sales and
    customer services and controlled all incoming
    inventory and restocking.

REFERENCES

Mr. Terry Martin, Instructor
Santa Rosa College, Microcomputer Lab

```
Santa Rosa, CA 95401
(415) 355-1002

Ms. Mary Scott, Supervisor
Peninsula Oil Co.
San Francisco, CA 95132
(415) 555-7400
```

Mrs. Carla Langley,
Professor
College of San Mateo
1700 W. Hillsdale
Blvd.
San Mateo, CA
94402
(415) 574-6000

Exercise 6.3

1. The screen should be clear, and the disk drive should be accessed where the file disk is located.

2. Type the following résumé.

3. Clear all tabs. Set a tab at 0.5 inches. Use the temporary indent feature for indenting paragraphs as shown.

4. Use the 1-inch defaulted margins.

5. Use left justification.

6. Use bold, underline, all capital letters, and special characters as shown.

7. Use the filename **6resume2**. Save the file without clearing the screen.

8. Print one copy using draft or high text quality.

```
                    Résumé
                  Carl Barton
                45 Fredrick Court
                Belmont, CA 94002


EDUCATIONAL BACKGROUND

San Jose City College
    Studied microcomputer courses--WordPerfect,
    MS/DOS, Telecommunications, and Desktop
    Publishing.

City College of Chicago
    Obtained a Certificate in Basic programming.

Completed U.S. Navy correspondence course.


WORK EXPERIENCE

U.S. Navy--4 years
    Have experience as a member of the flight crew
```

```
    for the P3 Orion; also worked as a ship board
    navigator, and computer operator.

Kentucky Fried Chicken--1 year
    Managed employees, handled inventory, and
    supervised kitchen operations.

Stanford Linear Accelerator--1 year
    Operated a 20-ton forklift, oscilloscope, and
    vacuum systems and was a machine operator.


REFERENCES

Available upon request.
```

Exercise 6.4

1. If necessary, retrieve **6resume2**.

2. Make the corrections as shown.

3. Use the filename **6resume2.rev**. Save the file without clearing the screen.

4. Print one copy using draft or high text quality.

```
                          Résumé
                        Carl Barton
                      45 Fredrick Court
                      Belmont, CA 94002


EDUCATIONAL BACKGROUND

San Jose City College        -- September 1989 - September 1990
    Studied microcomputer courses--WordPerfect,
    MS/DOS, Telecommunications, and Desktop
    Publishing.
                              -- February 1987 - December 1988
City College of Chicago       BASIC and FORTRAN  languages
    Obtained a Certificate in Basic programming.

Completed U.S. Navy correspondence course ✓ with
an emphasis in computer applications.

WORK EXPERIENCE

U.S. Navy--4 years
    Have experience as a member of the flight crew
    for the P3 Orion; also worked as a ship board
    navigator, and computer operator.

Kentucky Fried Chicken--1 year
    Managed employees, handled inventory, and
```

supervised⋎kitchen operations.
                all
<u>Stanford Linear Accelerator</u>--1 year
    Operated a 20-ton forklift, *oscilloscope*, and
    vacuum systems and was a machine operator.

REFERENCES

Available upon request.

_____

Exercise 6.5

1. The screen should be clear, and the disk drive should be
    accessed where the file disk is located.

2. Use the defaulted tabs and margins.

3. Use left justification.

4. Use bold, underline, all capital letters, and special characters
    as shown and type the following résumé.

5. Correct two spelling errors and three punctuation errors.

_____

                        Résumé
                    Kecia Howerton
                    166 Vine Street
                    Atlanta, GA 30314
                    (404) 388-2990

EDUCATION

Manhattan College--Graduated May 1990
    Studied micrcomputer applications--Lotus, dBase
    IV, Word and Ventura. Also studied BASIC, PASCAL
    and C programing languages.

EXPERIENCE

GTE Service Corporation--Summer Intern, 1989
    Project consisted of working with a small group
    of individuals to put together a computer-based
    Vertical Services costing model used to develop
    costs of new company telephone service.

Phoenix Fields Research--June 1988-May 1989 (Part-
time)
    Responsible for interviewing prospective panel
    members for the firm. Handled public relations
    as a hostess and supervised numerous focus
    groups.

Chemical Bank in IBM--June 1987-August 1987

Cashed checks, gave cash advances, and was
responsible for keeping accurate records
particularly for the vault and Automatic Teller
Machine.

ACTIVITIES

Member of the Voyagers Club the Newton Math
Society, and Tau Sigma Kappa (Computer Honor
Society).

REFERENCES

Available upon request.

---

6. Use the filename **6resume5**. Save the file and keep the document on the screen.

7. Use print procedure 2 and print one copy with high text quality.

8. Clear the screen.

Chapter 7

CREATE A TABLE

OBJECTIVES

After successfully completing this chapter, you should be able to:

● Create a table using the table editor.

● Align decimals by formatting.

● Center a table horizontally between left and right margins.

● Omit all table lines.

● Decrease cell size.

● Create a table with a title and column headings.

CREATE A TABLE

Creating a table is accomplished by using the table editor. The table editor creates rows and columns, similar to a spreadsheet, called a grid. (See Exhibit 7.1.) The columns are identified by letters, for example, A, B, C, and the rows are identified by numbers, for example, 1, 2, 3, etc.

The intersection of a column and row is called a cell. The cell address is the column and row where the cursor is located. The cell address is displayed on the status line. (See Exhibit 7.1.) If the cursor is located in the second column (B) and the third row, the cell location is B3. The cell address of the top left corner cell (A1) is "home." The table editor screen is obtained by pressing **Alt** and **F7**.

The outside lines of the table grid are created as double lines. The horizontal and vertical lines inside the table grid are single lines. The table lines are printed as displayed on the screen but can be changed by using the table editor.

```
┌─────────────┬─────────────┬─────────────┐
│             │             │             │
├─────────────┼─────────────┼─────────────┤
│             │             │             │
├─────────────┼─────────────┼─────────────┤
│             │             │             │
└─────────────┴─────────────┴─────────────┘




Table Edit:  Press Exit when done        Cell A1 Doc 1 Pg 1 Ln 1.14" Pos 1.12"
─────────────────────────────────────────────────────────────────────────────
Ctrl-Arrows Column Widths; Ins Insert; Del Delete; Move Move/Copy;
1 Size; 2 Format; 3 Lines; 4 Header; 5 Math; 6 Options; 7 Join; 8 Split: 0
```

EXHIBIT 7.1 Table editor

Any cell line (top, bottom, left, or right) can be set for single, double, dashed, dotted, thick, or no lines. To change the lines for one or more cells, highlight the cells(s), select Lines, choose the desired line(s) (top, bottom, etc.), and then select the type of line (single, dashed, etc.)

The column width of each cell varies depending on the number of columns created. The column width can be increased or decreased. The same amount of space should be placed between each column. For example, place one-half inch between the longest line in one column and the beginning of the next column. Changing the column width is accomplished by visually estimating the distance between columns while pressing the **Ctrl** and **left** or **right** arrow keys.

A table should be positioned horizontally centered on a page. Using Options in the table editor, the table can be centered horizontally. Also, by selecting the "Full" position, the table will be adjusted to "fill" the space between the left and right margins (i.e., the left column will begin at the left margin and the right column will end at the right margin).

The table editor is used to create, edit, and/or structure the cells such as changing or omitting table lines, totaling columns, moving columns, and inserting or deleting columns and rows. Exit the table editor (**F7**) to return the cursor to the normal editing screen. The normal editing screen is used to type text and figures in the cells. Also, any changes to the actual text and figures in the cells is accomplished while the cursor is located in the normal editing screen.

The table is defaulted to print with vertical line spacing of two. The spacing can be changed to single spacing by using Options; press **1** for space between text and lines, type zero for top, press **Enter** and **F7**. The table also displays on the screen with vertical line spacing of two. However, if the space between text and lines is changed to a zero top, the table prints with no space between lines. When the table is viewed through the Print menu (**Shift** and **F7**, **v**), the table is displayed with no space between lines.

▷ Use the Procedure to Create a Table and create a table with 3 columns and 4 rows.

▷ Type the following unformatted table text and figures. Remember that all text and figures are typed at the left of the cell—formatting will be accomplished later using the table editor.

▷ During the formatting process, you will:
    a.   Align figures at the decimal.
    b.   Omit all table lines.
    c.   Position the table to be centered horizontally.
    d.   Visually estimate and adjust the column widths to place one-half inch between columns.

Procedure to Create a Table

1. Press and hold the **Alt** key while tapping the **F7** key once (**Alt** and **F7**).

2. Press **2** for Tables.

3. Press **1** to create {*Layout, Tables, Create*}.

4. Type the number of desired columns or press **Enter** to accept 3 columns; press **Enter**.

5. Type the number of desired rows, for example, 4; press **Enter**. *Note:* The Table Edit menu and the columns and rows for the table display on the screen. (See Exhibit 7.1.)

6. Press **F7** to exit the Table Edit menu and return the cursor to the normal editing screen.

7. Always press the **tab** key to move the cursor from cell to cell and type the information into each column and row. Also

press the **tab** key after the last column entry.

Note: All words and numbers will begin at the left of the column. The decimals will be aligned when the columns are formatted in step 9.

Monitor Sales	$25,000.00	$28,500.50
Printer Sales	32,000.00	33,250.25
Computer Sales	85,000.00	89,100.50
Keyboard Sales	20,000.00	22,000.00

8. Press **Alt** and **F7** to enter the table editor. *Note:* If the table was created, saved, and retrieved, it is necessary to press **2** for tables and **2** for edit to obtain the Table Edit screen.

9. **Align decimals by formatting**
  a. Place the cursor in any cell of the column(s) where the decimal is to be aligned; for example, place the cursor in any cell in column B.
  b. Press **2** for format.
  c. Press **2** for column.
  d. Press **3** to justify.
  e. Press **5** for decimal align. Notice the figures are aligned at the decimal and are placed at the right side of each cell.

⇨ Repeat step 9 and align the figures in column C.

10. **Center the table horizontally (between the left and right margins)**
  a. Press **6** for options.
  b. Press **3** for position of table.
  c. Press **3** for center; press **F7** to exit and return the cursor to the table editor.

Note: The table does not display horizontally centered on the screen. To view the table, exit (F7), press Shift and F7, press v for view. Press F7 to exit the view screen. Press Alt and F7 to return to the table editor.

11. **Omit all table lines (borders)**
  a. Place the cursor in cell A1 (**Home** twice, **up** arrow key once).
  b. Press **Alt** and **F4** to block.
  c. Press the **right** arrow key and the **down** arrow key to

highlight all cells in the table. For example, press the **right** arrow key 2 times, press the **down** arrow key 3 times.

d. Press **3** for lines.
e. Press **7** for all.
f. Press **1** for none. All lines in the table are cleared.

12. **Decrease cell size to place approximately one-half inch between columns**

a. Place the cursor in any cell in the column that is to be decreased in width. For example, place the cursor in cell A1 (**Home** twice, **up** arrow key once).
b. Press and hold the **Ctrl** key and tap the **left** arrow key repeatedly to decrease the column width. For example, press and hold the **Ctrl** key while tapping the **left** arrow key 6 times. (Press **Ctrl** and **right** arrow keys to increase cell width.)
c. Move the cursor to any cell in the next column to be decreased in width. For example, place the cursor in cell B1.
d. Press and hold the **Ctrl** key and tap the **left** arrow key repeatedly to decrease the column width. For example, press and hold the **Ctrl** key while tapping the **left** arrow key 6 times. *Note:* Visually estimate that approximately one-half inch is between the longest line in the first column and the beginning of the second column.
e. Move the cursor to any cell in the next column to be decreased in width, e.g., cell C1.
f. Press and hold the **Ctrl** key and tap the **left** arrow key 6 times. *Note:* Visually estimate when there is approximately one-half inch between the longest line in the second column and the beginning of the third column.
g. Press **F7** to return the cursor to the normal editing screen.

⇨ Your formatted table should look similar to the following table:

Monitor Sales	$25,000.00	$28,500.50
Printer Sales	32,000.00	33,250.25
Computer Sales	85,000.00	89,100.50
Keyboard Sales	20,000.00	22,000.00

⇨ Use the filename **7ptable1**. Save the file and keep the document on the screen.

⮞ Print one copy using draft text quality.

⮞ Use the Procedure to Create a Table with a Title and Column Headings.

⮞ Type the following unformatted table text and figures. Remember all text and figures are typed at the left of the cell.

⮞ Omit all table lines; position the table to be centered horizontally. Visually estimate and adjust the column widths to place approximately one-half inch between columns.

Procedure to Create a Table with a Title and Column Headings

1. Use the Procedure to Create a Table steps 1–5 and create a table with 3 columns and 7 rows.

2. Join cells:
   a. Block the cells in row 1; for example, place the cursor in cell A1.
   b. Press **Alt** and **F4** to block; press the **right** arrow key twice to highlight all cells in row 1.
   c. Press **7** for join; press **y** for yes. Notice the vertical lines in row 1 have been eliminated.

3. Press **F7** to return to the normal editing screen.

4. Type the table title in uppercase letters; for example, SALARY DATA. *Note:* The title will be centered in step 7.

5. Always use the tab key to move the cursor from cell to cell and type the column headings and table entries in each column and row. *Note:* Press **F8** to underline before typing

SALARY DATA		
Name	Department	Annual Salary
Jeremy Ahern	Accounting	$35,500.80
Patricia Farrington	Sales	40,900.60
Georgia Miller	Personnel	37,630.20
Sam Perroni	Sales	39,380.70
Tanya Steiner	Accounting	35,750.50

each column heading. All table entries begin at the left of each column. The columns will be formatted in step 14.

6. Press **Alt** and **F7** for the table editor {*Layout, Table, Edit*}.

7. Place the cursor in cell A1; press **2**, **1**, **3**, and **2** to center the table title.

8. Block and highlight all cells. Follow step 11 in the Procedure to Create a Table and omit table lines.

9. *To insert a blank row*, place the cursor in the row where a row will be inserted above. For example, place the cursor in cell A2. *Note:* A row is inserted above the row where the cursor is located.
   a. Press the **Ins** key once.
   b. Press **1** for rows.
   c. Press **Enter** to accept number of rows: 1.

10. Follow step 10 under the Procedure to Create a Table and center the table horizontally.

11. Move the cursor to any cell in column 2. Decrease the cell width; press and hold the **Ctrl** key and tap the **left** arrow key approximately 9 times.

12. Move the cursor to any cell in column one. Press and hold the **Ctrl** key and tap the **right** arrow key twice. Visually estimate that one-half inch will be placed between columns.

13. Place the cursor in any cell in the third column. Press and hold the **Ctrl** key and tap the **left** arrow key approximately 3 times.

14. Block and highlight cells C3–C8. Center the column; press **2**, **2**, **3**, **2**. Notice that approximately one-half inch of space is displayed between columns two and three.

15. Press **F7** to return the cursor to the normal editing screen.

16. Place the cursor on the first character of the column heading "Name". (Reveal Codes **Alt** and **F3** and place the cursor on the **[UND]** code.) Visually estimate that to center the column heading over the longest line in the column the **space bar** is pressed 6 times. *Note:* The table editor center feature cannot be used to center the column heading, because the table editor centers the title over both the horizontal characters <u>and</u> spaces in the column.

▷ Your table should look similar to the following formatted table.

```
                          SALARY DATA

        Name            Department      Annual Salary
   Jeremy Ahern         Accounting       $35,500.80

   Patricia Farrington  Sales            40,900.60

   Georgia Miller       Personnel        37,630.20

   Sam Perroni          Sales            39,380.70

   Tanya Steiner        Accounting       35,750.50
```

▷ Use the filename **7ptable2**. Save the file and keep the document on the screen.

▷ Print one copy using draft text quality.

▷ Use the Procedure to Create a Table with a Subtitle and Print Table Lines.

▷ Create a table with 2 columns and 9 rows.

Procedure to Create a Table with a Subtitle and Print Table Lines

1. Press **Alt** and **F7, 2, 1** {*Layout, Tables, Create*}, and create a table; for example type 2 for columns and 9 for rows.

2. Block and join the two columns in the first row. Block and join the two columns in the second row.

3. Press **F7** to exit to the normal editing screen and type the information from the following unformatted table. Remember to use the **Tab** key to move from column to column; the table will be formatted later.

VARIOUS STATE'S POPULATIONS	
(Approximate)	
STATE	POPULATION
Hawaii	965,000
Idaho	944,000
Kentucky	3,660,000
Minnesota	4,076,000
Ohio	10,798,000
Texas	14,228,000

4. Return the cursor to the table editor (**Alt** and **F7**).

5. Center the title and subtitle. For example, block the first two cells (**Alt** and **F4**), press **2** for format, **1** for cell, **3** for justify, **2** for center.

6. Center each column heading. For example, place the cursor in the first column, third row, press **2, 1, 3, 2**.

7. Right align the decimals in the right column (**2, 2, 3, 3**).

8. Decrease the column width in each column in order to reduce the space between the columns. For example, place the cursor in column 1 and press the **Ctrl** and **left** arrow key approximately 12 times. Repeat for column 2.

9. View the table on the screen. Press **F7** to exit to the normal editing screen. Press **Shift** and **F7**, **v** to view the table. If more or less space is desired in the column widths, return the cursor to the table editor and increase or decrease the column width.

10. Center the table horizontally (**6, 3, 3, F7**). *Note:* If necessary, move the cursor from cell to cell to align the information in each cell. Your table should look similar to the following formatted table.

VARIOUS STATE'S POPULATIONS	
(Approximate)	
STATE	POPULATION
Hawaii	965,000
Idaho	944,000
Kentucky	3,660,000
Minnesota	4,076,000
Ohio	10,798,000
Texas	14,228,000

⇨ Use the filename **7ptable3**. Save the file and keep the document on the screen.

⇨ Use the print menu and print one copy using draft text quality.

SUMMARY

● A table is created using the table editor. By specifying the number of rows and columns desired, horizontal and vertical lines for the table are displayed on the screen (**Alt** and **F7**; **2**; **1**; type desired number of columns; **Enter**; type desired number of rows; **Enter**).

● The intersection of each column and row is called a cell. Each column is identified with a letter (A, B, C), and each row is identified with a number. The cell address is the location of the cursor.

● The column width can be increased or decreased by pressing the **Ctrl** and **right** or **left** arrow keys. The same amount of spacing should be placed between each column. Visually estimate and decrease the column widths in order to place one-half inch between columns.

● Formatting instructions are given in the table editor (**Alt** and **F7**, **2**, **2** to edit). The table can be positioned horizontally on the page (**6**, **3**, **3**, **F7**). The table decimals can be aligned (**Alt** and **F4**, highlight cells, **2**, **2**, **3**, **5**).

● The lines of the table can be omitted (**Alt** and **F4**, highlight cells, **3**, make desired choice—**7** for all). Also, the lines of a table can be changed to single, double, dashed, dotted, or thick.

● The cursor must be located in the normal editing screen to type text and figures. Exit the table editor by pressing **F7**.

● To type a table with a title and column headings, cells can be joined to eliminate the vertical lines (**Alt** and **F4** to block cells to be joined, **7**, **y**).

● A row can be inserted to place additional space between the column title and column headings (**Ins**, **1**, **Enter** to accept one row).

SELF-CHECK QUESTIONS

(True / False—Circle One)

T,F 1. A table is created by using the table editor.

T,F 2. To create a table press **Alt** and **F7, 1, 1**.

T,F 3. The intersection of a column and row is called a cell.

T,F 4. The width of the middle column cannot be decreased.

T,F 5. Text and figures are typed and edited in the table editor.

T,F 6. A column of figures can be aligned at the decimal in the table editor by placing the cursor in the figure column and pressing **2, 2, 3, 5**.

T,F 7. The most effective method of centering a table horizontally between the left and right margins is to use the **Ctrl** and **left** arrow keys.

T,F 8. Table lines can be omitted by blocking the table cells, and pressing **3** and **8**.

T,F 9. One new row can be inserted by pressing **Ins**, **1**, and **Enter**.

T,F 10. Visually estimate to place one-half inch between table columns.

ENRICHING LANGUAGE ARTS SKILLS

Spelling / Vocabulary Words

quarter   four parts of one whole part; one-quarter of a year is three months, or 1/4 of 12 months.
projected   to make a prediction by guessing.
data   a collection of information.

Dollar Signs in a Table

The dollar sign is typed beside the first column entry and is typed to the left of the first character in the longest column amount.

When the column is totaled, a dollar sign also precedes the total. Both dollar signs should align.

Example $ 234.50
                555.25
                620.50
           $1,410.25

EXERCISES

Exercise 7.1

1. The screen should be clear, and the disk drive should be accessed where the file disk is located.

2. Create a table with 2 columns and 4 rows. Increase the left-column cell width 4 spaces.

3. Type the following text and figures unformatted (i.e., type all text and figures at the left of the cells). Remember to use the **Tab** key to move from cell to cell.

4. Use the table editor to perform the following:
    a. Format the amount column for decimals.
    b. Omit all table lines.
    c. Position the table to be centered horizontally.
    d. Visually estimate and adjust the column widths to place approximately one-half inch between columns.

5. Use the filename **7table1**. Save the file and keep the document on the screen.

6. Print one copy using draft or high text quality. **Note:** The table will print double spaced.

```
First-Quarter Earnings Per Share     $1.92
Second-Quarter Earnings Per Share     2.35
Third-Quarter Earnings Per Share      2.20
Fourth-Quarter Earnings Per Share     1.85
```

Exercise 7.2

1. The screen should be clear, and the disk drive should be accessed where the file disk is located.

2.   Create a table with 2 columns and 5 rows. Increase the left-column cell width 7 spaces.

3.   Type the following text and figures unformatted (i.e., type all text and figures at the left of the cells). Remember to use the **Tab** key to move from cell to cell.

4.   Use the table editor to perform the following:
     a.   Format the amount column for decimals.
     b.   Omit all table lines.
     c.   Position the table to be centered horizontally.
     d.   Visually estimate and adjust the column widths to place approximately one-half inch between columns.

5.   Use the filename **7table2**. Save the file and keep the document on the screen.

6.   Print one copy using draft or high text quality.

Projected Sales	$135,350.50
Actual Sales	134,000.30
Sales over or under Projected Sales	1,350.20
Projected Sales for next year	175,555.90
Amount of Increase (Projected Sales)	40,205.40

Exercise 7.3

1.   The screen should be clear, and the disk drive should be accessed where the file disk is located.

2.   Create a table with 3 columns and 7 rows. Join the cells in row 1.

3.   Type the following unformatted text and figures (i.e., type all text and figures at the left of the cells). Remember to use the **Tab** key to move from cell to cell. Underline the column headings.

4.   Use the table editor to perform the following:
   a.   Center the table title.
   b.   Center each column heading.
   c.   Insert a blank row above row 2.
   d.   Format the amount column for decimals.
   e.   Position the table to be centered horizontally.
   f.   Omit all table lines.
   g.   Visually estimate and adjust the column widths to place approximately one-half inch between columns.
   h.   Decrease column B three spaces; decrease column C approximately five spaces.

5.   Use the filename **7table3**. Save the file and keep the document on the screen.

6.   Print one copy using draft or high text quality.

EMPLOYEE DATA		
Name	Location	Yearly Salary
Jerry Baylor	Building 10	$40,350.60
Verna Cox	Building 12	42,615.50
Gordon Pham	Building 16	44,590.40
Margery Samuelson	Building 11	41,400.30
Bernadine Yardley	Building 12	45,295.20

Exercise 7.4

1.   The screen should be clear, and the disk drive should be accessed where the file disk is located.

2.   Create a table with 4 columns and 8 rows. Join the cells in row 1; increase column A one space.

3.   Type the following unformatted text and figures (i.e., type all text and figures at the left of the cells). Remember to use the **Tab** key to move from cell to cell.

4.   Use the table editor to perform the following:
   a.   Center the table title.
   b.   Center each column heading.
   c.   Format the amount columns for decimals.
   d.   Position the table to be centered horizontally.

5.   Use the filename **7table4**. Save the file and keep the document on the screen.

6.   Print one copy using draft or high text quality.

SALES REPORT			
NAME	FIRST QUARTER	SECOND QUARTER	THIRD QUARTER
John Coates	$54,500.60	$53,500.50	$54,250.00
Ken Lim	51,600.70	49,900.00	50,650.60
Kerry Loustau	53,450.00	59,000.00	57,700.80
Marilyn Roberts	55,200.90	52,750.80	54,500.00
Rachel Stahl	48,680.00	49,500.00	51,320.00
Sheldon Vierra	45,290.00	48,600.00	50,590.00

Exercise 7.5

1. The screen should be clear and the disk drive should be accessed where the file disk is located.

2. Create a table with 4 columns and 7 rows.

3. Increase the left column by 3 spaces.

4. Use the normal editing screen and type all table entries at the left side of each column.

5. Use the table editor to perform the following:
   a. Join the first row of cells and center the table column.
   b. Center each column heading (press **2** for format, **1** for cell, **3** for justify, **2** for center).
   c. Right align the amount columns.

6. Correct three alignment errors.

YOGURT SALES			
FLAVOR	JULY	AUGUST	SEPTEMBER
Chocolate Fudge	$9,000	$9,980	$ 11,500
French Vanilla	9,900	10,600	12,000
Amaretto Cream	6,000	10,000	8,900
Raspberry Tart	5,000	6,000	4,300
Total	$29,900	$38,600	$37,700

7. Position the table to be centered horizontally.

8. Use the filename **7table5**. Save the file and keep the document on the screen.

9. Print one copy in draft or high text quality.

Chapter 8

EDIT A TABLE

OBJECTIVES

After successfully completing this chapter, you should be able to:

- Center a page vertically.
- Move a table column.
- Total a table column.
- Delete a table column.
- Print double underlines.

Once a table has been typed and printed, the table information can be edited. An edited table involves changes such as inserting or deleting text or numbers. Changes can also include relocating, deleting, or checking a column total for accuracy.

When preparing a table for a final printout, the table can be centered vertically on the page. A table centered vertically on the page leaves approximately the same amount of blank space in the top margin as in the bottom margin.

CENTER A PAGE VERTICALLY

Lines can be centered vertically on a page. The number of lines to be centered vertically should be less than 54 lines. Why? Because there are 66 vertical lines available on a 8½" × 11" page; the defaulted top and bottom margins together use 12 lines (6 vertical lines each). (See Exhibit 8.1.) Since 54 + 12 = 66, the number of lines in the table should be less than 54 for the vertical centering to be effective. The tables typed in this text will have 20 or less vertical lines; therefore, vertical centering will be useful.

EXHIBIT 8.1 Printing lines available on standard paper (66 lines)

118

If the table has less than 54 vertical lines and is to be printed on a page by itself, the Procedure to Center a Page Vertically can be used. The instruction to center a page vertically is referred to as centering a page between the top and bottom margin.

Procedure to Center a Page Vertically (Between the Top and Bottom Margins)

*Note: The cursor must be located in the normal editing screen. If the cursor is in the table edit screen, press **F7** to return the cursor to the editing screen.*

1. The cursor should be located at the beginning of the document. If the table has already been typed, move the cursor to the beginning of the document (press the **Home** key twice; press the **up** arrow key once).

2. Press and hold the **Shift** key while tapping the **F8** key once.

3. Press **2** for Page {*Layout, Page*}.

4. Press **1** for Center Page Top to Bottom; the word *No* is displayed; press **y** for yes.

5. Press the **F7** key once to return the cursor to the document screen.

COLUMN MOVES

A column can be relocated to another column location by using the move feature. The cursor must be in the table edit screen to move columns.

The usual move keys **Ctrl** and **F4** are used in the table edit screen to move a column. The cursor is located in the column to be moved and the column move is selected. Once the move procedure is performed, the moved column is retrieved in front of the column where the cursor is located.

▷ Retrieve the practice table 1 file named **7ptable1** that was typed in Chapter 7.

▷ Use the Procedure to Move Table Columns and move the last column to be the second column as shown.

▷ Center the table vertically on the page.

▷ Use the filename **8ptable1**. Save the table and keep the document on the screen.

⇨ Print one copy using draft text quality.

```
Monitor Sales  ▶ $25,000.00   $28,500.50
Printer Sales     32,000.00    33,250.25
Computer Sales    85,000.00    89,100.50
Keyboard Sales    20,000.00    22,000.00
```

Procedure to Move Table Columns

*Note: The cursor must be in the table edit screen (**Alt** and **F7**).*

| 1. | Place the cursor in any cell of the column to be moved.

| 2. | Press and hold the **Ctrl** key while tapping the **F4** key once (**Ctrl** and **F4**).

| 3. | Press **3** for column.

| 4. | Press **1** for move. The column to be moved is deleted from the screen. A vertical line may display on the screen, that's o.k.

| 5. | Move the cursor to the column that will be located to the right of the moved column. For example, the cursor is located in the column that will be located to the right of the moved column, therefore, the cursor is not moved.

| 6. | Press **Enter** to retrieve the column. *Note:* To omit the vertical line, block the column and select lines or none (**Alt** and **F4**, highlight column, **3** for lines, **7** for all, **1** for none).

TOTAL TABLE COLUMNS

Table columns can be totaled (added) in the table editor. The column to be totaled is blocked and the math feature is selected. The choice for adding columns is selected.

If the table lines are omitted and a column of numbers is totaled, a single underline is typed under the last number in the column to separate the last column entry from the total amount. The last column number can be blocked (**Alt** and **F4**) and underlined automatically by using the underline key (**F8**). Since the single underline should extend the width of the total amount, it may be necessary to place one or two spaces in front of the first digit in the underlined number.

```
┌─────────────────────────────────────────────┐
│  Cash in the Bank        $ 47,012.32         │
│  Accounts Receivable       13,290.60         │
│  Office Supplies            4,680.55         │
│  Equipment                 59,230.00         │
│  Building                 135,700.00         │
│  Total Assets                                │
│                                              │
└─────────────────────────────────────────────┘
```

EXHIBIT 8.2   Table with single underline

▷ Clear the screen (**F7, n, n**).

▷ Create a table with 2 columns and 6 rows. Use Exhibit 8.2 and type the table unformatted. Remember, all entries, including the figures, begin at the left side of the cell. *The figures will be formatted later.*

▷ Exit out of the table editor (**F7**); place the cursor on the "1" in the last column figure (135,700.00).

▷ Press the **space bar** once.

▷ Block (**Alt** and **F4**) the last figure including the space and press **F8** to underline.

▷ Use the Procedure to Total a Column to add the column of figures.

Procedure to Total a Column

Note: The cursor should be located in the table edit screen (Alt and F7).

1. Place the cursor on the figure in the first cell of the column to be totaled.

2. Turn on block (**Alt** and **F4**); press the **down** arrow key repeatedly to highlight the column including the blank cell where the total is to display.

3. Press **5** for math.

4. Press **4** for "+" to add the column. The total is displayed on the screen.

5. Press **Alt** and **F4** to turn block off. *Note:* Sometimes a new row may need to be created for the total amount. Create a new row by selecting **1** for size; **1** for row; type the total number of rows desired (for example, if there are 6 rows, type 7 for the new row); **Enter**.

▷ Format the amount column for decimal align (**2, 2, 3, 5**).

▷ Position the table to be centered horizontally (**6, 3, 3**).

▷ Visually estimate and adjust the column widths to place one-half inch between columns.

▷ Type a dollar sign in front of the total figure; place one space between the dollar sign and the first digit in the first column figure in order to align the dollar signs.

▷ Center the table vertically (optional).

▷ Use the filename **8ptable2**. Save the file and keep the document on the screen.

▷ Print one copy using draft print quality.

DOUBLE UNDERLINES

Double underlines are usually printed under total column amounts for emphasis. Once the column total has been calculated, an instruction to print double underlines is used. If the table lines have been omitted, a single underline is typed beneath the last column amount (before the column total amount).

▷ The file named **8ptable2** should be on the screen (retrieve the file, if necessary).

▷ Use the Procedure to Print Double Underlines and place double underlines below the total amount.

Procedure to Print Double Underlines

Note: The cursor must be located in the normal editing screen.

1. Place the cursor on the first character or number of the text/number to be double underlined. For example, place the cursor under the dollar sign ($) in the figure $259,913.47.

2. Press and hold the **Alt** key while tapping the **F4** key once to block {*Edit, Block*}.

3. Press the **right** arrow key to move the cursor and highlight the text/numbers to be double underlined.

4. Press and hold the **Ctrl** key while tapping the **F8** key once (**Ctrl** and **F8**).

5. Press **2** for appearance.

6. Press **3** for Double Underline {*Font, Appearance, Double Underline*}. *Note:* The double underlines are not displayed on the screen; a color monitor will display the amount in color.

7. Press **Shift** and **F7** {*File, Print*}, **6** to view the double underlines. Press **F7** to exit the view screen.

8. Press **Alt** and **F3** {*Edit, Reveal Codes*} to reveal codes. The double underline code **[DBL UND]** is displayed before the text/numbers to be double underlined; the **[dbl und]** code follows the text/numbers to be double underlined.

▷ Use the filename **8ptable3**. Save the file and keep the document on the screen.

▷ Print one copy using draft or high text quality.

DELETE A TABLE COLUMN

Table editing can include deleting an entire column. The cursor is placed in the column to be deleted. The **Del** key is pressed and the column selection is chosen. After a column is deleted, the columns will automatically recenter horizontally (if the table position has been formatted for center).

▷ Clear the screen (**F7**, **n**, **n**).

▷ Create a table with 3 columns and 7 rows. Join the top row of cells (**Alt** and **F7**, highlight row, **7**, **y**).

▷ Type the following unformatted table text and figures. Remember, all entries begin at the left of the column until formatted.

▷ Use the table editor (**Alt** and **F7**) to perform the following:
a. Center the table title (**2**, **1**, **3**, **2**).

> b.   Format the amount columns for decimal align (**2, 2, 3, 5**).
> c.   Position the table to be centered horizontally.
> d.   Visually estimate and adjust the column widths to place one-half inch between columns.

EMPLOYEES' ANNUAL SALARIES		
DEPARTMENT	FULL TIME	PART TIME
Accounting	$45,000	$35,000
Personnel	40,000	32,000
Marketing	60,000	50,000
Finance	60,000	48,000
R&D	50,000	40,000

▷ Center the table vertically (optional).

▷ Use the filename **8ptable4**. Save the file and keep the document on the screen.

▷ Print one copy using draft text quality.

▷ Use the Procedure to Delete a Table Column.

▷ Delete the right column, including the column heading.

▷ Use the filename **8ptabl4r**. Save the file and keep the document on the screen.

▷ Print one copy using draft text quality.

Procedure to Delete a Table Column

*Note: The cursor must be located in the table edit screen (**Alt** and **F7**) {**Layout, Tables, Edit**}.*

1. Place the cursor in any cell in the column to be deleted.
2. Press the **Del** key once.
3. Press **2** for columns.
4. Press **Enter** to accept one column.

> *Note: The column is deleted and the remaining columns move to the middle of the screen (if the table position is set for center).*

- Editing a table can entail relocating, deleting, or inserting entries or columns, or checking a column total. The final copy of a table can be printed vertically centered on a page (**Home** twice, **up** arrow once, **Shift** and **F8**, **2**, **1**, **y**, **F7**). Also the table can be printed horizontally centered on a page by using the table editor (**Alt** and **F7**, **6**, **3**, **3**, **F7**).

- The move feature is used to relocate a column. The cursor must be located in the table editor to move a column. Block and highlight the column to be moved, press **Ctrl** and **F4**, **3**, **1**, move the cursor to the column that will be to the right of the moved column, press **Enter**.

- Columns of numbers can be added automatically and the total displayed on the screen. The cursor must be in the table edit screen. Block the column to be totaled, press **5** for math, press **4** for plus (+). The total will display on the screen. *Note:* If necessary, create a new row (**1**, **1**, type number of rows desired, **Enter**).

- A table column can be deleted when the cursor is in the table edit screen (**Alt** and **F7**). Place the cursor in any cell of the column to be deleted. Press the **Del** key, **2** for columns, press **Enter** to accept one column.

- Double underlines are printed below the column total to emphasize the total figure (**Alt** and **F4**, press **right** arrow key to highlight the total figure, **Ctrl** and **F8**, **2**, **3**; **Shift** and **F7**, **6** to view the double underlines on the screen).

Note: The cursor must be in the normal editing screen to use the double underline feature.

SELF-CHECK QUESTIONS

(True / False—Circle One)

T,F 1. To center a table between the top and bottom margins, press **Shift** and **F8**, **2**, **1**, **y**, and **F7**.

T,F 2. There are 55 vertical lines available on an 8½" by 11" page.

T,F 3. To move a column, the column is first blocked and highlighted.

T,F 4. To total a column, the cursor must be located in the table edit screen.

T,F 5. A column is deleted by using the **Del** key while in the table edit screen and pressing **2** and **Enter**.

T,F 6. Once a table column is deleted and the table position is selected for center, the remaining columns are recentered horizontally.

T,F 7. After the double underline instruction is given, the double underlines are displayed on the screen.

T,F 8. If a table uses 54 vertical lines, the instruction to center the table between the top and bottom margins should be used.

T,F 9. Editing a table can include inserting, deleting, or relocating table columns.

T,F 10. All table lines can be omitted.

ENRICHING LANGUAGE ARTS SKILLS

Spelling / Vocabulary Words

accounts payable   a bill or account that is to be paid.
FICA   Federal Insurance Contribution Act; commonly known as social security.
retaining   to hold or keep in one place.

Single Underline in a Table

Type a single underline below the last column amount and before the total amount. The single underline should extend the width of the amount that has the most characters, including the dollar sign.

Example $1,550.50
                600.00
              _820.50_
            $2,971.00

Exercise 8.1

1. The screen should be clear, and the disk drive should be accessed where the file disk is located.

2. Create a table with 2 columns and 8 rows. Join the cells in row 1.

3. Type the following unformatted table text and figures (i.e., type all entries at the left of each cell).

LIZARDO COMPANY	
Accounts Payable	$19,678.88
Salaries Payable	20,450.45
Federal Income Tax Payable	6,230.33
State Unemployment Tax Payable	240.44
FICA Tax Payable	1,277.99
Notes Payable	47,878.09
Total Liabilities	

4. Use the table editor to perform the following:
   a. Omit all table lines; center the table title.
   b. Insert a blank row between the title and the first column entries.
   c. Right align the amount column.
   d. Position the table to be centered horizontally.
   e. Visually estimate and adjust the column widths to place approximately one-half inch between columns.
   f. Use the Procedure to Total a Column to place the total amount in the last cell.

5. Type a single underline below the next-to-the last figure in the column.

6. Center the page vertically.

7. Use the filename **8table1**. Save the file and keep the document on the screen.

8. Print one copy using draft or high text quality.

Exercise 8.2

1. Retrieve **8table1**.

2. Edit the table as shown.

3. Place double underlines beneath the total amount.

4. Use the filename **8table2r**. Save the file without clearing the screen.

5. Print one copy using draft or medium text quality.

LIZARDO COMPANY

Accounts Payable	$ ~~19,670.00~~ *18,750.00*
Salaries Payable	20,450.45
Federal Income Tax Payable	6,230.33
State Unemployment Tax Payable	240.44
FICA Tax Payable	1,277.99
Interest Payable	*950.55*
Notes Payable	47,878.09
Total Liabilities	$95,756.18

recalculate the total ↗

Exercise 8.3   Part I

1. The screen should be clear, and the disk drive should be accessed where the file disk is located.

2. Create a table with 3 columns and 7 rows.

3. Join the cells in the first row.

4. Exit (**F7**) the table editor. Type the table entries unformatted as shown.

MAINTENANCE EXPENDITURE ACTIVITY		
MAINTENANCE ITEM	BEGINNING BALANCE	ENDING BALANCE
Retaining walls	$5,672.00	$1,873.25
Painting	4,580.75	1,200.50
Roofs	9,000.00	5,000.00
Carports	1,750.00	878.00
Other	2,777.50	1,718.30

5. After the table entries are entered, press **Alt** and **F7** to obtain the table editor.
   a. Center the title and each column heading (**2, 1, 3, 2**).
   b. Align on the decimal in the amount columns.
   c. Visually estimate and adjust the column widths to place approximately one-half inch between columns.
   d. Center the table horizontally.

Note: If necessary, move the cursor to each cell to display the numbers aligned properly in each column. Your table should look like the following table:

MAINTENANCE EXPENDITURE ACTIVITY		
MAINTENANCE ITEM	BEGINNING BALANCE	ENDING BALANCE
Retaining walls	$5,672.00	$1,873.25
Painting	4,580.75	1,200.50
Roofs	9,000.00	5,000.00
Carports	1,750.00	878.00
Other	2,777.50	1,718.30

6. Use the filename **8table3**. Save the file and keep the document on the screen.

7. Print one copy using draft text quality.

8. Use the table editor to perform the following:
   a. Move the third column in front of the middle column.
   b. Block the first row and join cells.
   c. Block the table and select all lines for single.

9. Use the filename **8table3r**. Save the file and keep the document on the screen.

10. Print one copy using draft or high text quality.

Exercise 8.3 Part II (Optional)

1. The file named **8table3r** should be displayed on the screen.

2. Delete the right column.

3. Block the table and select lines, right, single.

4. Use the filename **8table3.del**. Save the file and keep the document on the screen.

5. Print one copy using draft or high text quality.

Exercise 8.4

1. The screen should be clear, and the disk drive should be accessed where the file disk is located.

2. Create a table with 2 columns and 6 rows. Join the cells in row 1.

3. Type the following unformatted table text and figures.

COSTS FOR SOFTWARE	
Gladwriter	$595.00
Shipping and handling	8.50
Sales tax (7%)	41.65
Express service	3.50
Total amount due	

4. Use the table editor to perform the following:
   a. Center the table title.
   b. Format the amount column for decimals.
   c. Total the amount column.
   d. Position the table to be centered horizontally.
   e. Visually estimate and adjust the column widths to place approximately one-half inch between the columns.

5. Place a dollar sign ($) in front of the total figure.

6. Position the table to be centered vertically (optional).

7. Use the filename **8table4**. Save the file and keep the document on the screen.

8. Print one copy using draft or high text quality.

Exercise 8.5

1. The screen should be clear and the disk drive should be accessed where the file disk is located.

2. Create a table with 4 columns and 6 rows. Join the first row of cells.

3. Increase the left column by 3 spaces.

4. Use the normal editing screen and type *all* table entries at the left side of each column.

5. Use the table editor to perform the following:
    a. Center the table title.
    b. Center the left column heading; right align the remaining column headings.
    c. Align the decimals by formatting.
    d. Omit all table lines.
    e. Position the table to be horizontally centered.

6. Correct five punctuation/alignment errors.

FIRST QUARTER SALES

BOOKS	JANUARY	FEBRUARY	MARCH
Fiction	$3,300.60	$3,850.00	$5,500.00
Biographies	3,000.80	3,600.60	4,200.00
Science fiction	2,780.00	7,450.00	3,730.00
Total	$9,081.40	$14,901.20	$13,430.00

---

7. Place double underlines under each total amount.

8. Position the table to be centered vertically.

9. Use the filename **8table5**. Save the file and keep the document on the screen.

10. Print one copy using draft or high text quality.

Chapter 9

CREATE NEWSPAPER AND PARALLEL COLUMNS

OBJECTIVES

After successfully completing this chapter, you should be able to:

● Define and keyboard newspaper columns.

● Keyboard and edit text columns.

● Define and keyboard parallel columns.

● Edit parallel columns.

CREATE COLUMNS

Columns created as newspaper and/or parallel columns are text columns. When columns are created, the number of columns and the spaces to be placed between columns are specified, and the margins are automatically determined by the WordPerfect program.

DEFINE AND KEYBOARD NEWSPAPER COLUMNS

First, columns are defined; second, the column feature is turned on; and third, the text is keyboarded. As text is keyboarded, the lines automatically wrap around from line to line. When the bottom line of the column is reached, the text will automatically "snake" to the top of the next column. (The bottom line is

COMPUTER HARDWARE

A computer keyboard is similar to a standard typewriter keyboard and includes letter, number, symbol, and function keys. Function keys are ten additional keys located on the top or side of the keyboard and are used to give instructions to the computer and to the program. The ten function keys are identified and labeled F1-F10.

Computer keyboards are made with several variations. Some computer keyboards have function keys placed on the top of the keyboard. Other keyboards have the function keys placed on the left side of the keyboard. Enhanced keyboards include two additional function keys; F11 and F12.

Enhanced keyboards generally have two sets of arrow keys (cursor movement keys). In addition, the home, end, page down, page up, insert, and delete keys are duplicated. These keys are duplicated because when using the number keys located on the "ten-key pad" the Num Lock key must be on. When the Num Lock key is on, the home, page up, and arrow keys etc., are not operational.

The Enter key is located on the right side of the alphabetic keys. The Enter key is used in word processing to end a short line or to end a paragraph. The Enter key is also used to complete a program instruction and to end a response to a computer prompt.

A control key is always used in combination with another key to give a program command. The control key is usually located on the left side of the keyboard. The control key is held down while pressing another key.

A computer monitor (screen) displays characters, symbols, and numbers. The screen is an input and output device; that is, a device used to see the characters during or after typing. Many screens are available for use with a computer. A home TV screen may be connected to a computer and used as a monitor; however, the resolution (quality of the characters displayed) is generally not as clear as a monitor made specifically for a computer system. A screen designed to clearly display characters, symbols, and numbers should be used for computer applications such as word processing, desktop publishing, and graphics.

The disk drive is a device connected to or housed inside the computer that writes to and reads the disk. The disk drive is used to transfer information between the computer and the disk. Most computers contain one or more disk drives.

EXHIBIT 9.1   Newspaper columns

```
Text Column Definition

    1 - Type                                Newspaper

    2 - Number of Columns                   2

    3 - Distance Between Columns

    4 - Margins

    Column    Left      Right     Column    Left      Right
     1:       1"        4"         13:
     2:       4.5"      7.5"       14:
     3:                            15:
     4:                            16:
     5:                            17:
     6:                            18:
     7:                            19:
     8:                            20:
     9:                            21:
    10:                            22:
    11:                            23:
    12:                            24:

Selection: 0
```

EXHIBIT 9.2   The text column definition menu

defaulted at 9.63 inches.) Snaking is the process of wrapping text vertically from column to column and page to page. See the newspaper columns example in Exhibit 9.1.

The instruction to define newspaper columns can be given before or after the text is typed. Once newspaper columns have been printed, it may be desirable to select left justification (**Shift** and **F8**; **1, 3, 1, F7**) and possibly use the hyphenation procedure to assist in aligning words more evenly at the end of the lines.

▷ Use the Procedure to Define Newspaper Columns and prepare for typing the columns in Exhibit 9.1.

Procedure to Define Newspaper Columns

1. Before typing text, press and hold the **Alt** key while tapping the **F7** key once (**Alt** and **F7**).

2. Press **1** for Columns; press **3** for Define {*Layout, Columns, Define*}.

3. The Text Column Definition menu is displayed. (See Exhibit 9.2.) The default is set for newspaper-type columns.

4. The number of columns is defaulted at 2. *Note:* To change the number of columns, press **2** and type the number of columns desired; press **Enter**.

5. The left and right margins for the columns are determined automatically and displayed on the screen.

6. Press **Enter** to accept the column definitions and exit.

7. Press **1** for Columns On.

8. Press **Alt** and **F3** to reveal codes; the column codes are displayed: **[Col Def:Newspaper;2,1". . .] [Col On]**. Press **Alt** and **F3** again to exit reveal codes.

9. Continue with the Procedure to Keyboard and Edit Text Columns.

▷ Use the Procedure to Keyboard and Edit Text Columns.

▷ Type the columns shown in Exhibit 9.1. *Note:* Turn on widow/orphan protection (**Shift** and **F8**, **1**, **9**, **y**, **F7**). See Chapter 13, page 209.

▷ Set justification for left.

▷ Use the filename **9pcols**. Save the file and keep the document on the screen.

▷ Print one copy using draft text quality.

Procedure to Keyboard and Edit Text Columns

1. Reveal Codes (**Alt** and **F3**); place the cursor on the **[Col Def newspaper; 2,1 . . .]** code.

2. Center (**Shift** and **F6**) and type the title; press the **Enter** key three times. *Note:* In order for the title to be centered over both columns, the title must be typed in front of the Column Definition code.

3. Move the cursor to the right of the **[Col On]** code; exit Reveal Codes (**Alt** and **F3**).

4. Keyboard the text to be printed in columns. The text will wrap around from line to line and snake from column to column. *Note:* If the defaulted margins are used, the text of the first column will end on the line located at approximately 9.83 inches. If there is more than one page of col-

umn text, the second column will also end on the line located at approximately 9.83 inches.

5. a. To move the cursor from the left column to the right column, press **Ctrl** and tap **Home** once {*Search, Go To*}, then press the **right** arrow key once. To move the cursor from the right column to the left column, press **Ctrl** and tap **Home** once; then press the **left** arrow key once. The cursor remains on the same horizontal line. *Note:* **Ctrl** and **Home** is referred to as "Go To."

   b. To move the cursor from page to page, press the **PgUp** or **PgDn** key.

6. To edit columns use the insert, delete, replace, move, and copy functions.

7. After the columns are typed, press **Alt** and **F7**; press **1** for columns; press **2** to turn columns off.

DEFINE AND KEYBOARD PARALLEL COLUMNS

Parallel columns are blocks of related information that are typed in columns side by side so the information can be read across the page from left to right. Parallel columns are used for programs, itineraries, résumés, lists, and so on. (See Exhibit 9.3.)

```
              Appointment Itinerary for Seattle Trip


    10:00 a.m.-11:30 a.m.        Meeting with Albert Graham of
                                 Barry and Associates to dis-
                                 cuss joint consultant ser-
                                 vices proposal for the State
                                 of Washington.

    12:00-2:00 p.m.              Lunch with Marlene Smith and
                                 Roland Temple at Luciano's.
                                 Discuss plans for new market
                                 research study.

    3:00 p.m.-5:00 p.m.          Strategic planning committee
                                 meeting in conference room
                                 202.
```

EXHIBIT 9.3 Parallel columns

Parallel columns wrap text around within each column similar to newspaper columns. However, related groups of short lines remain side by side. For example, if a group of lines in column 1 fills three vertical lines and the related group of lines in column 2 fills five vertical lines, the first line of each group remains on the same vertical line and two blank lines remain at the end of the lines in column 1.

⇨ Use the Procedure to Define Parallel Columns and prepare for typing the parallel columns in Exhibit 9.3.

Procedure to Define Parallel Columns

1. Before typing text, press and hold the **Alt** key while tapping the **F7** key once (**Alt** and **F7**).

2. Press **1** for Columns; press **3** for Define {*Layout, Column, Define*}.

3. The Text Column Definition menu is displayed. (See Exhibit 9.2.)

4. Press **1** for Type.

5. Press **3** for Parallel with Block Protect. (Block Protect will keep all lines of one block together on the same page.) *Note:* If the distance between columns is to be changed, press **3**; type the desired distance and press **Enter**.

6. Press **3** for distance between columns; type **.2**; **Enter**. Notice that the margins are automatically determined.

7. Press **Enter** to accept the column definition.

8. Press **1** for Columns On.

9. Press **Alt** and **F3** to reveal codes; the column codes are displayed: **[Col Def:Parallel/Block Pro;2,1 . . .]** **[Block Pro:On]** **[Col On]**.

⇨ Use the Procedure to Keyboard and Edit Parallel Columns.

⇨ Set justification for left.

⇨ Type the parallel columns shown in Exhibit 9.3.

⇨ Use the filename **9parcols**. Save the file and keep the document on the screen.

⇨ Print one copy using draft text quality.

Procedure to Keyboard and Edit Parallel Columns

1. Reveal Codes (**Alt** and **F3**); place the cursor on the **[Col Def:Parallel/Block Pro;2,1 . . .]** code.

2. Center (**Shift** and **F6**) and type the title; press the **Enter** key three times. *Note:* In order for the title to be centered over both columns, the title must be typed in front of the Column Definition code.

3. Move the cursor to the right of the **[Col On]** code; exit Reveal Codes (**Alt** and **F3**).

4. Keyboard the text to be printed in the first column. For example, type 10:00 a.m.–11:30 a.m. To move the cursor to the next column, press and hold the **Ctrl** key while tapping the **Enter** key once. Type the group of lines in column 2. Press **Ctrl** and **Enter** to return the cursor to the first column.

5. To move the cursor, see the Procedure to Keyboard and Edit Text Columns, page 136.

6. After the columns are typed, press **Alt** and **F7**; press **1** for Columns; **2** to turn Columns Off.

SUMMARY

- Newspaper and parallel columns are classified as text columns. The number of columns desired and the amount of space to be placed between columns are typed, and WordPerfect computes the margins for each column automatically (**Alt** and **F7**, **1**, **3**, make selections; if necessary, **F7**, **1**).

- Newspaper columns are paragraphs of text that wrap around from line to line and "snake" from column to column and page to page. Columns are defined and turned on before or after typing text (**Alt** and **F7**, **1**, **3**, make desired selections, **F7**, **1**).

- Parallel columns are blocks of related text that are printed in columns side by side (**Alt** and **F7**, **1**, **3**, **1**, **3**, **F7**, **1**).

- While typing parallel columns, press the **Ctrl** and **Enter** keys to move the cursor to the right column or to return the cursor to the left column.

- Once columns have been typed, the cursor can be moved from column to column (**Ctrl** and **Home**, **right** arrow key or **left** arrow key).

- After typing columns, the columns are turned off (**Alt** and **F7, 1, 2**).

SELF-CHECK QUESTIONS

(True / False—Circle One)

T,F 1. Parallel and newspaper columns are text columns.

T,F 2. Newspaper columns can be created before or after text is typed.

T,F 3. Once columns are defined and turned on, any typed information will display in columns.

T,F 4. Press **Ctrl** and **Home** to snake columns.

T,F 5. WordPerfect automatically wraps text in columns.

T,F 6. Columns are turned on by pressing **Alt** and **F7, 1, 1**.

T,F 7. Reveal codes to display the Column Definition code and the Column On code on the screen.

T,F 8. After text has been typed, the cursor can be moved between columns by pressing **Home** and the **right** or **left** arrow key.

T,F 9. Parallel columns require that the number of vertical lines in the left column group equal the number of vertical lines in the right column group.

T,F 10. Once columns are typed, turn columns off by pressing **Alt** and **F7, 1**, and **2**.

ENRICHING LANGUAGE ARTS SKILLS

Spelling / Vocabulary Words

fiber optics   a small bar-like glass tube through which light is passed.

microwave   electromagnetic radiation that has an extremely short wavelength.

extra vehicular activities (EVAs)   activities that take place in space outside of the space shuttle.

Abbreviations for Time

Type a.m. and p.m. with lowercase letters and no spaces.

Example Today the meeting will begin at 10:30 a.m.

EXERCISES

Exercise 9.1

1. The screen should be clear, and the disk drive should be accessed where the file disk is located.

2. Type the following newsletter article using newspaper columns.

3. Use the widow/orphan control (**Shift** and **F8, 1, 9, y, F7**.)

4. Set justification for left.

5. Use the filename **9.cols1**. Save the file without clearing the screen.

6. Print one copy using draft or high text quality.

A Space Champion

Aleta Jackson is a mover in more than one sense. She was born in St. Louis, Missouri, but in adulthood made Tucson, Arizona, her home. Last year, she moved to Washington, D.C., to become a member on the staff of the National Space Society. She recently bought a house in D.C. even while planning to make another big move as soon as possible: to the Moon.

She explains how that idea began. "My mother gave me a Tom Corbett, Space Cadet book to keep me occupied while undergoing the unspeakable inquisitional tortures of a 50's perm. The perm didn't take; space flight did." Resolving to become space bound, she ordered her life toward that goal.

"My bedroom in my parents' house looked east," she said, "and I have always been a night person, so on many evenings I could be found by my window, gazing longingly at the Moon. I knew we'd get there within my lifetime; I also expected to spend my adult life on the Moon. When Kennedy announced that we were going to the Moon, it was to me simply the adults of the world doing their jobs. What I still care most about is that humans get off the Earth on a viable, permanent basis.

I want to retire up there!"

"Perhaps that's why I get angry and impatient with how slowly things are going," she continued. "I'm not getting any younger, and the Moon seems to be getting further away instead of nearer." Aleta is too much of an action person to be satisfied with only reading and dreaming about space. She is often an official at the National Association of Rocketry meets, and, in the past, won a collection of trophies as a combat flier of model airplanes. She joined the Society of Creative Anachronism in 1973 out of fascination with the recreation of technology that has application today and in the future. "You can learn about the future by studying the past," she said.

Her first job was as a draftsman and electronics packaging designer for McDonnell Douglas Corporation and the Engineering Department of the Indiana Institute of Technology. Currently she is the Chapters' Administrator for the National Space Society.

"As Chapters' Administrator I intend to cultivate quality and encourage people to look beyond now to tomorrow's potential."

Exercise 9.2

1. The screen should be clear, and the disk drive should be accessed where the file disk is located.

2. Type the following program using parallel columns.

3. Use 0.3 inches for the distance between columns.

4. Set justification for left.

5. Use the filename **9cols2**. Save the file without clearing the screen.

6. Print one copy centered vertically on the page. (See Chapter 8 for centering a page vertically, page 117.) Use draft or high text quality.

```
               CRETA's Tenth Annual Conference
                     Boston, Massachusetts

The Management of Technology       Dr. Marion Sanderson
                                   Vice Provost
                                   Information Technology
                                   University of Virginia
                                   Charlottesville, Virginia

Managing a Telecommunications      Michael Gordon, President
Business                           Integrated Technology, Inc.
                                   Nashville, Tennessee

Fiber Optics Technology            Dr. Daniel Jacobs
                                   University of Nebraska
                                   Lincoln, Nebraska

ISDN: Concepts, Issues and         Patricia Nichols, President
Migration Strategies               Information Technology
                                   Services
                                   Princeton, New Jersey

Microwave Technology               Dr. Arnold Wallia
                                   Digital Microwave, Inc.
                                   Needham Heights,
                                   Massachusetts

Voice Processing                   Ronald Jimenez
                                   Executive Vice President
                                   Telecommunications Corp.
                                   Ann Arbor, Michigan
```

Exercise 9.3

1.   The screen should be clear, and the disk drive should be accessed where the file disk is located.

2.   Type the following glossary using parallel columns.

3.   Use 0.3 inches for the distance between columns.

4.   Set justification for left.

5.   Use the filename **9cols3**. Save the file without clearing the screen.

6.   Print one copy using draft or high text quality.

```
               DISKETTE GLOSSARY TERMS

Double-density              Twice as much information
                           can be saved on a double-
                           density disk as compared
                           to a single-density
                           diskette.

Double-sided               The diskette is guaranteed
                           that both sides can be
                           used for saving files.

Envelope                   The paper covering that
                           encloses the diskette. The
                           envelope is used to
                           protect the disk from
                           damage during handling.

Index hole                 The small hole located
                           above the large center
                           hole that tells the
                           read/write head the
                           location of the beginning
                           of a track.

Single-density             A specification for the
                           amount of information that
                           can be saved on a
                           diskette.

Single-sided               The diskette manufacturer
                           guarantees that only one
                           side of the diskette has
                           been tested for quality.

Write-protect-notch        The small notch located on
                           the right side of the
                           diskette. When this notch
                           is covered, information
                           can be retrieved from the
                           diskette but no
                           information can be saved
                           on the disk.
```

Exercise 9.4

1. The screen should be clear, and the disk drive should be accessed where the file disk is located.

2. Type the following newsletter article using newspaper columns. **Note**: Your line endings will be different from those shown.

3. Use the widow/orphan control (**Shift** and **F8**, **1**, **9**, **y**, **F7**).

4. Set justification for left.

5. Use the filename **9cols4**. Save the file without clearing the screen.

6. Print one copy using draft or high text quality.

THE DREAM IS ALIVE

"This is Launch Control with a preflight audio test. Flight Director, how do you read me? Mission Director, you are go for air-to-ground audio check. All positions begin prelaunch check lists."

Is this really Mission Control preparing to launch a Space Shuttle? Yes, if you are participating in a simulated space shuttle mission at the Alabama U.S. Space Academy.

It is raining outside, but inside the tent-shaped three-domed Space Camp building "space cadets" are learning the basic principles of propulsion, receiving flight assignments, and training for tomorrow's shuttle mission.

Dodging the raindrops, the space trainees skip over to the Marriott for a quick lunch. After lunch,

huddled under a sheet ready for laundry, the trainees dash over to the 67-foot domed theater to watch a film. The theater screen and audio system engulf the audience in the super-70-mm film image while astronauts practice maneuvers and emergency procedures, and orbit the earth.

Outside the theater and inside the museum, trainees experience the multi-axis maneuvering pod that turns 60 revolutions per minute and never revolves in any one specific direction more than twice. Who is made of the "right stuff?" Everyone. Dizziness and stomach somersaults are not experienced since there is not enough time for the brain to register the equilibrium change.

A new day begins at *5:00 a.m.* when an alarm clock rings in the dormitory-- both mission crews are awake. The mission pilot and commander must review the launch and landing procedures in order to prepare for the next shuttle launch.

At *3:00 p.m.* the air is filled with excitement as the *Atlantis* crew enters the space shuttle simulator ready for the two-hour shuttle mission. "This is Mission Director. All positions report satisfactory audio and the air-to-ground wind check is complete." The countdown begins and there is lift-off!

Mission specialists prepare to exit the space shuttle. Mission scientists begin laboratory experiments inside the space lab module. Mission Control's launch director, flight director, and mission director are busy communicating--with each crew member. A remote control camera takes pictures of the *Extra Vehicular Activities.*

The shuttle has completed its mission and will be landing soon. "The landing convoy is along the runway," reports Mission Control's public relations announcer. The pilot broadcasts that the descent has begun, the Air Force base is in sight, and we have touchdown!

Exercise 9.5

1. The screen should be clear, and the disk drive should be accessed where the file disk is located.

2. Type the following information using parallel columns.

3. Set justification for left.

4. Correct two spelling errors and four punctuation errors.

5. Use the filename **9cols5**. Save the file without clearing the screen.

6. Print one copy using draft or high text quality.

IRVIN'S ANNUAL CONFERENCE SPEAKERS

Dr. Judith Martin
University of North
Carolina

Dr. Martin, Division
Director of Information
Technology, has a
specialty in technology
management.

Mr. Roy Larson
Michigan State
University

Mr. Larson, Vice
President of Integrated
Technology, has a
specialty in fiber
optecs.

Dr. Patrick Calantone
Bentley College

Dr. Calantone is a
Professor in the CIS and
Business Technology
Division.

Ms. Claudia Sager
University of
Wisconsin, Madison

Ms. Sager Vice President
of Information Services
is an expert in
administrative systems.

Dr. Charles Quelch
Florida Atlantic
University

Dr. Quelch Associate
Professor has special
training as a
telecommunications
specialist.

Dr. Linda Malhotra
Digital Services, Inc.

Dr. Malhotra, President
is owner and manager of
micrwave systems.

Mr. Val Chang
Information Processing
Associates

Mr. Chang Chief
Commander, has expertise
in electronic mail.

Chapter 10

CREATE FORM LETTERS, MERGE ADDRESSES, AND PRINT FORM LETTERS

OBJECTIVES

After successfully completing this chapter, you should be able to:

● Create a form letter.

● Create a primary file.

● Create a secondary file.

● Merge the form letter and variable list.

● Print merged letters.

FORM LETTERS

A form letter is a standard letter sent to many individuals. A letter that is to be sent to more than one individual or company can be typed once, merged with a list of names and addresses, and printed. A form letter can be used for collecting overdue accounts, requesting donations, sales information, and so on. The variable information in a form letter includes names, addresses, dollar amounts, dates, and so on and can be referred to as a variable list.

```
{DATE}



{FIELD}1~
{FIELD}2~
{FIELD}3~ {FIELD}4~ {FIELD}5~

Dear {FIELD}6~:

We have received your request for an adjustment to your
mobile telephone service account.  Your account has been
reviewed and ${FIELD}7~ has been credited to account number
{FIELD}8~.  This amount will be reflected on your next
monthly mobile telephone statement under the category of
"Other Charges and Credits."

If you have any further questions, please call Customer Ser-
vice at 800-922-4884.  Thank you for choosing Intertex
Mobilnet as your cellular service provider.

Sincerely,



Mandy Chriss, Director
Customer Service
```

EXHIBIT 10.1 Primary file for form letter

CREATE A FORM LETTER

A primary file and secondary file are originated to create a form letter. The primary file is the typed form letter that includes the text and variable information codes. (See Exhibit 10.1.) The form letter includes the spacing, text, field codes, and information that is to be printed in each letter.

A field is one part of the information that varies in each form letter. For example, the recipient's name is one field, the street address is one field, the city name is one field, and so on. Field codes are placed in the primary file to indicate the location for each field.

The secondary file is a list of variable information such as name, address, state, zip code, dollar amount, and so on. (See Exhibit 10.2.) The secondary file includes codes that correlate with the codes in the primary file.

```
MRS MARGARET KONE{END FIELD}
908 SMITH AVE{END FIELD}
MENLO PARK{END FIELD}
CA{END FIELD}
94025{END FIELD}
MRS KONE{END FIELD}
15.35{END FIELD}
415-369-2269{END FIELD}
{END RECORD}
================================================================
MR JAMES BROWDER{END FIELD}
100 MAIN STREET{END FIELD}
ROHNERT PARK{END FIELD}
CA{END FIELD}
94428{END FIELD}
MR BROWDER{END FIELD}
42.55{END FIELD}
707-480-4008{END FIELD}
{END RECORD}
================================================================
MS RHONDA SMITH{END FIELD}
80 SOUTHLAND AVE{END FIELD}
CUPERTINO{END FIELD}
CA{END FIELD}
95014{END FIELD}
MS SMITH{END FIELD}
106{END FIELD}
415-968-5522{END FIELD}
{END RECORD}
================================================================
```

EXHIBIT 10.2   Secondary file variable list

▷ Use the Procedure to Create a Primary File.

▷ Type the primary file form letter shown in Exhibit 10.1.

▷ Use the filename **10letter.pf**. Save the file and keep the document on the screen.

▷ Print one copy using draft text quality.

Procedure to Create a Primary File

1. Clear the screen (**F7**, **n**, **n**).

2. Press **Shift** and **F9** for merge codes. (See Exhibit 10.3.)

3. Press **6** for more {*tools, merge codes, more*}; press the **down**

{DATE}	Places the date code in the primary file. The current date will be printed in the letter. (**Shift** and **F9; d**).
{END RECORD}	Places a code at the end of a variable list (record) for one document. The code represents the end of one set of variable information (**Shift** and **F9; e**)
{FIELD}	Places field codes in the primary field and the secondary field. Each field is numbered, e.g., FIELD 1, FIELD 2, etc. The field code, {FIELD}1~, in the primary file refers to the first line of information in the secondary file. The second field, {FIELD}2~, in the primary file refers to the second line of information in the secondary file, etc. (**Shift** and **F9; f**).
{END FIELD}	Places a code at the end of each line (field) in the secondary file (**F9**).

EXHIBIT 10.3   Merge codes

arrow key and highlight {**DATE**}; press **Enter**. The {**DATE**} code is displayed on the screen. *Note:* The {**DATE**} code will place the current date in the letter. (The current date must have been set when the computer was turned on.)

4. Press the **Enter** key five times.

5. Press **Shift** and **F9**.

6. Press **F** for Field {*tools, merge codes, field*}; the **Field:** prompt is displayed.

7. Press **1**; press **Enter**; {FIELD}1~ is displayed. Press **Enter**. *Note:* When the letter and addresses are merged, the first field will be replaced with the recipient's name.

8. Press **Shift** and **F9** again.

9. Press **F** for Field; the **Field:** prompt is displayed.

10. Press **2**; press **Enter**; {FIELD}2~ is displayed. Press **Enter**. The second field will be replaced with the street address.

11. Press **Shift** and **F9**; press **F** for Field; press **3**; press **Enter**; {FIELD}3~ is displayed. Type a comma and press the **space bar** once. The third field will be replaced with the city name.

12. Press **Shift** and **F9**; press **F** for Field; press **4**; press **Enter**; {**FIELD**}4~ is displayed. Press the **space bar** once. The fourth field is for the state.

13. Press **Shift** and **F9**; press **F** for Field; press **5**; press **Enter**; {**FIELD**}5~ is displayed. Press the **Enter** *twice*. The fifth field is for the zip code.

14. Type *Dear*; press the **space bar** once; press **Shift** and **F9**; press **F** for Field; press **6**; press **Enter**; {**FIELD**}6~ is displayed; type the colon (**Shift** and **;**). The sixth field is for the title and surname.

15. Press the **Enter** key twice; type the body of the letter.

16. When another variable is to be typed in the letter, press **Shift** and **F9**; press **F** for Field; press **7**; press **Enter**; (or press the number of the field desired); the {**FIELD**}7~ is displayed. Press the **space bar** or type the punctuation that will follow the variable. (See Exhibit 10.1.)

17. Continue typing the remainder of the letter.

➪ Use the Procedure to Create a Secondary File.

➪ Type the secondary file variable list from Exhibit 10.2.

➪ Use the filename **10name.sec**. Save the file and keep the document on the screen.

➪ Print one copy using draft text quality. *Note:* Each name and variable information will print on a separate page.

Procedure to Create a Secondary File

1. Clear the screen (**F7**, **n**, **n**).

2. Type the name of the first recipient; press **F9**. The code {**END FIELD**} is displayed, and the cursor automatically returns to the beginning of the next line. (See Exhibit 10.2.)

3. Type the street address; press **F9**. The code {**END FIELD**} is displayed, and the cursor automatically returns to the beginning of the next line.

4. Type the city name; press **F9**. The code {**END FIELD**} is displayed, and the cursor automatically returns to the beginning of the next line.

5. Type the two-letter state abbreviation; press **F9**. The code {**END FIELD**} is displayed, and the cursor automatically returns to the beginning of the next line.

6. Type the zip code; press **F9**. The code {**END FIELD**} is displayed, and the cursor automatically returns to the beginning of the next line.

7. Type the title and surname of the recipient; press **F9**. For example, type **Mrs. Kone**. The code {**END FIELD**} is displayed, and the cursor automatically returns to the beginning of the next line.

8. Type the first variable; press **F9**. For example, type **15.35**. The code {**END FIELD**} is displayed, and the cursor automatically returns to the beginning of the next line.

9. Type the second variable; press **F9**. For example, type **415-369-2269**. The code {**END FIELD**} is displayed, and the cursor automatically returns to the beginning of the next line.

10. Press **Shift** and **F9**; type **2** for End Record. *Note:* The {**END RECORD**} marks the end of a set of variables (a record) for one letter. The double lines (horizontal line of equal signs) indicate a hard page break. The hard page break is discussed in Chapter 13, page 200. (See Exhibit 10.2.)

11. Continue to type the next name, address, and variables. Repeat steps 2–10.

⇨ Use the Procedure to Merge the Form Letter and Variable List.

⇨ Merge the files named **10letter.pf** and **10name.sec**.

Procedure to Merge the Form Letter (Primary File) and Variable List (Secondary File)

Note: Clear the screen (F7, n, n).

1. Press **Ctrl** and **F9**.

2. Press **1** for Merge.

3. The prompt **Primary File** is displayed.

4. Type the name of the primary file, for example, **10letter.pf**; press **Enter** (or press **F5**; **Enter**; highlight filename; press **1**).

5. The prompt **Secondary File** is displayed.

6. Type the name of the secondary file, for example, **10name.sec**; press **Enter** (or press **F5**; **Enter**; highlight filename; press **1**).

7. All letters are displayed on the screen with the cursor located after the last letter. Press the **Home** key twice; press the **up** arrow key once to locate the cursor at the beginning of the first form letter.

8. Proofread the letters and check that the addresses, names, and variable information are placed correctly in the letter.

   Note: Saving the merged file is optional.

⇨ Use the Procedure to Print the Merged Letters.

⇨ Print one copy using draft text quality.

Procedure to Print the Merged Letters

1. The merged letters should be displayed on the screen.

2. Press **Shift** and **F7** to print.

3. Press **1** for Full Document.

   Note: All letters will print.

SUMMARY

- Form letters are created once and sent to more than one individual. The form letter is typed once and is referred to as a primary file. When the form letter is typed, a date code is placed at the beginning of the letter in order for the current date to be printed (**Shift** and **F9**, **6**, highlight {**DATE**}, **Enter**.)

- The form letter is combined (merged) with a list of names and addresses of individuals or companies who will receive the letter. Any information that will be different in each individual's letter, such as an amount or employee number, will also be typed with the name and address. Therefore, the record of changeable information is often referred to as a variable list. WordPerfect identifies the variable list as the secondary file.

● When the primary (letter) file is created, the customary letter format is utilized. At the location in the letter where variable information is to be printed, a field code is entered. The field codes are consecutively numbered when entered into the letter (**Shift** and **F9, f,** press field number, **Enter**).

● When the secondary file is created, each part of the variable information ends with a {**END FIELD**} code (**F9**). An end record code follows the last line in a group of variable information (**Shift** and **F9, 2**).

● After the primary and secondary files are created, the two files can be merged and displayed on the screen (**Ctrl** and **F9, 1,** type name of primary file, **Enter**, type name of secondary file, **Enter**). The merged file displays all the letters with the variable information located in the desired positions.

● The merged file can be saved and printed using the normal saving and printing procedures.

SELF-CHECK QUESTIONS

(True/False—Circle One)

T,F 1. A form letter is sent to more than one individual or company.

T,F 2. Variable information contains filenames and the date code.

T,F 3. The secondary file is a list of variable information.

T,F 4. The primary file is the form letter sent to many individuals.

T,F 5. The **Shift** and **F9, 6,** highlight {**DATE**} and **Enter** is pressed to place a date code in the primary file.

T,F 6. Each item in the variable file must end with a {**END RECORD**} code.

T,F 7. In the secondary file, each group of variable information ends with {**END FIELD**}.

T,F 8. The primary file and secondary file are merged by pressing **Ctrl** and **F9,** and **1**.

T,F 9. Form letters can be used for collecting overdue accounts.

T,F 10. The form letter includes the spacing, text, and information that is to be printed in every letter.

ENRICHING LANGUAGE ARTS SKILLS

Spelling/Vocabulary Words

delinquent   neglect of responsibility.
elegant   luxurious; gracious manner.
inquiry   a request or question.

Nonrestrictive Clause

A nonrestrictive clause is a clause that is not essential to the meaning of the sentence and therefore is set off by a comma.

Example   We will meet Thursday at 2:00 for our monthly sales meeting, which was postponed last month.

EXERCISES

Exercise 10.1

1. The screen should be clear, and the disk drive should be accessed where the file disk is located.

2. Create a primary file using the form letter, as shown; use seven fields. (See Exhibit 10.1.)

3. Use the defaulted margins.

4. Use the filename **10exer1.pf**. Save the file without clearing the screen.

5. Print one copy of the form letter using draft text quality.

```
{DATE}


{FIELD}1~
{FIELD}2~
{FIELD}3~, {FIELD}4~ {FIELD}5~

Dear {FIELD}6~:

According to our records, your account is
delinquent in the amount of ${FIELD}7~.

Payment must be received within seven business days
from the date of this letter. If payment is not
received, your service will be permanently
disconnected and your account referred to a local
collection agency.

Your prompt attention to this matter will be very
much appreciated.

Sincerely,



Justin Stenerson
Collection Manager

JS/xxx
letter1.pf/d2
```

Exercise 10.2

1. The screen should be clear, and the disk drive should be accessed where the file disk is located.

2. Create a secondary file using the variable information as shown.

3. Use the filename **10exer2.sec**. Save the file without clearing the screen.

4. Print one copy using draft text quality. *Note:* Each name and variable information will print on a separate page.

```
Mr. Scott McCoy {END FIELD}
286 Foxmont Drive {END FIELD}
Santa Rosa {END FIELD}
```

```
CA {END FIELD}
95401 {END FIELD}
Mr. McCoy {END FIELD}
359.90 {END FIELD}
{END RECORD}
================================================
Ms. Barbara Mulvaney {END FIELD}
92 Freedom Circle {END FIELD}
Belmont {END FIELD}
CA {END FIELD}
94002 {END FIELD}
Ms. Mulvaney {END FIELD}
423.30 {END FIELD}
{END RECORD}
================================================
Ms. Maureen Loy {END FIELD}
228 Fair Street {END FIELD}
Petaluma {END FIELD}
CA {END FIELD}
94952 {END FIELD}
Ms. Loy {END FIELD}
287.70 {END FIELD}
{END RECORD}
================================================
```

Exercise 10.3

1. The screen should be clear, and the disk drive should be accessed where the file disk is located.

2. Merge the form letter **10exer1.pf** with the variable list **10exer2.sec**.

3. Use the filename **10merge3**. Save the file without clearing the screen.

4. Print one copy of each merged letter using draft or high text quality.

Exercise 10.4

1. The screen should be clear, and the disk drive should be accessed where the file disk is located.

2. Create a primary file using the form letter, as shown; use six fields. (See Exhibit 10.1.)

3. Use the defaulted margins.

4. Use the filename **10exer4.pf**. Save the file and clear the screen.

(Use Date Code)

{FIELD}1~
{FIELD}2~
{FIELD}3~, {FIELD}4~ {FIELD}5~

Dear {FIELD}6~:

Thank you for your recent *inquiry* to the Cocoa
Beach Chamber of Commerce.

When you visit Florida's Space Coast, we invite you
to stay with us at the Chamberlin Hotel. We offer
our guests an *elegant* 200-room hotel, *located
directly on the Atlantic Ocean.*

Spaceport USA, featuring the new Imax Theater, is
20 minutes north of the Chamberlin. Also, we are 10
minutes south of Port Canaveral where you will find
adventure aboard deep sea charters, one-day cruise
ships, and three-day cruise ships to the Bahamas.

If additional information is needed, please contact
me at 800-886-4400. On behalf of the Chamberlin
Hotel staff, we welcome you to the Space Coast.

Sincerely,

Toni Johannes
Sales Director

TJ/xxx
client/d5

---

5. Create a secondary file, using the names and addresses, as shown.

6. Use the filename **10exer4.sec**.

7. Save the file and clear the screen.

```
Linda and Fred Davila {END FIELD}
102 Crystal Springs Rd. {END FIELD}
San Mateo {END FIELD}
CA {END FIELD}
94402 {END FIELD}
Linda and Fred {END FIELD}
{END RECORD}
================================================
Ms. Marsha Donnelly {END FIELD}
85 East Valley Drive {END FIELD}
Santa Clara {END FIELD}
CA {END FIELD}
95050 {END FIELD}
Ms. Donnelly {END FIELD}
{END RECORD}
================================================
Mr. Ned Hashemi {END FIELD}
350 Terrace Ct. {END FIELD}
Spokane {END FIELD}
WA {END FIELD}
99220 {END FIELD}
Mr. Hashemi {END FIELD}
{END RECORD}
================================================
```

8. Merge the form letter **10exer4.pf** with the variable list **10exer4.sec**.

9. Use the filename **10merge4**. Save the file without clearing the screen.

10. Print one copy using draft or high text quality.

Exercise 10.5

1. The screen should be clear, and the disk drive should be accessed where the file disk is located.

2. Create a primary file using the following form letter; use six fields.

3. Correct one spelling error and four punctuation and/or grammar errors.

4. Use the filename **10exer5.pf**. Save the file and clear the screen.

(Use Date Code)

{FIELD}1~
{FIELD}2~
{FIELD}3~, {FIELD}4~ {FIELD}5~

Dear {FIELD}6~:

As a new Farris Buick car owner you are cordially
invited to attend our new owner clinic next
Thursday at 7:30 P.M.

Refreshments will be served, and a free car care
kit is available for you and your family. Our
customer relations Manager will be on hand to
discuss warranty coverage, demonstrate maintenance
checks and answer any of your questions.

The Farris Buick Sales staff is eager to make your
car purchase and ownership a positive experience.
Please join us at our new facilty on Mission
Avenue.

Sincerely,

Sammy Goodwin
Customer Services

SG/xxx
owner.ltr/d2

---

5.   Create a secondary file using the following names and ad-
     dresses.

6.   Use the filename **10exer5.sec**. Save the file and clear the
     screen.

Mr. and Mrs. Bud Hanger {END FIELD}
4002 Spruce Street {END FIELD}
Philadelphia {END FIELD}
PA {END FIELD}
19104 {END FIELD}

```
Mr. and Mrs. Hanger
{END RECORD}
=============================================
Ms. Doris Scott {END FIELD}
2550 Chestnut Street {END FIELD}
Philadelphia {END FIELD}
PA {END FIELD}
19104 {END FIELD}
Ms. Scott {END FIELD}
{END RECORD}
=============================================
David and Carol Yavas {END FIELD}
3305 Oak Street {END FIELD}
Philadelphia {END FIELD}
PA {END FIELD}
19104 {END FIELD}
David and Carol {END FIELD}
{END RECORD}
=============================================
```

7. Merge the form letter **10exer5.pf** with the variable list **10exer5.sec**.

8. If desired, use the filename **10merge5**. Save the file without clearing the screen.

9. Print one copy using draft or high text quality.

Chapter 11

CREATE AND PRINT MAILING LABELS AND ENVELOPE ADDRESSES

OBJECTIVES

After successfully completing this chapter, you should be able to:

- Create one- and three-column mailing labels.

- Create a primary file for mailing labels.

- Use merge to create the mailing label file.

- Define and print mailing labels.

- Create a label definition.

- Create envelope addresses.

- Create an envelope definition.

- Block an address and print.

- Create and print a mailing list using three-column, predefined labels.

MAILING LABELS AND ENVELOPE ADDRESSES

Mailing labels are short forms on which names and addresses are printed. Mailing labels come in various sizes. One commonly used size is 4 × 1 inch. Generally, the labels are self-adhered to backing paper that is 11 inches in length. The self-adhesive mailing label is removed from the backing paper and placed on an envelope.

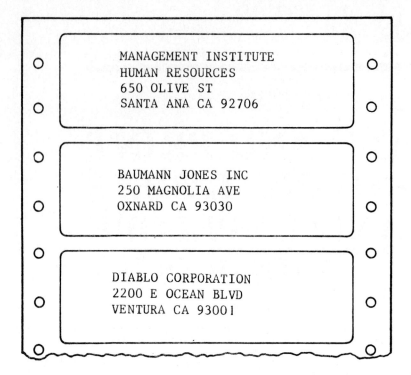

MANAGEMENT INSTITUTE
HUMAN RESOURCES
650 OLIVE ST
SANTA ANA CA 92706

BAUMANN JONES INC
250 MAGNOLIA AVE
OXNARD CA 93030

DIABLO CORPORATION
2200 E OCEAN BLVD
VENTURA CA 93001

EXHIBIT 11.1   One-column mailing labels

The 8½″ × 11″ paper on which the labels are adhered is usually connected between each page. The paper is perforated between each page and is referred to as continuous form paper.

Mailing labels are designed with one, two, or three columns per page. Procedures for printing one- and three-column mailing label forms are discussed in this book. A mailing label address is printed on the second or third line two to three spaces from the left edge of the form. (See Exhibit 11.1.)

Envelope addresses can be printed in one of three ways. First, addresses can be printed directly on envelopes that are manually placed in the printer. Second, an address can be copied from a letter address, blocked, and printed on an envelope. Third, a mailing label form can be defined, the address typed on the screen, and the label printed on an envelope.

The U.S. Post Office requests that addresses be typed in all capital letters with no punctuation and for a large (No. 10, 9½ × 4⅛ inch) envelope be placed on approximately line 14, 4 inches from the left edge of the envelope. (See Exhibit 11.2) The placement and form of the address is requested in order to allow an OCR (optical character reader) to scan the address electronically and sort the mail quickly, thus expediting the mail service.

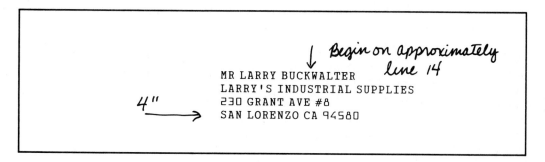

EXHIBIT 11.2   Envelope address

CREATE MAILING LABELS

Mailing labels are easily created from the secondary file that was originated to merge addresses with form letters. (See Exhibit 11.3.) First, a primary file is created with field code numbers and second, the new primary file and secondary file are merged.

```
MRS MARGARET KONE{END FIELD}
908 SMITH AVE{END FIELD}
MENLO PARK{END FIELD}
CA{END FIELD}
94025{END FIELD}
MRS KONE{END FIELD}
15.35{END FIELD}
415-369-2269{END FIELD}
{END RECORD}
==========================================================
MR JAMES BROWDER{END FIELD}
100 MAIN STREET{END FIELD}
ROHNERT PARK{END FIELD}
CA{END FIELD}
94428{END FIELD}
MR BROWDER{END FIELD}
42.55{END FIELD}
707-480-4008{END FIELD}
{END RECORD}
==========================================================
MS RHONDA SMITH{END FIELD}
80 SOUTHLAND AVE{END FIELD}
CUPERTINO{END FIELD}
CA{END FIELD}
95014{END FIELD}
MS SMITH{END FIELD}
106{END FIELD}
415-968-5522{END FIELD}
{END RECORD}
==========================================================
```

EXHIBIT 11.3   Original secondary file

```
{FIELD}1~
{FIELD}2~
{FIELD}3~ {FIELD}4~ {FIELD}5~
```

EXHIBIT 11.4 Primary file used to create mailing labels

The primary file consists of selected field numbers from the original secondary file. (See Exhibit 11.4.) The selected field numbers are the fields that represent the name, address, city, state, and zip code of each addressee.

Before the primary and secondary files are merged, the names and addresses are changed to uppercase letters with no punctuation to comply with U.S. Post Office requirements. The merged file is used to print the names and addresses on mailing labels. The merged file is saved as a separate file (See Exhibit 11.5.)

▷ Use the Procedure to Create a Primary File for Mailing Labels.

▷ Use the filename **11pmerge**.

▷ Your file should look similar to Exhibit 11.4.

Procedure to Create a Primary File for Mailing Labels

1. Press **Enter** to create one blank line. *Note:* The blank line places the first line of the address on line 2 of the label.

2. Press **Shift** and **F9** for Merge Codes.

```
MRS MARGARET KONE
908 SMITH AVE
MENLO PARK CA 94025
=======================================================
MR JAMES BROWDER
100 MAIN STREET
ROHNERT PARK CA 94428
=======================================================
MS RHONDA SMITH
80 SOUTHLAND AVE
CUPERTINO CA 95014
```

EXHIBIT 11.5 Merged file used to print mailing labels

3. Press f{*Tools, Merge codes, Field*}; the **Field:** prompt is displayed.

4. Press **1**; press **Enter** twice.

5. Press **Shift** and **F9**; press **f**; press **2**; press **Enter** twice.

6. Press **Shift** and **F9**; press **f**; press **3**; press **Enter** once; and press the **space bar** once.

7. Press **Shift** and **F9**; press **f**; press **4**; press **Enter** once; press the **space bar** once.

8. Press **Shift** and **F9**; press **f**; press **5**; press **Enter**. *Note:* These field numbers must be identical to the field numbers used in the original secondary file that was created to merge with a form letter.

9. Press **F10** to save the file. For example, use the filename **11pmerge**. Press **Enter**. *Note:* The primary file should look similar to Exhibit 11.4.

10. Clear the screen (**F7, n, n**).

⮕ Use the Procedure to Use Merge to Create a Mailing Label File. Use the primary file **11pmerge** previously created and merge the **10name.sec** (secondary file) created in Chapter 10 from Exhibit 10.2.

⮕ Use the filename **mail.lab**. Save the file and keep the document on the screen.

⮕ Use Print Screen (**Shift** and **PrtSc**) and print one copy of the **mail.lab** file. *Note:* Use plain paper to print the file.

⮕ Clear the screen (**F7, n, n**).

Procedure to Use Merge to Create a Mailing Label File

1. Press **Ctrl** and **F9**.

2. Press **1** for Merge {*tools, merge*}; the **Primary file:** prompt is displayed.

3. Type the name of the primary file. For example, type **11pmerge**; press **Enter** (or press **F5**; highlight the primary filename; press **1**).

4. The **Secondary file:** prompt is displayed.

| 5. | Type the name for the original secondary file. For example, type **10name.sec**; press **Enter** (or press **F5**; highlight the primary filename; press **1**).

| 6. | The names and addresses are displayed on the screen. *Note:* The mailing label file will have only the information needed from the original secondary file.

| 7. | Change addresses to all uppercase letters and no punctuation:
    a. Place cursor at the beginning of the document (press **Home** twice; press **up** arrow key once).
    b. Block entire file. (Press **Alt** and **F4**; press **Home** twice; press the **down** arrow key once.)
    c. Press **Shift** and **F3** to Switch.
    d. Press **1** for Uppercase.
    e. Delete all punctuation. Place the cursor at the beginning of the document. Press **Alt** and **F2**; **n**; type a period; press **F2**; press the **Del** key once; press **F2**. *Note:* All periods will be deleted. Your screen should look similar to Exhibit 11.5.

Note: If necessary, delete all commas.

| 8. | Use the filename **mail.lab**. Save the labels and clear the screen (**F7**, **y**, **type document name**, **Enter**).

DEFINE AND PRINT MAILING LABELS

Before the mailing labels are printed, a mailing label form is defined. The mailing label form paper size, label size, number of labels, and distance between labels is defined. (See Exhibit 11.6.) Once the mailing label form is defined, the Format: Paper Size/ Type is selected. (See Exhibit 11.7.)

⇨ Use the Procedure to Create a Label Definition.

⇨ Use one column of labels, 3 rows, 4 inches wide, and zero distance between columns.

Procedure to Create a Label Definition

| 1. | Press **Shift** and **F8** to display the Format menu.

| 2. | Press **2** for page {*Layout, Page*}.

```
Format: Labels

    1 - Label Size
                    Width           2.63"
                    Height          1"

    2 - Number of Labels
                    Columns         3
                    Rows            10

    3 - Top Left Corner
                    Top             0.5"
                    Left            0.188"

    4 - Distance Between Labels
                    Column          0.125"
                    Row             0"

    5 - Label Margins
                    Left            0"
                    Right           0"
                    Top             0"
                    Bottom          0"

Selection: 0
```

EXHIBIT 11.6 Format labels menu

```
Format: Paper Size/Type
                                                    Font  Double
Paper type and Orientation   Paper Size   Prompt Loc   Type  Sided  Labels

Envelope - Wide              9.5" x 4"    No   Manual  Land  No
Labels                       8.5" x 11"   No   Contin  Port  No     1 x 10
Labels                       8.5" x 11"   No   Contin  Port  No     3 x 10
Legal                        8.5" x 14"   No   Contin  Port  No
Legal - Wide                 14" x 8.5"   No   Contin  Land  No
Standard                     8.5" x 11"   No   Contin  Port  No
Standard - Wide              11" x 8.5"   No   Contin  Land  No
[ALL OTHERS]                 Width ≤ 8.5" Yes  Manual        No




1 Select; 2 Add; 3 Copy; 4 Delete; 5 Edit; N Name Search: 1
```

EXHIBIT 11.7 Paper Size/Type menu

3. Press **7** for Paper Size/Type.

4. Press **2** to add.

5. Press **4** for labels.

6. Press **8**; press **y** for yes.

7. Press **1** for label size.

8. Press **4** for width; **Enter** twice.

9. Press **2** for Number of labels.

10. Press **1** for columns; **Enter** twice.

11. Press **4** for Distance between labels.

12. Press **0** columns; **Enter** twice.

13. Press **F7** twice; the cursor returns to the Format Paper Size/Type listing.

14. The cursor should be located on labels 1 × 10. (See right column.)

15. Press **1** to select; (Wait a moment); press **F7**. *Note:* Reveal Codes (**Alt** and **F3**). The code **[Paper Sz/Typ:8.5″×11″, Labels,4″×1″]** is displayed. Exit Reveal Codes (**Alt** and **F3**).

▷ Retrieve the **mail.lab** file. (If necessary, press **y** to retrieve into current document.) Print on plain paper; print on one column mailing labels (optional).

▷ Save the **mail.lab** file.

CREATE ENVELOPE ADDRESSES

One of three methods can be used to print envelope addresses. First, the type-through program can be used to type directly from the keyboard to the printer. Second, an envelope definition can be created and the address printed. Third, the address on the letter can be blocked (highlighted) and printed as a block.

▷ Use the Procedure to Create an Envelope Definition.

▷ Use plain paper; use of an envelope is optional. If using plain paper, draw a 9½ × 4⅛-inch envelope outline on the printout to check placement of the address (optional).

▷ Type your friend's or relative's name and address.

Procedure to Create an Envelope Definition

1. Press **Shift** and **F8**.

2. Press **2** for Page {*Layout, Page*}; **7** for Paper Size/Type.

3. Press **2** to add; the Paper Type menu displays.

4. Press **5** for Envelope.

5. Press **1** for Paper Size; the Paper Size menu displays.

6. Press **5** for Envelope.

7. Press **3** for Font type.

8. Press **2** for Landscape. *Note:* Landscape uses the 11½ side of the paper as the top edge of the paper. This is useful when printing on laser printers that rotate their fonts.

9. Press **5** for location.

10. Press **3** for manual. *Note:* The printer will beep when an envelope is to be placed in the printer feed tray.

11. Press **Enter** to return the cursor to the Format: Paper Size/ Type menu.

12. Press **1** to select.

13. Press **F7** to return the cursor to the editing screen.

14. *Set margins:*
   a.   Press **Shift** and **F8**; **1** for line; **7** for margins.
   b.   Type **4** for left margin; **Enter**.
   c.   Type **zero** (0) for right margin; press **Enter** twice.
   d.   Press **2** for page; press **5** for margins.
   e.   Type **zero** (0) for top; **Enter**; type **zero** (0) for bottom; press **Enter**.
   f.   Press **Enter** to return the cursor to the Format menu.
   g.   Press **4** for Other.
   h.   Press **1** for Advance.
   i.   Press **3** for Line.
   j.   Press **2** for two inches; **Enter**.
   k.   Press **F7** to return the cursor to the editing screen.

15. Type your name and address in uppercase letters and no punctuation.

16. Print one copy: **Shift** and **F7**; **1** to print. *Note:* A beep will sound and the message **Action required in Printer Control**

is displayed at the bottom of the screen.

17. Press **Shift** and **F7**; **4** for Control Printer; **g** for Go. Press **F7** to exit.

▷ Use the Procedure to Type Directly from the Keyboard and Print an Address.

▷ Use plain paper; use of an envelope is optional. If using plain paper, draw a 9½ × 4⅛-inch envelope outline on the printout to check placement of the address (optional).

▷ Type your name and address.

Procedure to Type Directly from the Keyboard and Print an Address

*Note: The type-through printing feature is available on a separate disk. The floppy disk with the type-through program can be used to print directly from the keyboard. Also, the **TYPETHRU.EXE** file can be copied to the WordPerfect directory on your hard disk drive and can be used to print from the keyboard. This feature is not available for laser printers.*

1. *Using a floppy disk:*
   a. Place the floppy disk containing the type-through program in disk drive A: or B:
   b. Exit to DOS: Press **Ctrl** and **F1**, **1**.
   c. Type the disk drive letter where the type-through program is located, for example, **a:** or **b:**; press **Enter**.
   d. Type **typethru**; press **Enter**.
   Using a hard disk drive:
   a. Exit to DOS: Press **Ctrl** and **F1**, **1**. If necessary, type **c:**; press **Enter**.
   b. Type **typethru**; press **Enter**.

2. The Line Type-Through Printing menu is displayed. (See Exhibit 11.8.)

3. Use plain paper or place an envelope in the printer at the vertical line where the address is to be printed. For example, place the print device on line 14 for a number 10 (large) envelope (approximately 2 inches from the top edge of the envelope).

4. Press the **space bar** approximately 40 times (for 10-pitch) printers or 48 times (for 12-pitch printers) to move the cursor

```
Line Type-Through Printing

Function Key          Action

Move                  Retrieve the Previous Line for Editing
Format                Do a Printer Command
Enter                 Print the Line
Exit/Cancel           Exit Without Printing
Setup                 Setup New Printer Selection

Selected Printer      Dos Text Printer
Port                  LPT1:
```

EXHIBIT 11.8   The Type-Through screen

over 4 inches. Notice the **Pos . . .** is displayed at the lower right corner of the screen.

5. Type the name of the individual in uppercase letters who is to receive the letter; press **Enter**. The name is printed after the **Enter** key is pressed.

6. Space over 40 (or 48) times to move and position the cursor.

7. Type the street address in uppercase letters; press **Enter**.

8. Space over 40 (or 48) times and type the city, state (in uppercase letters), and zip code.

9. Press **F7** to exit.

10. If using a floppy disk:
   a.   Type **c:**; press **Enter**. (If necessary, type the name of the directory where WordPerfect files are located, for example, **c:\wp51**).

   Note: If using a hard disk drive, go to step 11.

11. Type **exit**; press **Enter** to return to the editing screen.

   *Note: The printer begins printing where the print head is located. When using type-through, the margins set with the format key (**Shift** and **F8**) are not in effect. Corrections can be made before the **Enter** key is pressed.*

Procedure to Block the Address and Print

1. Place an envelope in the printer. Align the printing device with the line on the envelope where the address is to be printed.

2. Place the cursor on the first character of the address to be printed; press **Ctrl** and **Enter** to insert a hard page. (See hard page breaks, Chapter 13, page 200). *Note:* The portion of the document to be printed as a block will print on the exact line as the original; that is, if the address begins on line 7 on the screen, the printer will move to line 7 before printing the block. Therefore, place a hard page before the text to be blocked and printed, so that printing will begin where the printing device is aligned on the envelope.

3. Without moving the cursor, press **Shift** and **F8** to obtain the Format menu.

4. Press **1** for Line {*Layout, Line*}.

5. Press **7** for Margins (left and right).

6. For a 10-pitch printer, type **4**; for a 12-pitch printer, type **4.7**.

7. Press **Enter** three times to return the cursor to the Format menu.

8. Press **2** for Page.

9. Press **5** for Margins (top and bottom).

10. Type **0** (zero); press **Enter**.

11. Type **0** (zero); press **Enter**. *Note:* The top and bottom margins are changed to zero.

12. Press **F7** to exit. *Note:* The entire letter will be indented 4 or 4.7 inches—that's fine.

13. Place the cursor on the first character of the address to be printed.

14. Press **Alt** and **F4** for Block {*Edit, Block*}.

15. Press **Enter** three or four times to highlight each line in the address.

16. Press **Shift** and **F7** {*File, Print*}.

17. The prompt **Print block? (Y/N) No** is displayed.

18. Press **y** for yes. *Note:* A **Please Wait** message is displayed and the address is printed.

19. Reveal Codes (**Alt** and **F3**) {*Edit, Reveal Codes*} and delete the left/right and top/bottom margin codes and the hard page code.

20. Press **Alt** and **F3** to exit the Reveal Codes.

▷ Type the following letter.

▷ Use the Procedure to Block the Address and Print, page 175.

▷ Block and print the letter address using plain paper. Printing on an envelope is optional. If using plain paper, draw a 9½ × 4⅛-inch envelope outline on the printout to check placement of address. (Optional)

▷ Save and print one copy of the letter. (Optional)

```
(Use current date)



Ms. Lois Richards
228 Shoreline Drive
Brooksville, FL 34602

Dear Ms. Richards:

Thank you for your recent telephone call concerning
the appraisal report.

A brief review of the appraisal indicates that your
property is worth substantially more than was the
case last year. The appraisal shows the fair market
value to be $325,000.

The recent appraisal indicates that as a matter of
economics the property should be sold and the
profit invested in other assets.

Let me know if I can be of further assistance.

Sincerely,


Donna Hill
```

➪ Type the following names and addresses in uppercase letters with no punctuation. After each address press **Ctrl** and **Enter** to obtain a page break. The page break instruction places a double row of equal signs across the screen. Page breaks are discussed in Chapter 13, page 200.

➪ Use the filename **create.lab**. Save the file and keep the document on the screen.

```
MR CHARLES REYER
COMPUTER SUPPLIES INC
340 28TH AVENUE
SAN MATEO CA 94402

MS TANYA KOJO
HOME REAL ESTATE
788 MAIN STREET
PASADENA CA 91106

MRS PATRICIA WHEELER
SOUTHLAND ESTATES
3400 DEER CREEK ROAD
PALO ALTO CA 94304

MR SAMUEL GONZALES
LYON PERSONNEL SERVICES
1360 KIFER ROAD
SUNNYVALE CA 94086

MS CLAUDIA FISHER
NSE MANUFACTURING
403 W TRIMBLE ROAD
SAN JOSE CA 95131
```

➪ Use the Procedure to Create a Mailing List, Use Predefined Labels and Print Three-Column Mailing Labels.

Procedure to Create a Mailing List, Use Predefined Labels and Print Three-Column Mailing Labels

1. Place the cursor at the beginning of the file (**Home** twice and **up** arrow key once; press **Alt** and **F10**.

2. Type filename including the location of the file, for example, **c:\wp51\labels.wpm**. *Note:* The file named **labels.wpm** is a macro file (see macros in Chapter 15) and is provided with the WordPerfect program. WordPerfect files are usually placed in the directory named **wp51** (WordPerfect Version 5.1).

3. Place the cursor on the **5260 Avery 1″ × 2⅝″** selection.

4. Press **1** to Select. (Wait a moment.)

5. Press **1** for Continuous.

6. The Format Paper Size/Type list displays; press **1** to select. (Wait a moment.)

7. Press **Shift** and **F7**, **v** to view the labels. (If necessary, press **1** for 100%.) The addresses should display in three columns.

8. Press **F1** to Cancel; press **1** to print the labels.

SUMMARY

- When letters are sent to many individuals or companies, mailing labels can be printed for the addresses. Mailing label forms are used for the printed addresses.

- The mailing labels are self-adhered to continuous form backing paper. Once the mailing labels are created, many labels can be printed quickly as the mail label forms automatically feed through the printer.

- Mailing addresses are typed in all capital letters, single-spaced, and with no punctuation in order to be machine-sorted efficiently at U.S. Post Offices. For a No. 10 envelope, the address should be printed on approximately line 14 and 4 inches from the left edge of the envelope.

- Mailing labels can be created from the secondary file that was used to merge addresses and variable information with form letters. A primary file is created to merge only the names and addresses from the former secondary (variable list) file. The merge procedure is used to create the mailing label file from the original secondary (variable list) file.

- A mailing label is defined by paper size, label size, number of labels, and distance between labels. Once the mailing label form is defined, the Format Paper Size/Type is selected. (See Exhibit 11.7.)

- Envelope addresses are printed by typing directly from the keyboard to the printer, creating an envelope definition, or by blocking and highlighting a letter address.

- Mailing labels can be created by using predefined labels that are provided with the WordPerfect program. The file named **labels.wpm** contains files for a number of standard forms that are available for Avery and 3M labels.

● An envelope address can be printed from the letter address. A page break is inserted, the margins are set, and the letter address is blocked. An envelope is placed in the printer and the address is printed.

SELF-CHECK QUESTIONS

(True / False—Circle One)

T,F 1. Mailing labels are short forms that are self-adhered to continuous form backing paper.

T,F 2. When a label definition is created, the label size, number of labels, and the distance between labels is specified.

T,F 3. Envelope addresses should be typed in upper- and lowercase letters and with punctuation in order to meet U.S. Post Office requirements.

T,F 4. An address is printed on a No. 10 envelope on approximately line 10 and two inches from the left edge of the envelope.

T,F 5. A mailing label can be defined and created using a file named **labels.wpm**.

T,F 6. An address from a letter can be blocked, and printed on an envelope.

T,F 7. The primary file created for mailing labels contains field numbers that must match the field numbers used in the secondary (address) file.

T,F 8. Use the **Ctrl** and **F9**, and **1** to merge the primary file and secondary file in order to create a mailing label file.

T,F 9. The **Ctrl** and **Enter** keys are pressed between each address when creating a mailing list.

T,F 10. WordPerfect has various predefined label sizes for Avery and 3M labels.

ENRICHING LANGUAGE ARTS SKILLS

Spelling / Vocabulary Words

fictitious   an assumed or imaginary name.
rendered   to have given assistance or performed a job.

Words Often Confused

personnel and **personal**
personnel   the group of workers employed by a company.
personal   pertaining to one's own self or private business.

EXERCISES

Exercise 11.1

1.   The screen should be clear, and the disk drive should be accessed where the file disk is located.

2.   Using the secondary file named **10exer2.sec** that was typed in Chapter 10, page 159, create a primary file for mailing labels.

3.   Name the primary file **11exer1.pf**. Save the file and clear the screen.

4.   Merge the primary file (**11exer1.pf**) with the secondary file (**10exer2.sec.**). Use the Procedure to Use Merge to Create a Mailing Label File. Save the new file; use the filename **11Labels**.

5.   With the file named **11Labels** on the screen, press **Home** 3 times and the **up** arrow key once. Use the Procedure to Create a Label Definition; use 1 column, 3 rows, 4 inches wide, and zero between columns.

6.   Save and replace the file named **11Labels**.

7.   Print one-column mailing labels. Use plain paper or 4 × 1 inch labels. If using plain paper, draw 4 × 1 inch label outlines on the printout to check placement of the address. (Optional)

Exercise 11.2

1.   Create an envelope definition; set a left margin at 4 inches and zero right, top, and bottom margins.

2.   Type the following addresses. Print on plain paper or on No. 10 envelopes. (Optional)

3.   (Optional). Use the type-through program and print the addresses directly from the keyboard to the printer.

```
MR BARRY YOUNG
FEATHERVIEW SALES DIVISION
2380 SCOTT BLVD
SANTA CLARA CA 95051

MR EUGENE CLAIRE
PARAMOUNT MOTORS
880 BARTER BLVD
CHARLOTTESVILLE VA 22901
```

Exercise 11.3

1. The screen should be clear.

2. Type the following letter.

3. Block the letter address, switch to all uppercase letters (**Shift** and **F3**, **1**). Delete the punctuation.

4. Print the address on a No. 10 envelope (9½ × 4⅛ inches) or on plain paper. If using plain paper, draw 9½ × 4⅛ inch envelope outlines on the printout to check placement of addresses. (Optional)

5. (Optional). Use the filename **11exer3**. Save the file and clear the screen.

(Use current date)

Mr. David Sanchez
Huntington News
P. O. Box 8099
Los Angeles, CA 90060-0859

Dear Mr. Sanchez:

Three original copies of the Fictitious Business Name Statements are enclosed along with a check in the amount of $250 in payment of your fees for services rendered.

Please file a Fictitious Business Name Statement with the County Clerks in Los Angeles, Fresno, and San Bernardino counties by the end of next week.

If you have questions, please telephone me at (818) 555-8800.

Yours very truly,

Maria Byler

Encs.

Exercise 11.4

1. The screen should be clear.

2. Type the following mailing list; press **Ctrl** and **Enter** after each name and address.

3. Use the Procedure to Create a Mailing List, Use Predefined Labels and Print Three-Column Mailing Labels. *Note*: If the message ". . . already defined, set-up? Yes (No)" displays, press **y** for yes.

4. Use the filename **11exer4**. Save the file and keep the document on the screen.

5. Print on plain paper or print on 3-column mailing labels that are 1″ × 2⅝″. (Optional)

```
MR STEPHEN WALKER
VALLEY VIEW ESTATES
890 FOOTHILL BLVD
YORK PA 17403

MRS CONNIE PARISH
TELECOMMUNICATIONS INC
P O BOX 15
BOISE MD 83707

MS BONNIE MAI
INTEGRATED SERVICES CORP
2600 CINCINNATI AVE
ROCKLIN CA 95677

MR GEORGE MCDONALD
SYSTEMS SUPPORT COMPANY
650 14TH STREET SW
LOVELAND CO 80537
```

Exercise 11.5

1. The screen should be clear.

2. Use the type-through procedure to print the following addresses. Print on plain paper. Printing on envelopes is optional.

3. Correct two spelling errors and three punctuation errors.

```
MR HAROLD KOHLI              MRS TINA BOOTS
ADVENT SYSTEMS               PERSONNAL DIRECTOR
90 MAYFAIR STREET            P O BOX 1703
YONKERS, NY 10710            LAKE CITY FL 32056

MR AND MRS CLAIR RYAN        MS JENNIFER MERCHANT
RYAN CONSTRUCTION, CO        ACOUNTS PAYABLE
865 LAKE STREET              877 BETNER RD.
GREENWICH CT 06831           MANSFIELD OH 49907
```

Chapter 12

CREATE
A ONE-PAGE
DOCUMENT

OBJECTIVES

After successfully completing this chapter, you should be able to:

- Create a document.

- Format a document.

- Create a one-page document single spaced and left justified.

- Create a one-page document double spaced with full justification.

A one-page document can be an article, essay, minutes, agenda, or any type of document that describes an event or provides information. Examples of business documents are investment, insurance, and sales documents. Documents are often referred to as reports, research papers, or manuscripts.

CREATE A DOCUMENT

The document can be created with single spacing or double spacing. If the document is single spaced, the paragraphs begin at the left margin with a blank space between paragraphs. (See Exhibit 12.1.) If the document is double spaced, the paragraphs are indented approximately five spaces from the left margin. (See Exhibit 12.2.) The paragraphs of a single- or double-spaced document can be full justified or left justified.

↓ 1" (default)

ACCOUNTING POLICIES SUMMARY
↓ 3

1"
→

The Berryessa Homeowners Association is a
Washington non-profit corporation and is
comprised of owners of 50 townhouse units in
Richland, Washington. The Articles of
Incorporation were filed on March 7, 1987.
↓ 2

1"
←

The association's Board of Directors are
required to maintain and protect the common
areas owned by the association members. The
common areas include the building exteriors,
recreation areas, roads, and landscaping.
↓ 2

The authority and responsibilities for the
association are obtained from a Declaration of
Covenants, Conditions, and Restrictions which
were executed and recorded on January 20,
1987.
↓ 2

The majority of the policy decisions are made
by the seven-member Board of Directors. The
policy decisions are made in accordance with
the governing documents.
↓ 2

Property and equipment purchased are
capitalized at cost and are depreciated over
the estimated useful life of four to ten years
using the straight-line method of
depreciation.
↓ 2

Routine annual maintenance of building and
grounds is charged to expenses in the year
incurred. Major maintenance expenditures such
as painting, roofs, and paving are charged to
expenses at an estimated annual amount on a
straight-line method. The amount computed is
based on estimates of expected life and
estimated cost. This account is reduced in the
year the actual expenditure occurs.

EXHIBIT 12.1 Single-spaced document with left justification

↓ 1"

ACCOUNTING POLICIES SUMMARY

↓ 1 or 2 (set on vertical line spacing of 2)

The Berryessa Homeowners Association is a Washington non-profit corporation and is comprised of owners of 50 townhouse units in Richland, Washington. The Articles of Incorporation were filed on March 7, 1987.

↓ 1

1" →

The association's Board of Directors are required to maintain and protect the common areas owned by the association members. The common areas include the building exteriors, recreation areas, roads, and landscaping.

← 1"

↓ 1

The authority and responsibilities for the association are obtained from a Declaration of Covenants, Conditions, and Restrictions which were executed and recorded on January 20, 1987.

↓ 1

The majority of the policy decisions are made by the seven-member Board of Directors. The policy decisions are made in accordance with the governing documents.

↓ 1

Property and equipment purchased are capitalized at cost and are depreciated over the estimated useful life of four to ten years using the straight-line method of depreciation.

↓ 1

Routine annual maintenance of building and grounds is charged to expenses in the year incurred. Major maintenance expenditures such

(continued)

EXHIBIT 12.2 Double-spaced document with full justification

> as painting, roofs, and paving are charged to
> expenses at an estimated annual amount on a
> straight-line method. The amount computed is
> based on estimates of expected life and
> estimated cost. This account is reduced in the
> year the actual expenditure occurs.
>
> 1"

EXHIBIT 12.2 (continued)

FORMAT A DOCUMENT

Standard 8½ × 11-inch paper has 66 vertical lines available. Since the top and bottom margins are each 1 inch (6 lines per inch), 12 lines are used with 54 lines remaining for printing. (See Exhibit 12.1.)

The title is centered and typed in all capital letters. Two or three blank lines follow the title.

A document is formatted with 1-inch top, bottom, left, and right margins. (See Exhibit 12.1.) All margins in WordPerfect are defaulted to 1-inch.

⇨ Use the Procedure to Create a One-Page Document Single Spaced and Left Justified.

⇨ Type the one-page document in Exhibit 12.1.

⇨ Use single spacing and left justification.

⇨ Use the filename **12pdoc1**. Save the file and keep the document on the screen.

⇨ Print one copy using draft print quality.

Procedure to Create a One-Page Document Single Spaced and Left Justified

1. Use left justification: **Shift** and **F8**, **1**, **3**, **1**; press **F7** once.

2. Press **Shift** and **F6** to center the title.

3. Type the title in all capital letters; press **Enter** three times.

4. Type the first paragraph. Press the **Enter** key twice after the paragraph.

5. Repeat step 4 for each paragraph.

▷ Use the Procedure to Create a One-Page Document Double Spaced and Full Justification.

▷ Type the following document (Statement of Partnership) with double spacing and full justification. *Note:* If the default is set for full justification, no change is necessary.

▷ Indent the enumerated items as shown. *Note:* Use hard spaces within dates and persons' names. (Hard spaces are discussed in Chapter 6, page 90.)

▷ Use the filename **12pdoc2**. Save the file and keep the document on the screen.

▷ Print one copy using draft print quality.

Procedure to Create a One-Page Document Double Spaced and Full Justification

1. Change the line spacing to 2 (**Shift** and **F8, 1, 6, 2**; press **F7** twice).

2. Press **Shift** and **F6** to center the title.

3. Type the title in all capital letters; press **Enter** two times. *Note:* When using double spacing, two **Enter/Returns** will create three blank lines between title and text.

4. Press the **Tab** key once. Type the first paragraph. Press the **Enter** key once after the paragraph.

5. Repeat step 4 for each paragraph.

STATEMENT OF PARTNERSHIP

The undersigned partners of the partnership identified below declare and state that:
1. The name of the partnership is MITSUTOME, CORSO, DICKINSON, & HANSEN.
2. The names of the partners are DARREL R. MITSUTOME, MARY LOU CORSO, GREGORY DICKINSON, JR., and DOROTHY S. HANSEN.

3. The persons named in paragraph 2 of this Statement are all of the partners of said partnership.
4. Any conveyance, encumbrance or transfer of an interest in the real property of the partnership other than a lease of any portion thereof for a period of six (6) years or less (including the total period of any options granted thereunder) must be signed on behalf of the partnership by each of the partners, DARREL R. MITSUTOME, MARY LOU CORSO, GREGORY DICKINSON, JR., and DOROTHY S. HANSEN, acting together. No other signature shall be required.
This statement was executed on July 25, 1990 at Sacramento, California.

SUMMARY

- Business documents such as agendas, reports, meeting minutes, and so on, that are one page in length are printed with one-inch right, left, top, and bottom margins.

- A one-page document can be printed single- or double-spaced. Paragraphs are indented when the document is printed double spaced and are not indented when printed single spaced.

- A document title is typed in all capital letters and centered.

- One-page documents can be printed with left or full justification.

SELF-CHECK QUESTIONS

(True/False—Circle One)

T,F 1. A one-page document is printed with one-inch margins.

T,F 2. The title of a report is typed in upper- and lowercase letters.

T,F 3. Paragraphs for a double-spaced document are indented approximately five spaces from the left margin.

T,F 4. The document title is followed by two or three blank lines.

T,F 5. All margins in WordPerfect are defaulted for one inch.

T,F 6. A double-spaced document should always be printed with full justification.

T,F 7. A standard 8½″ × 11″ paper has 66 vertical lines available for printing.

T,F 8. A single-spaced document should be printed with indented paragraphs and left justified lines.

T,F 9. Typical business documents include investment, insurance, and sales documents.

T,F 10. A standard one-inch top margin is 6 vertical lines.

ENRICHING LANGUAGE ARTS SKILLS

Spelling/Vocabulary Words

liability   a debt; a disadvantage.
cumulative   a collection or adding together of items.
compensation   a benefit for having provided something; a payback.

Coordinating Conjunction

A comma is placed before a coordinating conjunction (*and, or, because*) that joins two independent clauses, i.e., clauses that are complete sentences.

Example   We will respond promptly to the questionnaire, because our company would like to maintain a good working relationship with our clients.

No comma is placed before a conjunction if one or both clauses are dependent.

Example   We mailed 500 surveys yesterday and expect to obtain a 1 percent response by the end of June.

EXERCISES

Exercise 12.1

1. The screen should be clear, and the disk drive where the disk is located should be accessed.

2. Type the following document single spaced with left justi-
    fication.

3. Use the filename **12exer1**. Save the file without clearing the
    screen.

4. Print one copy using draft or high text quality.

NOTES FOR GENERAL PARTNER

*Perkins Management and Investment Company (PMIC),
the general partner, has unlimited liability for
obligations of the Partnership and has significant
contingent liabilities as general partner in other
limited partnerships.*

The general partner will receive a 2% interest in
taxable income and loss generated by operations and
all cash distributions prior to sale or refinancing
of the Partnership property. The general partner
also will receive a 15% subordinated interest in
the net distributed cash proceeds obtained from the
sale or refinancing of all or any portion of the
Partnership property.

No proceeds from the sale or refinancing of
the property shall be allocated to the general
partner until the limited partners have received
distributions equal to the total amount of their
adjusted capital contributions plus an 8.5% per
annum cumulative return.

The general partner will receive an allocation of
18% of the remaining gain upon the sale or other
disposition of the Partnership property. The
allocation after the gain from the sale will be
allocated first to partners with negative balances
in their capital accounts until no partner has a
negative balance. In addition, the limited partners
must receive allocations of gain equal to the total
amount of their adjusted capital contributions plus
an 8% per annum *cumulative* return.

Any loss recognized by the Partnership on the sale
or other disposition of all or any part of the
Partnership property will be allocated 2% to the
general partner and 98% to the limited partners.

PMIC and its subsidiaries also receive compensation
in the form of commissions on the formation of
the Partnership and purchase and sale of the
Partnership property and fees for management
and administration of Partnership affairs. This
compensation is not determined by arm's length
negotiations, but PMIC considers the commissions
and fees charged to be comparable to those that

would have been negotiated in arm's length
transactions.

In addition, the Partnership paid $19,500 last year
to PMIC Air Transport Services for reimbursement
of travel expenses incurred on behalf of the
Partnership. The Partnership also paid $7,880 last
year for reimbursement of insurance and data
processing costs incurred on behalf of the
Partnership.

Exercise 12.2

1. The screen should be clear, and the disk drive where the
    disk is located should be accessed.

2. Type the following document single spaced with full justi-
    fication.

3. Use the filename **12exer2**. Save the file without clearing the
    screen.

4. Print one copy using draft or high text quality.

HUMAN RESOURCES DEVELOPMENT

The goal of Mansfield Funds is to service our
shareholder and broker communities in order to lead
the mutual fund industry. Each employee is informed
of our goals the first day on the job. Mansfield
Funds' employees are committed to excelling in
their work both personally and as a company team.
The employees provide a quality of service that
sets industry standards.

The Mansfield Human Resources Department is
dedicated to enhancing the employer/employee
relationship through various programs. Our major
goal this past year was to develop a new Wage and
Salary Administration Program for the over 1200
employees who now work at Mansfield. One major goal
is to initiate internal equity among all positions
within the company, and to give management the
ability to address all *compensation* issues in a
fair and consistent manner.

*Our technical training program has been expanded to
include over 20 new courses to supplement
Mansfield's on-the-job training, because we
recognize the customer's desire to receive service
from knowledgeable and informed employees.* The new
Leadership Skills Training Course is offered to all

```
levels of management including management trainees.

The Management Trainee Program increased from 70
employees last year to 90 employees this year.
Selections this year were made from over 500
applicants from a variety of colleges and
universities and from the ranks of our own
employees.

The structure of the Management Trainee Program
has two new features. First, all trainees rotate
through core courses that ensure they will receive
at least 10 months of training in our key service
and systems operation areas. Second, all trainees
will participate in a mentor program that pairs a
new trainee with a colleague who is in the second
year of the program.

Mansfield Funds recognizes the importance of
considering the personal needs of our employees.
The Employee Support Program provides free
counseling to employees. Also we provide a complete
health benefit program, an education reimbursement
plan, and promotions from within the company.

Employees are motivated by the incentive plan that
rewards outstanding employees each month for
superior achievement. Employees of the month for
the past six months are Marion Reese, Accounting
Systems; Verdelle Martin, Human Resources; Victor
Madison, Dealer Services; Herman Easton, Data
Input; Bill Justis, Word Processing; and Leslie
Norton, Adjustments.
```

Exercise 12.3

1. The screen should be clear, and the disk drive where the disk is located should be accessed.

2. Type the following document double spaced with full justification.

3. Use the filename **12exer3**. Save the file without clearing the screen.

4. Print one copy using draft or high text quality.

```
            EMPLOYMENT SAFETY CONDITIONS


     The Board of Directors acknowledges that in
providing the services of this company, it assumes
liability for the safety of employees while they
```

are in and on the facilities performing company
responsibilities.

     The Board of Directors is to provide, publish,
and post rules for safety and the prevention of
accidents and furnish protective devices where they
are required for the safety of the employees. In
addition the company is to provide safe and
appropriate equipment necessary for the operations
of the company.

     The company shall at all times maintain
standards of safety and sanitation in conformance
with law, and the union and the company shall
cooperate to eliminate hazards and correct any
conditions adversely affecting the health and
safety of employees.

Exercise 12.4

1.   The screen should be clear, and the disk drive where the
     disk is located should be accessed.

2.   Type the following agenda. Use the spacing as shown with
     left justification.

3.   Use the filename **12exer4**. Save the file without clearing the
     screen.

4.   Print one copy using draft or high text quality.

```
                    AGENDA
            INTERNATIONAL SPACE EXPO
            STEERING COMMITTEE MEETING


DATE:    January 25, 19xx

TIME:    7:00 p.m.

PLACE:   College of San Mateo, Building 30, Room
         128

Objectives:

1. Formally organize this Steering Committee.

2. Review the concept and goal of the space expo.

3. Identify key local industry resources available
```

and plan how to utilize them.

4. Brainstorm exhibits and exhibitors to
   participate with the fair.

5. Identify the major tasks to be completed and
   assign the responsibilities to specific persons.

AGENDA

7:00 p.m.   Call to order and introductions

7:10 p.m.   Review meeting objectives and purpose
             of space expo

7:30 p.m.   Review of current plans and budget

7:45 p.m.   Discussions of local resources
             available and corporate sponsorships

8:00 p.m.   Brainstorm on possible exhibits and
             exhibitors

8:30 p.m.   Review major tasks and assign
             responsibilities

9:00 p.m.   Adjourn

Exercise 12.5

1. The screen should be clear, and the disk drive where the disk is located should be accessed.

2. Type the following document double spaced with left justification.

3. Correct two spelling errors and four punctuation errors.

4. Use the filename **12exer5**. Save the file without clearing the screen.

5. Print one copy using draft or high text quality.

NEWSPRINT

California ports have been receiving newsprint for more than three quarrters of a century. Since the beginning of the 1920s Pacific Marine Incorporated has been handling newsprint with devoted service, remarkable damage control and a quality of newsprint handling knowledge that no other west coast marine company can match.
Pacific Marine handles almost every ton of newsprint that is offloaded in California--from San

Francisco to San Diego. Less damage occurs in
Pacific Marine's operations compared to any other
marine company.

At Pacific Marine, valuable newsprint cargos
are guarded against paper tears and the newsprint
freight is protected from ground damage. Safety,
efficiency, and productivity are maintained during
all operations.

Vacuum lifts are used on the docks that were
designed and built specifically for Pacific
Marine's operations. The vacuum systems can't
release a load until it is set down.

Pacific Marine constantly reviews and
reevaluates advanced technology newsprint handling
systems. Suggestions are made to the steamship
lines regarding refinements and improvements that
would improve services.

Paper manufacturers are consulted to ensure
that packaging is compatible with vacuum handling.
Also, fully trained personal from clerks to
superintendents are highly motivated. Pacific
Marine is the west's number one paper products
handler.

Chapter 13

CREATE A MULTIPLE-PAGE DOCUMENT

After successfully completing this chapter, you should be able to:

● Create a multiple-page document.

● Number pages.

● Create headers and footers.

● Create footnotes.

● Control widow and orphan lines.

A multiple-page document is comparable to a one-page report and can be an article, essay, minutes, agenda, or any type of document that describes an event or provides information. A multiple-page document is two or more pages. Examples of multiple-page business documents are investment, insurance, and sales documents.

CREATE A MULTIPLE-PAGE DOCUMENT

Like a one-page document, a multiple-page document can be created with single spacing or double spacing. Also, the pages of a mulitple-page document are formatted the same as a one-page document with 1-inch margins. (See Exhibits 12.1 and 12.2.)

Each page of a multiple-page document is separated by a page break. A page break is a line of hyphens that is placed on the screen to indicate that the number of vertical lines on the page have reached 9.83 inches on the display screen (approximately 54 printed lines). As text is typed, the text automatically wraps around to the next page and WordPerfect inserts a page break between the pages. The automatic page break is called a soft page. When codes are revealed, **[SPg]** indicates the location of the automatic page break.

If a new page is desired before the lines on the screen reach 9.83 inches, a hard page break is used to create a new page. A hard page break is placed in a document by pressing the **Ctrl** and **Enter** keys. A hard page break displays a row of equal signs across the screen. When codes are revealed the **[Hpg]** code indicates the hard page break location.

▷ Use the Procedure to Create a Multiple-Page Document.

▷ Type the following multiple-page document.

Procedure to Create a Multiple-Page Document

1. Set the vertical line spacing for 2 (**Shift** and **F8; 1, 6, 2**). *Note:* Single spacing can also be used.

2. Center (**Shift** and **F6**) and type the title in all capital letters.

3. Press the **Enter** key once.

4. Type the subtitle in lowercase letters with the first letter of each major word capitalized.

5. Press the **Enter** key twice.

6. Indent each paragraph five spaces (if line spacing of 2 is set); press the **Enter** key once after each paragraph. If using line spacing of one, the paragraphs are not indented and the **Enter** key is pressed twice after each paragraph. (See Exhibit 12.1.)

```
              REUSABLE EXTERNAL TANKS

              On-Orbit Tank Servicing

     Once on orbit, the external tank is prepared
for habitation. The orbiter could orient the tank
aft end toward the sun to maximize boil-off of
residual hydrogen after the hatch was opened and to
minimize loss of oxygen. External tank servicing
during extravehicular activities could be carried
out by two or three astronauts, one using a Manned
Maneuvering Unit for external inspection and for
```

transporting equipment between the orbiter cargo
bay and tank hatches, and one or two astronauts
stationed inside the tanks to remove and install
equipment. It is expected the servicing would take
approximately two days to accomplish, one day for
each end of the tank.

Part of the on-orbit servicing procedure would
be removal of the internal oxygen and hydrogen
propellant feedlines and baffles. The oxygen tank
has an X-shaped vortex baffle that would be
disassembled and removed. The hydrogen feedline
suction bell and interior feedline would be removed
at a flange installed where the feedline passes
through the aft tank wall. Both tank openings would
be fitted with covers carried aboard the orbiter.

Ladders, deck supports, deck segments, and
interior wall panels could be carried in the
orbiter cargo bay and added as needed on orbit. The
decking could be a lightweight structural grid
similar to that used on Skylab, with triangular
openings to provide receptacles for boot sole
twist-to-lock cleats and for cargo tiedown. Clips
could be fitted to the underside of the deck grid
to accept ceiling panels.

Small segments of the decking would surround
all four hatches to allow astronauts to be anchored
by their cleated boots while working the hatches or
guiding cargo through the hatch openings. The
decking also could be installed before flight where
it would not disturb fluid flow at the feedline
inlets.

Decks, ceiling, and wall panel sections could
be carried in the orbiter cargo bay in 32-inch-wide
sections, small enough for bundled sections to be
guided through the hatch openings.

A forced-air circulation system could be added
to those tanks that would be used for living
accommodations and in factory modules that were not
completely automated. Heat dissipation could be
accomplished with freon radiators similar to those
on the orbiter cargo bay doors mounted directly to
the outside of the tank, or could be connected to
radiators as on the Space Station.

The air circulation ducting manifold, fan,
filters, and cooling coils could be modular, with
one unit used within the oxygen tank and two in
the hydrogen tank. These could be carried aloft
collapsed to 10-foot-long modules in the orbiter
cargo bay, fitted through the tank hatches, and
then extended to 45 feet, and mounted to the deck
section edges opposite the ladder in the central
access opening.

▷ Use the filename **13pexer**. Save the file and keep the file on
the screen.

▷ Print one copy of the document using full justification and
draft text quality.

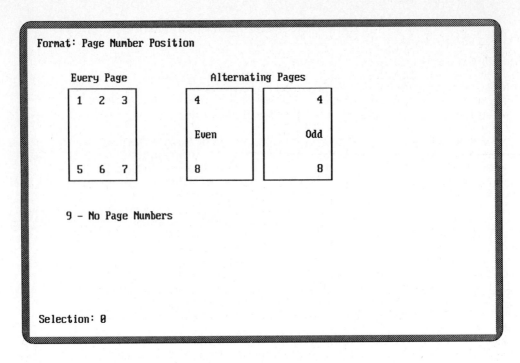

```
Format: Page Number Position

    Every Page                 Alternating Pages
    ┌─────────────┐        ┌──────────┐  ┌──────────┐
    │ 1   2   3   │        │ 4        │  │        4 │
    │             │        │          │  │          │
    │             │        │ Even     │  │     Odd  │
    │             │        │          │  │          │
    │ 5   6   7   │        │ 8        │  │        8 │
    └─────────────┘        └──────────┘  └──────────┘

    9 - No Page Numbers




Selection: 0
```

EXHIBIT 13.1   Page number position screen

PAGE NUMBERING

Each page of a multiple-page document should be numbered. By using the page number instruction once, numbers will print on each page. Numbers can be printed at the top or bottom of the page. WordPerfect has eight possible number positions (See Exhibit 13.1.) The default for WordPerfect is no page numbering.

▷ The **13pexer** document should be on the screen.

▷ Use the Procedure to Number Pages.

Procedure to Number Pages

1. Place the cursor at the beginning of the file (press **Home** three times; press the **up** arrow key once). *Note:* Pressing the **Home** key three times places the cursor in front of all codes.

2. Press **Shift** and **F8**.

3. Press **2** for Page {*Layout, Page*}.

4. Press **6** for Page Numbering; the Format: Page Numbering menu is displayed.

5. Press **4** to select the Page Number Position.

6. Press **6** to select the bottom center position.

7. Check that the New Page Number is 1.

202

8. Press **F7** once to return the cursor to the editing screen.

9. Reveal Codes (**Alt** and **F3**); the code **[Pg Numbering: Bottom Center]** is displayed; exit reveal codes (**Alt** and **F3**). *Note*: To display the page number, press **Shift** and **F7, 6** for view.

➪ Use the filename **13pexer.rev**. Save the file and keep the document on the screen.

➪ Print one copy using justification and draft text quality.

HEADERS AND FOOTERS

Generally, a multiple-page document includes headers and/or footers, that is, a title that is printed at the top or bottom on each page. (See Exhibits 13.2 and 13.3.) A header is printed at the top of a page; a footer is printed at the bottom of a page. Headers and footers often include page numbers. Headers and footers are displayed on the screen by using the view feature (**Shift** and **F7, 6**).

➪ The **13pexer.rev** document should be on the screen.

➪ Delete the page number and bottom center codes: move the cursor to the beginning of the file (press **Home** three times; press the **up** arrow once). Reveal Codes (**Alt** and **F3**); place the cursor on the bottom center code; and press **Del**. Exit reveal codes (**Alt** and **F3**).

➪ Use the Procedure to Create a Header and create the following header:

REUSABLE EXTERNAL TANKS   ^B

Procedure to Create a Header

1. On page 1, place the cursor at the beginning of the document (**Home** three times; **up** arrow key once). Generally, a title is printed on the first page, and headers are printed on the second and following pages.

2. Press **Shift** and **F8**.

3. Press **2** for Page {*Layout, Page*}.

4. Press **3** for Headers.

5. Press **1** for Header A.

triangular openings to provide receptacles for boot sole twist-to-lock cleats and for cargo tiedown. Clips could be fitted to the underside of the deck grid to accept ceiling panels.

Small segments of the decking would surround all four hatches to allow astronauts to be anchored by their cleated boots while working the hatches or guiding cargo through the hatch openings. The decking also could be installed before flight where it would not disturb fluid flow at the feedline inlets.

Decks, ceiling, and wall panel sections could be carried in the orbiter cargo bay in 32-inch-wide sections, small enough for bundled sections to be guided through the hatch openings.

A forced-air circulation system could be added to those tanks which would be used for living accomodations and in factory modules that were not completely automated. Heat dissipation could be accomplished with freon radiators similar to those on the orbiter cargo bay doors mounted directly to the outside of the tank, or could be connected to radiators as on the Space Station.

The air circulation ducting manifold, fan, filters, and cooling coils could be modular, with one unit used within the oxygen tank and two in the hydrogen tank. These could be carried aloft collapsed to 10-foot-long modules in the

EXHIBIT 13.2   A document with a header

204

REUSABLE EXTERNAL TANKS
On-Orbit Tank Servicing

Once on orbit, the external tank is prepared for habitation. The orbiter could orient the tank aft end toward the sun to maximize boil-off of residual hydrogen after the hatch was opened, and to minimize loss of oxygen. External tank servicing during extravehicular activities could be carried out by two or three astronauts, one using a Manned Maneuvering Unit for external inspection and for transporting equipment between the orbiter cargo bay and tank hatches, and one or two astronauts stationed inside the tanks to remove and install equipment. It is expected the servicing would take approximately two days to accomplish, one day for each end of the tank.

Part of the on-orbit servicing procedure would be removal of the internal oxygen and hydrogen propellant feedlines and baffles. The oxygen tank has an X-shaped vortex baffle which would be disassembled and removed. The hydrogen feedline suction bell and interior feedline would be removed at a flange installed where the feedline passes through the aft tank wall. Both tank openings would be fitted with covers carried aboard the orbiter.

Ladders, deck supports, deck segments and interior wall panels could be carried in the orbiter cargo bay and added

EXHIBIT 13.3 A document with a footer

6. Press **2** for Every Page; a partially blank screen is displayed.

7. Type the header information. For example, type REUSABLE EXTERNAL TANKS in all capital letters; press **Alt** and **F6** to move the cursor to the right side of the screen. *Note:* Moving the cursor to the right of the screen permits flush-right alignment of text, that is, the text will end at the right margin.

8. Press **Ctrl** and **b** to give the page-numbering instruction.

9. Press **Enter** once.

10. Press **F7** once to exit and return the cursor to the Format: Page screen.

11. Press **8** for Suppress (this page only); press **5** for Suppress Header A; press **y** for yes; press **F7** once to exit and return the cursor to the document screen.

12. Reveal Codes (**Alt** and **F3**); the header code and the suppress code are displayed: **[Header A: Every page REUSABLE . . . [Flsh Rt]^B[HRt][Suppress:HA]**.

13. Exit Reveal Codes (**Alt** and **F3**).

⇨ Use the filename **pexer13.hdr**. Save the file and keep the document on the screen.

⇨ Print one copy using full justification and draft text quality.

⇨ Delete the header and suppress codes: Reveal Codes (**Alt** and **F3**); move the cursor to the beginning of the document; place the cursor on the header code; press **Del**; place the cursor on the suppress code; press **Del**. Press **Alt** and **F3** to exit reveal codes.

⇨ Use the Procedure to Create a Footer and create the following footer:

REUSABLE EXTERNAL TANKS   PAGE #

Procedure to Create a Footer

1. On page 1, place the cursor at the beginning of the document (press **Home** three times; press the **up** arrow key once).

2. Press **Shift** and **F8**.

3. Press **2** for Page {*Layout, Page*}.

4. Press **4** for Footers.

5. Press **1** for Footer A.

6. Press **2** for Every Page; a partially blank screen is displayed. *Note:* This will print the footer on every page.

7. Type the footer information. For example, type REUSABLE EXTERNAL TANKS in all capital letters; press **Alt** and **F6** to move the cursor to the right side of the screen.

8. Type PAGE; press the space bar once.

9. Press **Ctrl** and **b** to give the page-numbering instruction.

10. Press **Enter** once.

11. Press **F7** twice to exit and return the cursor to the document screen.

12. Reveal Codes (**Alt** and **F3**); the footer code is displayed: **[Footer A: Every page; REUSABLE . . . [Flsh Rt]PAGE ^B[HRt]]**.

13. Exit Reveal Codes (**Alt** and **F3**).

➪ Use the filename **13footer**. Save the file and keep the document on the screen.

➪ Print one copy using full justification and draft text quality.

CREATE FOOTNOTES

A multiple-page document can have footnotes or endnotes. Footnotes and endnotes provide the name, date, and page number of the resource from which the information being discussed was obtained. Footnotes and endnotes can also be referred to as reference notes. Footnotes are sequentially numbered and typed at the bottom of the page where the information is referenced. (See Exhibit 13.4.) Endnotes are numbered and are printed on a page that will be placed at the end of the document. Footnote procedures are discussed in this textbook.

➪ The **13footer** document should be displayed on the screen.

getting richer and, in some cases, the poor are getting poorer.

With replicating assemblers, wealth per capita will rapidly increase if we can harness even a small portion of the nanotechnology potential (provided, of course, human populations are still limited to slower doubling times). A capital base doubling on a time scale of a year or less would make us almost arbitrarily wealthy, at least until we run into resource limits.

Nanotechnology offers an opportunity for widespread personal wealth on a scale (in terms of materials and energy) that can only be compared to today's gross world product.

The changes expected from wealth on this scale make the sum of all the technological and social changes since we started chipping flint look tame. How would even vast wealth get us into space? Being rich won't automatically get us into space, but the few of us who want to go there will no longer have to get a government or a large corporation to pay our way. We won't have to sell our dreams to anyone, but we will have to keep them, and that may not be an easy task!¹

---

¹H. Keith Henson, "Megascale Engineering and Nanotechnology," Space-Faring Gazette, February 1988, p. 7.

EXHIBIT 13.4   A document with footnote

▷ Delete the footer code.

▷ Use the Procedure to Number Pages and number pages at the bottom center.

▷ Use the Procedure to Create Footnotes and type the following footnote:

Robert L. Price, "Reusable External Tanks," <u>Space-Faring Gazette</u>, August 1987, p. 12.

Procedure to Create Footnotes

| 1. | The cursor should be located at the space after the information that is to be footnoted. For example, locate the cursor one space to the right of the period in the last sentence of the document. |

| 2. | Press **Ctrl** and **F7** for Footnotes. |

| 3. | Press **1** for Footnote. |

| 4. | Press **1** to Create {*Layout, Footnote, Create*}; a partially blank screen is displayed and the cursor is located to the right of the number 1. *Note:* If this is the second footnote, the cursor would be located to the right of the number 2. |

| 5. | Type the footnote information: for example, type **Robert L. Price, "Reusable External Tanks," <u>Space-Faring Gazette</u>, August 1987, p. 12.** |

| 6. | Press **F7** to exit; the number 1 is displayed to the left of the cursor. |

| 7. | Reveal Codes (**Alt** and **F3**) to view the footnote code: **[Footnote:1;[Note Num]Robert L. Price . . .].** |

| 8. | View the footnote (**Shift** and **F7, 6**). Press **PgDn**, if necessary. |

▷ Use the filename **13fnote**. Save the file and keep the document on the screen.

▷ Print one copy with left justification and use draft text quality.

WIDOW AND ORPHAN LINES

A widow line is the last line of a paragraph that prints at the top of the next page and the preceding paragraph lines print at the bottom of the previous page. An orphan line is the first line of a paragraph that prints at the bottom of the page and the remaining paragraph lines print at the top of the next page.

A minimum of two lines of a paragraph should be printed at the bottom or top of a page. The widow/orphan protection will assure that a minimum of two lines are printed on each page.

Procedure to Use Widow/Orphan Protection

1. Place the cursor at the beginning of the file (press **Home** three times; press the **up** arrow key once).

2. Press **Shift** and **F8**.

3. Press **1** for Line {*Layout, Line*}.

4. Press **9** for Widow/Orphan Protection.

5. Press **y** for yes.

6. Press **F7** once to return the cursor to the document screen.

Note: A footer can invalidate the widow/orphan protection.

SUMMARY

- A multiple-page document is formatted similar to a one-page document with one-inch margins, single or double spacing, and printed with full justified or left justified lines.

- Multiple-page documents are separated by page breaks. When the text reaches 9.83 inches, a soft page break is displayed automatically on the screen.

- A hard page break can be placed in a document before the lines reach 9.83 inches on the screen. Press **Ctrl** and **Enter** to create a hard (required) page break.

- Pages can be numbered consecutively. The page number can be printed at the top or bottom of the page and located on the left, center, or right side of the horizontal line (**Shift** and **F8**, **2**, **6**, **4**, press the number of the desired page number location, **F7**).

- A header is title information that is printed at the top of page 2 and the following pages. A footer is title information that is printed at the bottom of each document page. Headers and footers can also contain page numbers (**Shift** and **F8**, **2**, **3** for headers or **4** for footers, **1** for Footer A or Header

A, **2**, type the header/footer information, **F7** twice). Press **Ctrl** and **b** to give the page-numbering instruction in a header or footer.

● Footnotes provide the name, date, and page number of the resource from which the information being discussed was obtained. Footnotes are printed at the bottom of the page where the information is referenced (**Ctrl** and **F7**, **1**, **1**, type the footnote information, **F7**).

● A widow line is a line that prints singly on the top of a page; an orphan line is a line that prints singly on the bottom of a page. Widows and orphans should be avoided. WordPerfect can be given an instruction to print a minimum of two paragraph lines at the bottom and top of each page. This instruction is called widow/orphan protection (**Shift** and **F8**, **1**, **9**, **y**, **F7**).

SELF-CHECK QUESTIONS

(True / False—Circle One)

T,F 1. Page numbers can be consecutively numbered by pressing **Shift** and **F8**, **2**, **6**, **4**, press the figure for the page number location, press **F7**.

T,F 2. A multiple-page report is printed with single or double spacing.

T,F 3. A header should be printed on all pages of a document.

T,F 4. The footer information is typed once and is printed on all pages of a multiple-page document.

T,F 5. A hard page break is placed in a document by pressing the **Ctrl** and **Enter** keys.

T,F 6. To request that page numbering be included in the header or footer, press the **Ctrl** and **b** keys.

T,F 7. A footnote is a footer with page numbers.

T,F 8. Footnotes are consecutively numbered in a multiple-page document and printed on the page where the information is referenced.

T,F 9. Before creating a footnote, the cursor should be located at the space after the information that is to be referenced.

T,F 10. The widow and orphan protection is obtained by pressing **Shift** and **F8**, **1**, **9**, **y**, and **F7**.

ENRICHING LANGUAGE ARTS SKILLS

Spelling/Vocabulary Words

commercial pertaining to business that is usually performed for a profit.
replicating copying; reproducing.
nanotechnology a very, very small application of science especially as it relates to industrial goals.

Independent Adjectives

Two adjectives that modify the same noun are separated by a comma.

Example The large, colorful picture will be hung in the lobby.

EXERCISES

Exercise 13.1

1. The screen should be clear, and the disk drive where the disk is located should be accessed.

2. Type the following meeting minutes using the vertical spacing as shown and left justified lines.

3. Use page numbering at the bottom center of the pages.

4. Use widow/orphan protection.

5. Use the filename **13exer1**. Save the file without clearing the screen.

6. Print one copy using draft or high text quality.

```
        PINE VIEW HOMEOWNERS ASSOCIATION MINUTES
                Board of Directors Meeting
                     March 10, 19xx


Members Present:

Karen Phelps, Bob Marrone, Ted Caplan, Angela
Perrochet, Bertha Crutcher, and Mitch Nimmo

1. Treasurer's report: Bertha Crutcher circulated
   the treasurer's report, which was accepted and
   is appended to these minutes. She reported that
```

some members are two months behind in paying
dues. Under conditions of the CC&Rs it will be
determined what percentage of past-due costs
will be charged.

2. President's report: Bob Marrone reported that
correspondence has been received from the
Gridley Insurance Company, indicating a possible
commercial insurance premium surcharge. It is
unclear whether Pine View Association will
be required to pay a surcharge, based on a
percentage of .002 to .007 of earned premium.

The board received a letter from Bob Marrone
expressing his regret at having to resign as
President of the Board because of his move to
a new home in Shore Park Estates. The Board
accepted his resignation and expressed great
appreciation for his service as president.

3. Maintenance report: Angela Perrochet reported
that there are seven units with roof leaks.
These are currently being repaired. The roof
repair has priority over the painting. Angela
noted that all work on the retaining wall near
Rich Gibson's unit was completed by Rich,
although Pine View paid for the materials. The
Board expressed appreciation for all of Rich's
donated labor.

4. Landscaping report: The gardener has purchased
and planted 25 new plants at the entrance, near
unit 2505, at the clubhouse on Pine View Lane. A
search continues for a new sprinkler timer clock
for the clubhouse area. Most logs left from the
pine tree removal at 2122 have been removed. The
lawns have been fertilized, the pine tree at
1899 trimmed, and the tennis court area weeded.
More eucalyptus trees have been pruned.

Karen Phelps is taking over landscaping
maintenance for the year, including supervision
of the gardeners. She is also donating personal
time to clearing weedy landscaping adjacent to
the Community Church building. The Board is
looking forward to her capable assistance.

5. Report on the tennis court: Ted Caplan
recommends purchasing a new net and including
the cost in next year's budget. He is still
trying to obtain a better quality resurfacing
than has previously been considered. There is
still $500 remaining in the budget for court
repairs.

6. Report by Mitch Nimmo: There is still a problem
with homeowners parking in spaces reserved for
guests and on the street. Angela volunteered to
make GUEST stencil markers to make these
reserved spaces more obvious.

7. Homeowners are needed to serve on the Board
of Directors. A letter will be circulated
to homeowners urging them to recognize the

```
importance and responsibility that all members
of the Association share in its governance and
maintenance.
```

Exercise 13.2

1. The file named **13exer1** should be displayed on the screen. If necessary, retrieve the file.

2. Create a header to be printed on the second page of the minutes. Print the header information **BOARD OF DIREC- TORS MEETING** at the left side of the document and flush align the date **March 10, 19xx** at the right side.

3. Use the filename **13exer2**. Save the file and keep the document on the screen.

4. Print one copy using draft or high text quality.

Exercise 13.3

1. The screen should be clear, and the disk drive where the disk is located should be accessed.

2. Type the following document using double spacing and full justification.

3. Create a footer to print page numbers at the bottom right of each page.

4. Use Widow/Orphan Protection.

5. Use the filename **13exer3**. Save the file without clearing the screen.

6. Print one copy using draft or high text quality.

```
                     NANOTECHNOLOGY

                   The Ultimate Tool


     The key to nanotechnology is the replicating
assembler, a microscopic, complex device with the
capacity for building anything, including copies of
itself, that can be built out of atoms. Its size
and speed of operation can be estimated. After all,
natural replicators are all around us. They seem to
be about the same order of magnitude in size,
complexity, and doubling time as the artificial
```

ones will be. Microorganisms in ideal conditions
(often the case in industrial vats) can double in
about 20 minutes.

When people figure out how to make, feed, and
control replicating assemblers, the base of our
"industrial capital" (roughly equal to wealth) will
depend on something that replicates in 20 minutes.
Planning, design, transportation, and so on, will
slow down the pace, but even a factor of 10,000
slower would leave us with more than a doubling per
year.

All of us survivors of "limits to growth" know
about exponential increase. Human populations do it
with minimum doubling times of about 15 years; the
industrial base in the developed world does it in
about 20 years. The ratio between industrial growth
rates and population equals the increasing (or
decreasing) wealth per capita. Because of
differential birth rates, rich societies really are
getting richer and, in some cases, the poor are
getting poorer.

With replicating assemblers, wealth per capita
will rapidly increase if we can harness even a
small portion of the nanotechnology potential
(provided, of course, human populations are still
limited to slower doubling times). A capital base
doubling on a time scale of a year or less would
make us almost arbitrarily wealthy, at least until
we run into resource limits.

Nanotechnology offers an opportunity for
widespread personal wealth on a scale (in terms of
materials and energy) that can only be compared to
today's gross world product.

The changes expected from wealth on this scale
make the sum of all the technological and social
changes since we started chipping flint look tame.
How would even vast wealth get us into space? Being
rich will not automatically get us into space, but
the few of us who want to go there will no longer
have to get a government or a large corporation to
pay our way. We will not have to sell our dreams to
anyone, but we will have to keep them, and that may
not be an easy task!

Exercise 13.4

1. The file named **13exer3** should be displayed on the screen. If
    necessary, retrieve the file.

2. Delete the footer code.

3. Create a footnote. Place the footnote after the last paragraph
    in the document. The footnote information is as follows: **H.
    Keith Henson, "Megascale Engineering and Nanotechnol-
    ogy," Space-Faring Gazette, February 1988, p. 7.**

4. Create a header to be printed on the second page. Print the

header information **NANOTECHNOLOGY** at the left side of the document and flush align the page number at the right side.

5. Use the filename **13exer4**. Save the file and keep the document on the screen.

6. Print one copy using draft or high text quality.

Exercise 13.5

1. The screen should be clear, and the disk drive where the file disk is located should be accessed.

2. Type the following document using double spacing, left justification, and widow/orphan protection.

3. Create a footer to print numbers at the bottom center of each page.

4. Correct two spelling errors and four punctuation errors.

5. Use the filename **13exer5**. Save the file without clearing the screen.

6. Print one copy using draft or high text quality.

STONERIDGE HOMEOWNER'S ASSOCIATION

The Stoneridge Homeowner's Association is an Oregon nonprofit corporation, and is comprised of owners of 55 townhouse units in Rocky Mount, North Carolina. The Articles of Incorporation were filed on August 8, 1989.
The association's Board of Directors is required to maintain and protect the common areas owned by the association's members. The common areas include the building exteriors, recreation areas, roads, and landscaping.
The authority and responsibilities for the association are obtained from the Declaration of Covenants, Conditions, and Restrictions which were executed and recorded on September 13, 1989.
The majority of the policy decisions are made by the seven member Board of Directors. The policy decisions are made in accordance with the governing documents.
Routine annual maintenance of buildings and grounds is charged to expenses in the year incurred. Major maintenance expenditures such as painting, roofing, and paving, are charged to

expenses at an estimated annual amount on a
straight line method. The amount computed is based
on estimates of expected life and cost. The expense
account is reached in the year actual expenditure
occurs.

While the estimates of future expenditures are
based upon generally accepted daeta and seem
reasonable under the circumstances, no assurance
can be given that actual expenditures will match
the accrued libility at the time the expenditure
occurs.

The Board of Directors meet in the small
arched building on the third Tuesday of each month.
Special meetings of members can be called at any
time by the President or upon written request of
20 percent of all members.

Chapter 14

CREATE
AN OUTLINE
AND A TABLE
OF CONTENTS

OBJECTIVES

After successfully completing this chapter, you should be able to:

● Create and format an outline.

● Create and format a table of contents.

● Mark text for a table of contents.

● Define and generate a table of contents.

CREATE AN OUTLINE

An outline is a list of ideas expressed in phrases or sentences. The outline can provide a brief summary for writing a document such as a report. The ideas listed in an outline are enumerated in levels. WordPerfect can automatically number eight outline levels.

A standard outline numbering style is shown in Exhibit 14.1. The standard number style is WordPerfect's default and is identified as the "Current Definition" in the Paragraph Number Definition menu. (See Exhibit 14.2.) Also, other numbering styles such as paragraph, legal, bullets, etc. can be selected in the Paragraph Number Definition menu. If the standard outline numbering style is used, no changes are made in the Paragraph Number Definition menu.

219

```
I.    FIRST LEVEL

      A.    Second level
            1.    Third level
                  a.    Fourth level
                        (1)  Fifth level
                              (a)  Sixth level
                                    i)    Seventh level
                                          a)    Eighth level

II.   SECOND LEVEL
```

EXHIBIT 14.1   Outline style with eight levels

⇨ Use the Procedure to Create an Outline for the sample outline in Exhibit 14.1.

⇨ Use the filename **poutline.c14**. Save the outline and keep the document on the screen.

⇨ Print one copy using draft text quality.

Procedure to Create an Outline

1. Center and type the title in all capital letters; press the **Enter** key three times.

2. Press **Shift** and **F5** for Outline.

3. Press **4** for Outline, press **1** for Outline On {*Tools, Outline, On*}. The prompt **Outline** is displayed at the bottom left of the screen.

4. Press the **Enter** key once; the Roman numeral **I** is displayed.

5. Press **F4** for Indent; type the information in all capital letters; press **Enter** twice. The Roman numeral **II** is displayed.

6. Press the **Tab** key once; the **A** is displayed, replacing the Roman numeral **II**.

7. Press **F4** for Indent; type the information; press **Enter**.

8. Press the **Tab** key once; the **1** is displayed.

9. Press **F4**; type the information; press the **Enter** key once.

```
Paragraph Number Definition

    1 - Starting Paragraph Number          1
        (in legal style)
                                        Levels
                            1   2   3   4    5    6    7    8
    2 - Paragraph           1.  a.  i.  (1)  (a)  (i)  1)   a)
    3 - Outline             I.  A.  1.  a.   (1)  (a)  i)   a)
    4 - Legal (1.1.1)       1   .1  .1  .1   .1   .1   .1   .1
    5 - Bullets             •   o   -   ■    *    +    ·    x
    6 - User-defined

    Current Definition      I.  A.  1.  a.   (1)  (a)  i)   a)
    Attach Previous Level       No  No  No   No   No   No   No

    7 - Enter Inserts Paragraph Number      Yes

    8 - Automatically Adjust to Current Level  Yes

    9 - Outline Style Name




Selection: 0
```

EXHIBIT 14.2 Paragraph Number Definition menu

10. Press the **Tab** key once; the **a** is displayed.

11. Press **F4**; type the information; press the **Enter** key once.

12. Press the **Tab** key once; the **(1)** is displayed.

13. Press **F4**; type the information; press the **Enter** key once.

14. Press the **Tab** key once; the **(a)** is displayed.

15. Press **F4**; type the information; press the **Enter** key once.

16. Press the **Tab** key once; the **i)** is displayed.

17. Press **F4**; type the information; press the **Enter** key once.

18. Press the **Tab** key once; the **a)** is displayed.

19. Press **F4**; type the information.

*Note: To obtain Roman Numeral II, return the cursor to the first outline level by pressing **Shift** and **Tab** as many times as necessary.*

20. Press **Shift** and **F5**; press **4** for Outline; **2** for Outline Off {*tools, Outline, Off*}. *Note:* The word **Outline** is no longer displayed at the bottom of the screen.

Make Adjustments and Corrections to an Outline

- To return the cursor from a lower level to the next higher level, press **Shift** and **Tab**.

- To correct outline level numbering, press the backspace key to return the cursor to the line above and press **Enter** again.

- To delete a number or letter, use the normal delete keys.

- If the **Outline** message is no longer displayed on the screen, press **Shift** and **F5 4, 1** to turn outline on.

- If a second outline is to be created in the same document, Reveal Codes (**Alt** and **F3**), place the cursor after the **[Outline Off]** code. Turn on outline (**Shift** and **F5, 4, 1**).

CREATE A TABLE OF CONTENTS

A table of contents lists the main topics that are written in a report, newspaper, book, and so forth. The topic is usually followed by "leaders" (periods) and the page number where the topic is located. (See Exhibit 14.3.)

The table of contents is created from the text that has been previously typed. The main topics are usually typed centered or at the left margin and are referred to as major headings or side

```
                     TABLE OF CONTENTS


INTRODUCTION  . . . . . . . . . . . . . . . . . . . . . .    1
         Statement of the Problem . . . . . . . . . . . .    1
         Significance of the Problem  . . . . . . . . . .    2
         Definitions of Terms . . . . . . . . . . . . . .    3


HYPOTHESES  . . . . . . . . . . . . . . . . . . . . . . .    3


REVIEW OF RELATED LITERATURE  . . . . . . . . . . . . . .    4


PROCEDURES USED . . . . . . . . . . . . . . . . . . . . .    5


SUMMARY AND CONCLUSIONS . . . . . . . . . . . . . . . . .    5
         Restatement of the Problem . . . . . . . . . . .    7
         Principle Findings and Conclusions . . . . . . .    8
         Recommendations for Further Research . . . . . .    8


BIBLIOGRAPHY  . . . . . . . . . . . . . . . . . . . . . .   10


APPENDIX  . . . . . . . . . . . . . . . . . . . . . . . .   11
         Chart I . . . . . . . . . . . . . . . . . . . . .   12
         Chart II . . . . . . . . . . . . . . . . . . . . .   13
```

EXHIBIT 14.3 Table of contents

headings. Before the table of contents can be generated, the table of contents must be defined and the headings must be marked.

Defining the table of contents involves specifying the number of levels desired. The topics that are to be placed in the table of contents are marked in the text and one of the levels that has been previously defined is selected. Each level of the table of contents is indented by the number of spaces between the defaulted tabs. Tabs could be changed if the defaulted five-space indentation is not desired.

▷ Type the following five paragraphs and side headings as shown.

▷ Use the filename **14ptoc**. Save the file and keep the document on the screen.

▷ Print one copy of the document using draft text quality.

```
Definition of Responsibilities of Residents

The CC&Rs Article V limits responsibility as
follows: Paint, repair, replace and care for roofs,
gutters, downspouts, exterior building surfaces,
decks, and garages.


Application of Definitions of Responsibilities

The Board of Directors will provide a reasonable
level of maintenance. Reasonable means maintaining
an appearance that is acceptable by the average
person.


Obligations of the Resident

The resident must notify the maintenance committee
of any conditions where there is damage or where a
condition may lead to interior damage.


The Exterior Maintenance Committee

The Board of Directors shall create a committee of
three persons, at least one of whom shall be a
current member of the board.


Responsibilities of the Exterior Maintenance
Committee

The Exterior Maintenance Committee is responsible
for providing emergency and preventive services for
maintaining the exterior structure.
```

⇨ Use the Procedure to Mark Text and mark the side headings in the previous paragraphs to be listed in the table of contents.

Procedure to Mark Text

1. Place the cursor on the first character of the first heading to be listed in the table of contents.

2. Press **Alt** and **F4** for Block; press **Home** once and press the **right** arrow key once to highlight the first heading.

3. Press **Alt** and **F5** for Mark Text.

4. Press **1** for ToC.

5. Press **1** for ToC Level; **Enter**. *Note:* Reveal Codes (**Alt** and **F3**) to display the marked text codes **[Mark:ToC,1][End Mark:ToC,1]**.

6. Place the cursor on the first character of the next heading to be listed in the table of contents.

7. Continue to block and mark each heading that is to be listed in the table of contents by repeating steps 2–6.

⇨ Use the Procedure to Define and Generate a Table of Contents.

⇨ Generate a table of contents for the file named **14ptoc**.

⇨ Save the file; use the filename **14ptoc.toc**.

⇨ Print one copy of the table of contents using draft text quality.

Procedure to Define and Generate a Table of Contents

1. Place the cursor at the beginning of the document that contains the marked headings. (Press **Home** three times; press **up** arrow key once.)

2. Press **Ctrl** and **Enter** to create a page break. *Note:* The table of contents will be created on the new page.

3. Notice that page 1 of the original document is now page 2 and must be renumbered to become page 1 again. Press **Shift** and **F8**; press **2**; **6**; **1**; **1**; **Enter**; **F7**. *Note:* **Pg 1** is displayed at the bottom right of the screen.

4. Move the cursor to the new page above the page break: Press **Home** three times; press **up** arrow key once. Notice that there are two pages designated as page 1.

5. Press **Alt** and **F5** for Mark Text.

6. Press **5** for Define.

7. Press **1** for Define Table of Contents {*Mark, Define, Table of Contents*}.

8. Table of Contents Definition menu is displayed.

9. The number of levels (**1**) is defaulted.

10. Press **F7** to accept the default and return the cursor to the document screen. *Note:* The Procedure to Define and Generate a Table of Contents is performed only *once*.

11. Press **Alt** and **F5**.

12. Press **6** for Generate {*Mark, Generate*}.

13. Press **5** for Generate Tables, Indexes, and so on.

14. A prompt is displayed: **Existing Tables, lists, and indexes will be replaced. Continue?Yes(No)**.

15. Press **Enter** to accept the yes.

16. A **Generation in Progress** message is displayed.

17. The table of contents is displayed on the screen. *Note:* The title and any needed spaces can be inserted after the table of contents is generated.

Note: If sentences and/or paragraphs are inserted or deleted in the document, generate a new table of contents. Generating a new table of contents does not require the remarking of text or the redefining of table characteristics.

SUMMARY

- The ideas in an outline are enumerated by levels. WordPerfect automatically creates up to eight outline levels. The defaulted tabs can be used for indenting outline items or the tabs can be changed.

- The outline title is typed in all capitals followed by three **Enters**. The first outline level information is typed in all capital letters followed by two **Enters**. The second and following outline level information is typed with the first letter of the word capitalized and the remaining words in all lowercase letters followed by one **Enter**.

- The outline is turned on at the location in the document where the outline is to be typed (**Shift** and **F5**, **4**, **1**, press **Enter**, press **F4** to indent, type the outline idea, **Enter** twice after the first level or once after other levels, press **Tab** key to obtain next level—each time the **Tab** key is pressed a new level is obtained, press **Enter** once). *Note:* To return the cursor from a lower level to the next higher level, press **Shift** and **Tab**.

- During the typing of an outline, corrections can be made in an outline level numbering by pressing the **backspace** key to return the cursor to the line above and pressing **Enter** again.

- If a second outline is to be typed in the same document, the cursor is placed after the **[Outline Off]** code and the outline feature is turned on again by pressing (**Shift** and **F5**, **4**, **1**).

- A table of contents is created to print major headings and side headings from a previously typed document and to indicate the page numbers where the headings can be located. The headings are blocked and marked, the table of contents is defined and generated (Mark Text: **Alt** and **F4**, **Home** and **right** arrow key, **Alt** and **F5**, **1**, **1**, **Enter**).

- A new first page is created for the generation of the Table of Contents. Since the original page 1 is now page 2, the page numbering instruction is changed on the original first page of the text to begin numbering from page 1 (**Shift** and **F8**, **2**, **6**, **1**, **1**, **Enter**, **F7**).

- To define and generate the Table of Contents: press **Home** three times and the **up** arrow once, **Alt** and **F5**, **5**, **1**, **1** (or type the number of levels desired), **F7**, **Alt** and **F5**, **6**, **5**, **Enter**).

SELF-CHECK QUESTIONS

(True / False—Circle One)

T,F　1. The title and first level information in an outline are typed in all capital letters.

T,F   2.   WordPerfect can enumerate ten outline levels automatically.

T,F   3.   To turn on the outline, press **Shift** and **F5, 4**.

T,F   4.   If a second outline is typed in one document, WordPerfect can be instructed to begin the numbering from the number 1 again.

T,F   5.   Main headings and side headings are marked before the table of contents is defined and generated.

T,F   6.   The amount of levels desired for the table of contents can be selected when the table of contents is defined.

T,F   7.   Before text is marked, the text is blocked and highlighted.

T,F   8.   Text is marked for a table of contents by pressing **Alt** and **F4, 2,** and **2**.

T,F   9.   If a document has information inserted and/or deleted, a new table of contents can be generated without re-marking or redefining text.

T,F 10.   To generate a table of contents, press **Alt** and **F5, 6, 5, Enter**.

ENRICHING LANGUAGE ARTS SKILLS

Spelling / Vocabulary Words

hygienist   a person who deals with the prevention of disease.
encroachment   to infringe on the rights of others.
easements   provide a right to others to make use of another individual's property.

Percentage Amounts

Use figures for numbers that are followed by the word percentage. Spell out the word percent unless the percentage amount is used in technical material.

Example   Salaries are 30 percent of the total budget.

EXERCISES

Exercise 14.1

1. The screen should be clear, and the disk drive where the disk is located should be accessed.

2. Type the following outline using the spacing as shown.

3. Use the filename **14exer1**. Save the file and keep the document on the screen.

4. Print one copy using draft or high text quality.

Contract for Services

I. Performance of Services

    A. Services performed for patients
    B. Services performed as a consultant

II. Extent of Services

    A. Services performed three days a week
    B. Services performed four days a week

III. Compensation for Services

    A. Full days
    B. Billing for services
    C. Compensation received for
       patients referred

IV. Invoices and Payment for Services

    A. Invoices for compensation
    B. Payment for services

V. Insurance

    A. Insurance maintained by
       contractor
    B. Consultant named on
       insurance policy

Exercise 14.2

1. The screen should be clear, and the disk drive where the disk is located should be accessed.

2. Type the following text using line spacing of 2.

3. Use the filename **14exer2**. Save the file and keep the document on the screen.

4. Define and mark the side headings; generate a table of contents. Remember to renumber page 2 as page 1. Use the title CONTRACT FOR SERVICES; center the title at the top of the table of contents.

5. Print one copy of the table of contents using draft or high text quality.

```
        CATHERINE KIRZNER, D.D.S., INC.
           CONTRACT FOR SERVICES
              WITH WILLIAM HOWE


     This agreement is made by and between
CATHERINE KIRZNER, D.D.S., INC., a Virginia
corporation and WILLIAM HOWE.

PERFORMANCE OF SERVICES
     Howe shall provide the following professional
services during the term of this agreement.

a. Performing services as a dentist for patients of
   Kirzner, Inc.; and

b. Performing services as a dental hygienist, and
   consulting with other dentists, dental
   hygienists and nurses, as requested by Kirzner,
   Inc.

EXTENT OF SERVICES
     Kirzner, Inc. and Howe estimate that Howe
shall perform the services called for in this
agreement on an average of four (4) days a week.

COMPENSATION FOR SERVICES
     For and in consideration of the satisfactory
performance of services, Kirzner, Inc. shall
compensate Howe as follows:

a. For at least six and one-half (6¹/₂) hours per
   day ("full day of work") of services, compensation
   shall be computed on a daily basis of $250 per
   day.

b. For less than a full day of work, compensation
   shall be computed on the same ratio that such
```

compensation bears to the daily rate.

INVOICES AND PAYMENT FOR SERVICES
     Invoices and payment for services shall be as
follows:

a. Howe's invoices for compensation are to be
   invoiced semimonthly.

b. Howe shall be paid within seven (7) days after
   submission of each invoice.

INDEPENDENT CONTRACTOR
     Howe is an independent contractor, responsible
for the methods and means used in performing his
services under this agreement, and is not a joint
venturer nor an employee of Kirzner, Inc.

OWNERSHIP OF PATIENT RECORDS, CHARTS, AND DOCUMENTS
     All patient records, charts, and other
documents prepared by Howe as instruments of
services, to the extent that they do not belong to
the patient, shall be the property of Kirzner, Inc.
as distinguished from the property of Howe.

INSURANCE
     Howe shall put into effect and maintain
insurance to protect himself and Kirzner, Inc. from
errors and omissions (professional malpractice) in
connection with the services performed by Howe.

Exercise 14.3

1. The screen should be clear, and the disk drive where the
    disk is located should be accessed.

2. Type the following outline using the vertical spacing as
    shown.

3. Use the filename **14exer3**. Save the file and keep the docu-
    ment on the screen.

4. Print one copy using draft or medium text quality.

              DECLARATION OF COVENANTS, CONDITIONS,
                    AND RESTRICTIONS

I.   DEFINITIONS

     A. Association
     B. Owner

```
      C. Properties
      D. Common area

 II.  PROPERTY RIGHTS

      A. Owner's easements of enjoyment
      B. Delegation of use
      C. Parking rights
      D. Easements
         1. For private sidewalk, yard, and patio use
         2. For encroachments of overhanging eaves,
            decks, and fireplaces

III.  MEMBERSHIP AND VOTING RIGHTS

      A. Every lot owner is an Association member
      B. All owners are entitled to one vote
      C. The Board will have rights to adopt
         reasonable rules

 IV.  ANNUAL AND SPECIAL ASSESSMENTS

      A. Lien and personal obligation of assessments
      B. Purpose of assessments
      C. Maximum annual assessments
         1. No more than 10% increase without a vote
         2. Increased assessment with a written
            consent of 51% of members
      D. Due dates for assessments
         1. Approved operating budget 60 days before
            beginning of year
            a. Estimate revenue and expenses on
               accrual basis
            b. Identify total cash reserves
         2. Financial statements prepared with
            accepted accounting principles
         3. Nonpayment of assessments

  V.  EXTERIOR MAINTENANCE

      A. Common area maintenance
      B. Exterior maintenance on lots
```

Exercise 14.4

1. The screen should be clear, and the disk drive where the disk is located should be accessed.

2. Type the following text using vertical line spacing of 2.

3. Use the filename **14exer4**. Save the file and keep the document on the screen.

4. Mark the centered headings as level 1 and mark the side headings as level 2. When the centered headings are marked, remember to not select the **[center]** code.

5. Define the table of contents with two levels and generate a table of contents. Remember to renumber page 2 as page 1.

6. Print one copy of the table of contents using draft or high text quality.

```
        HOUSTON RETIREMENT STRATEGY AND TRUST RECORD


                          GENERAL

Purpose
     This prototype pension plan and trust
constitute an employee pension benefit strategy
created for eligible employees.

Name of Plan
     The legal name of the plan shall be set forth
by the employer.

Approval of Internal Revenue Service
     Approval must be obtained through the District
Director of the Internal Revenue Service.

Amendment or Termination
     The strategy sponsor can amend any part of the
plan at any time. The employer has the right to
amend the choice of options in the Adoption
Agreement.


                        DEFINITIONS

Accrued Benefit
     Accrued benefit means the balance of the
enrollee's account.

Administrator
     The administrator means the employer or other
appointed entity.

Adoption Agreement
     The adoption agreement means that the detailed
specifications set forth by the agreement are an
integral part of this record.


                         FUNDING

Contribution Formula
     The employer contributes a specific amount for
each calendar year, and the amount distributed from
any net profits for the year will be approved by
the Board.

Forfeitures
     Forfeitures will be added to the employer's
```

contribution for the calendar year and allocated
therewith.

Voluntary Contributions
     The administrator shall allow each enrollee to
contribute to the trust not more than *10 percent* of
his/her compensation.

BENEFITS

Amount of Distribution
     An enrollee who terminates employment with the
employer shall be entitled to receive *100 percent*
of the amount credited to his/her employer
contribution account.

Form of Benefit
     Distribution of benefits under this strategy
shall be made by the current trustees and
distributed in one lump sum payment or in equal
monthly payments over a period of time.

Exercise 14.5

1. The screen should be clear, and the disk drive where the
    disk is located should be accessed.

2. Type the following outline using the vertical spacing as
    shown and left justification.

3. Correct four spelling errors and three punctuation/grammar
    errors.

4. Use the filename **14exer5**. Save the file and keep the docu-
    ment on the screen.

5. Print one copy using draft or high text quality.

PROFESSIONAL GROWTH PROGRAM

I.   TYPES OF ACTION

          A. Workshops and seminars
             1. Microomputer applications
             2. Computer programing
             3. Retirement/pinsions
          B. Retraining
          C. Advanced studies

              D. Research enquiries

II.   ELIGIBILITY AND FREQUENCY

III. SELECTION PROCESS

        A. Eligible employees will initiate the selection process
        B. Preliminary proposal submitted to a review committee
        C. Review committee will be composed of two directors and three regular employees

IV. TIMELINES

        A. Long-term projects must receive 80% of the committee members' approval 6 months in advance
        B. Short term projects must receive 70% of the committee members' approval 3 months in advance

V.   REPORT WRITING AND EVALUATION

        A. Submit report to chief executive officer
        B. Submit summary reports to Board of Trustees
        C. Evaluation performed within four weeks

CREATE DOCUMENTS WITH SPECIAL FEATURES: FONT CHANGES, MACROS, SUPERSCRIPTS, AND SUBSCRIPTS

OBJECTIVES

After successfully completing this chapter, you should be able to:

- Create a document and use font changes.
- Select a printer.
- Change font style and size.
- Create a macro.
- Define and describe a macro.
- Activate a macro.
- Edit a macro.
- Create superscripts and subscripts.

CREATE A DOCUMENT WITH FONT CHANGES

By using various styles and sizes of type, the appearance of a document can be enhanced. Also, type styles can be printed in

```
                          AGENDA
              INTERNATIONAL SPACE EXPO
              STEERING COMMITTEE MEETING


    DATE:        January 25, 19XX
    TIME:        7:00 p.m.
    PLACE:       College of San Mateo, Building
                 30, Rm. 128


    Objectives:

    1.   Formally organize this Steering Committee.

    2.   Review the concept and goal of the space expo.

    3.   Identify key local industry resources available and
         plan how to utilize them.

    4.   Brainstorm exhibits and exhibitors to participate
         with the fair.

    5.   Identify the major tasks to be completed and assign
         the responsibilities to specific persons.

                          AGENDA

    7:00 p.m.    Call to order and introductions

    7:10 p.m.    Review meeting objectives and purpose of
                 space expo

    7:30 p.m.    Review of current plans and budget

    7:45 p.m.    Discussion of local resources available
                 and corporate sponsorships

    8:00 p.m.    Brainstorm on possible exhibits and
                 exhibitors

    8:30 p.m.    Review major tasks and assign
                 responsibilities

    9:00 p.m.    Adjourn
```

EXHIBIT 15.1   Font style and size changes

boldface (see Chapter 6), italic, or both. For example, the heading of an agenda can be printed in bold with one type style and size and the times and agenda information can be printed in a different type style and size. (See Exhibit 15.1.)

A font is one size of a specific type style. Various sizes of a font can be selected. WordPerfect allows the user to select the type style (called font) and size from a font menu.

Printers will differ in their ability to print various type styles and sizes. For example, the Epson FX 80 dot matrix printer can print characters as large as five characters per inch (cpi) and as small as 17 cpi. In addition, the Epson FX 80 can print italics in 12 cpi. A laser printer, such as the Apple LaserWriter II, can print characters as small as 3 points (1 inch equals 72 points) and as large as 34 points or more. Also, the Apple LaserWriter can print a variety of typefaces such as Helvetica, Palatino, Schoolbook, and so on.

The printer must be selected before the font type and size are changed. Once the printer has been selected, the fonts can be chosen and the size can be assigned. The changed fonts are viewed through the view feature (**Shift** and **F7, 6**).

▷ Use the Procedure to Select the Printer for Font Changes and the Procedure to Change Font Style and Size.

▷ Type the agenda in Exhibit 15.1 or retrieve the file named **12exer4**, which was typed in Chapter 12. *Note:* Because of font changes, it may be desirable to press the space bar after each lead word—DATE:, TIME:, and PLACE:—instead of pressing the **Tab** key.

▷ Use the filename **15agenda**. Save the file and keep the document on the screen.

▷ Print one copy using draft text quality.

Procedure to Select the Printer for Font Changes

Note: The printer to be selected must be listed in the Select Printer list. The WordPerfect printer disks can be used to select additional printers.

1. Press **Shift** and **F7** for Print {*File, Print*}.
2. Press **s** for Select Printer.
3. Place the cursor on the printer to be selected.
4. Press **1** for Select.
5. Press **F7** to exit and return the cursor to the document screen.

Procedure to Change Font Style and Size

1. Place the cursor at the location in the document where the font change is to begin. For example, place the cursor under the *A* in *Agenda*.

2. Press **Ctrl** and **F8** for Font.

3. Press **4** for Base Font.

4. a. If using an Apple LaserWriter, place the cursor on **New Century Schoolbook Bold**. (If this selection is not available, make your choice of font.) Press **1** for Select, type **12** for point size; press **Enter**.

  b. If using a dot matrix printer, place the cursor on a selection that is approximately **5 cpi**. (If this selection is not available, make your choice of font.) Press **1** for Select.

5. Reveal Codes (**Alt** and **F3**) to see the font code. The code for the laser printer is similar to the following: **[Font:New Century Schoolbook bold 12 pt]**. The code for the dot matrix printer is similar to the following: **[Font:Roman 5cpi]**.

6. Exit Reveal Codes (**Alt** and **F3**). *Note:* This font and size will be in effect until WordPerfect encounters another font and size code.

7. Place the cursor under the *D* in *DATE*.

8. Press **Ctrl** and **F8**; and press **4** for Base Font.

9. a. If using an Apple LaserWriter, highlight **New Century Schoolbook**; press **1**; type **13** for point size; press **Enter**. If using a different laser printer, make a selection of your choice.

  b. If using a dot matrix printer, place the cursor on a selection that is approximately **6 cpi**; press **1** to select.

10. Place the cursor under the *O* in *Objectives*.

11. Press **Ctrl** and **F8**; and press **4** for Base Font.

12. a. If using an Apple LaserWriter, highlight **New Century Schoolbook Italic**; press **1**; type **10** for point size; press **Enter**. If using a different laser printer, make a selection of your choice.

b.   If using a dot matrix printer, place the cursor on a selection that is approximately **10 cpi**; press **1** to select.

13. Press **Shift** and **F7**, **6** to view the font changes.

Note: Various fonts will realign text; make spacing corrections if necessary.

CREATE A MACRO

A macro is a saved list of instructions or text that can be activated and recalled by using just a few keystrokes. Macros are shortcuts that assist in eliminating repetitious typing. For example, a frequently used business name such as Santa Barbara Building and Supply Company could be saved in a macro. Also, a macro could be created for deleting a line or sending a document to be printed.

First, a macro must be defined. Defining a macro is the process of naming the macro. Second, the macro is described. A macro is described by typing a brief description of what the macro will accomplish. Third, the actual macro text or instructions are typed.

Once the macro has been defined, described, and typed, the macro can be activated. Activating the macro is the process of recalling the macro at the location in the document where the macro is to be used or recalling the macro when the instructions are to be used.

⇨   Create the following macros using the Procedure to Define (Name) and Describe a Macro.

Define (Name)	Description	Macro Text
Peterson	Types Frank Peterson's name	FRANK L. PETERSON
Gentry	Types Robin Gentry's name	ROBIN S. GENTRY
Sugita	Types Bruce Sugita's name	BRUCE SUGITA, JR.
Co	Types company name	PETERSON, GENTRY, AND SUGITA

Procedure to Define (Name) and Describe a Macro

1. Press **Ctrl** and **F10** for Macro Define {*Tools, Macro, Define*}.

2. Type a name for the macro (1–8 characters) preceded by the disk drive letter where the file disk is located; for example, type a:peterson or b:peterson.

3. Press **Enter**; the word **Description** is displayed on the bottom of the screen.

4. Type a description of what the macro will accomplish. For example: Types Frank Peterson's name.

5. Press **Enter**; type the macro text. For example: FRANK L. PETERSON. *Note:* The words are displayed on the screen and the prompt **Macro Def** blinks on and off at the bottom of the screen.

6. Press **Ctrl** and **F10** to end the macro define process. *Note:* The macro saves automatically to the a or b disk drive that was typed in step 2.

7. Repeat steps 1–6 to type each macro. Clear the screen (**F7, n, n**).

▷ Change the vertical line spacing to 2 (**Shift** and **F8, 1, 6, 2, Enter, F7**).

▷ Type the following lease. Where indicated, activate the macros using the Procedure to Activate a Macro.

```
                ASSIGNMENT OF LEASE


     FOR GOOD AND OTHER VALUABLE CONSIDERATION,
receipt of which is hereby acknowledged, and in
connection with the formation of the general
partnership known as (Alt and F10; Co), effective
February 20, 19XX, (Alt and F10; Peterson), (Alt
and F10; Gentry), and (Alt and F10; Sugita) each
hereby assign to (Alt and F10; Co) his/her undivided
one-third interest ("Lessor's Interest") as Lessor,
in and to that certain lease dated January 1, 19XX
by and between PGS, Inc. an Oregon corporation, as
Lessor, and T.R. LYSONKI LUMBER COMPANY, an Oregon
corporation, as Lessee. Such lessor's interest was
assigned by PGS, Inc. to (Alt and F10; Peterson),
```

```
(Alt and F10; Gentry) and (Alt and F10; Sugita),
effective February 20, 19XX.
```

_____

(**Alt** and **F10**; Peterson)

_____

(**Alt** and **F10**; Gentry)

_____

(**Alt** and **F10**; Sugita)

Procedure to Activate a Macro

1. Place the cursor at the exact location in the document where the macro is to be typed.

2. Press **Alt** and **F10** for Macro Def {*Tools, Macro, Execute*}.

3. Type the macro name. For example: type Peterson. Press **Enter**. The macro text is displayed immediately on the screen.

➪ Use the filename **15macros**. Save the file and keep the document on the screen.

➪ Print one copy using draft text quality.

➪ Use the Procedure to Edit a Macro.

Procedure to Edit a Macro

1. Press **Ctrl** and **F10** for Macro Def.

2. Type the macro name; for example, type **a:gentry** or **b:gentry**; **Enter**.

3. The message is displayed: **Gentry.wpm Already Exists: 1 Replace; 2 Edit; 3 Description:0**.

4. Press **2** for Edit. A screen is displayed with the macro listed inside a box including any typing corrections made while typing the macro.

5. Make the desired changes; for example, move the cursor over and delete the initial **S**. Type the initial **T**.

| 6. | Press **F7** once to return the cursor to the document screen.

▷ Retrieve the edited macro: press **Alt** and **F10**; type **Gentry**; press **Enter**.

▷ Check to see if the initial in Gentry's name has been changed to a **T**.

CREATE SUPERSCRIPTS AND SUBSCRIPTS

Superscripts are characters that are printed a fraction above the line of type, and subscripts are characters that are printed a fraction below the line of type. (See Exhibit 15.2.) Superscripts and subscripts are used to print formulas, equations, degrees, and so on.

The superscript and subscript instructions are selected through the Font menu. The instructions to print superscripts and subscripts can be given while typing the characters or after typing the characters. The most efficient method is to give a superscript or subscript instruction after typing the characters. In this test the procedure to give a superscript and subscript instruction after typing the characters will be presented.

▷ Use the Procedure to Create a Superscript and the Procedure to Create a Subscript to type the equations and formulas in Exhibit 15.2. Type the equations and formulas only; it is unnecessary to type the column headings.

▷ Use the filename **15supsub**. Save the file and keep the document on the screen.

▷ Print one copy using draft text quality.

Algebraic Equations	Chemical Formulas
$(x + 2)^2$	H_2O
$(a + 3)^2$	NH_4
$(c - d)^2$	Na_2PO_4

EXHIBIT 15.2   Superscripts and subscripts

Procedure to Create a Superscript

1. Type the equation with the desired spacing. For example, type (x + 2)2.

2. Place the cursor under the last 2, which will become a superscript.

3. Press the **Alt** and **F4** for Block. Press the **right** arrow key once to highlight the superscript.

4. Press **Ctrl** and **F8** for Font.

5. Press **1** for Size.

6. Press **1** for Superscript {*Font, Superscript*}. *Note:* Some monitors can display the superscript character a fraction above the line and some monitors cannot. A color monitor displays the superscript character in color. View the superscript: **Shift** and **F7**; **V**. Press **F7** to return the cursor to the editing screen.

7. Reveal Codes (**Alt** and **F3**). The code **[SUPRSCPT]** is displayed on the left side of the superscript, and **[suprscpt]** is displayed on the right side of the superscript.

8. Exit Reveal Codes (**Alt** and **F3**).

Procedure to Create a Subscript

1. Type the formula with the desired spacing. For example, type H2O.

2. Place the cursor under the **2**.

3. Press the **Alt** and **F4** for Block. Press the **right** arrow key once to highlight the subscript.

4. Press **Ctrl** and **F8** for Font.

5. Press **1** for Size.

6. Press **2** for Subscript {*Font, Subscript*}. *Note:* Some monitors can display the subscript character a fraction below the line and some monitors cannot. A color monitor will display the subscript character in color. View the subscript: **Shift** and **F7**, **V**. Press **F7** to return the cursor to the editing screen.

7. Reveal Codes (**Alt** and **F3**). The code **[SUBSCPT]** will dis-

play on the left side of the subscript, and **[subscpt]** will display on the right side of the subscript.

8. Exit Reveal Codes (**Alt** and **F3**).

SUMMARY

- Printing in WordPerfect can be enhanced by using various styles and sizes of type. Also, documents can be printed with boldface, italics, or both.

- The size and type style in WordPerfect is selected through the font feature. Generally, dot matrix printers can print fonts as large as five characters per inch (cpi) or larger, and 17 cpi or smaller. A laser printer can print various sizes and styles of typefaces such as Helvetica, Palatino, and so on.

- More than one printer can be installed with the WordPerfect program. The printer is selected before the type style and sizes are chosen. (**Shift** and **F7**, **s**, place the cursor on the printer to be selected, **1**, **F7**).

- For a dot matrix printer, both the font size and style are selected with a single menu choice (**Ctrl** and **F8**, **4**, place the cursor on the desired choice, **1**). For a laser printer, the font style is selected from a menu and the font size is typed in by the user (**Ctrl** and **F8**, **4**, place the cursor on the desired style, **1**, type the desired font size, **Enter**).

- A macro is a word processing shortcut that is created and saved and then used at a later time. For example, a macro can be created for frequently used words that are long or difficult to spell. Also, a macro can be created to delete a paragraph or to turn justification off.

- A macro is defined (named), described, and activated. To define and describe the macro: **Ctrl** and **F10**, type a short name for the macro, **Enter**, type a brief description of what the macro will perform, **Enter**, type the macro text and/or instructions, **Ctrl** and **F10**. To activate the macro: **Alt** and **F10**, type the macro name, **Enter**.

- A macro can be changed by editing or replacing the macro content (**Ctrl** and **F10**, type the macro name, **2**, **2**, make the desired changes, **F7** twice).

- A superscript is a character that is printed a fraction above the line of type. A subscript is a character that is printed a fraction below the line of type. The instructions for printing superscripts or subscripts can be accomplished while typing the characters or after typing the characters (**Alt** and **F4**, press **right** arrow key to highlight the superscript/subscript character, **Ctrl** and **F8**, **1**, press **1** for a superscript or press **2** for a subscript).

SELF-CHECK QUESTIONS

(True / False—Circle One)

T,F 1. A single type style can print in various sizes.

T,F 2. Dot matrix printers have the capability to print all font type styles and sizes.

T,F 3. A printer is selected by pressing **Shift** and **F7**, **s**, place cursor on printer name, **1**, **F7**.

T,F 4. To select a font type and size for a dot matrix printer, press **Ctrl** and **F8**, **4**, place the cursor on the desired choice, press **1**.

T,F 5. A macro is a list of instructions or text that is saved and then activated by using very few keystrokes.

T,F 6. A macro can be written to set tabs or to delete a line.

T,F 7. During the creation of a macro, the macro is first activated and then described.

T,F 8. A superscript is a character that is printed one inch above the line of type.

T,F 9. After typing the character to be subscripted, block the character, and then press **Ctrl** and **F8**, **1**, **2**.

T,F 10. One method of editing a macro is to replace the contents of the macro.

ENRICHING LANGUAGE ARTS SKILLS

Spelling / Vocabulary Words

executive   a person of high-level authority in a company.
bylaw   a rule governing the internal business of an organization.
stock certificate   a document that indicates how many company stock shares are owned.

Speller Hint

The speller approves words that are correctly spelled. A correctly spelled word could be used incorrectly in a sentence. After using the speller, proofread the document for words used incorrectly.

Example   Words that are easily mistyped

you/your	book/took
of/off	to/too
from/form	hot/not

EXERCISES

Exercise 15.1

1. The screen should be clear, and the disk drive where the disk is located should be accessed.

2. Type the following agenda using left justification and the vertical spacing as shown.

3. a. If using a laser printer, set an instruction to print the heading lines in bold, 12 points, and your choice of font style. For the times and agenda items, use the same font style (not bold) and 10 points.
   b. If using a dot matrix printer, set an instruction to print the heading lines in bold, approximately 8.5 or 6.0 cpi. For the times and agenda items, use approximately 10 cpi and no bold.

4. Use the filename **15exer1**. Save the file and keep the document on the screen.

5. Print one copy using draft or high text quality.

```
                      AGENDA

     MANAGEMENT OF A WORD PROCESSING PROGRAM

                SEPTEMBER 15, 19xx

      REGIONAL OCCUPATION PROGRAM INSTRUCTORS


     9:30    Welcome/Introductions

     9:45    Management of a Word Processing Lab/Program

     10:30   Break--Coffee compliments of Judy Bramlin

     10:45   Changes in Teaching Formatting for Word
```

```
         Processing Programs and Systems

11:30    Sharing of Lab Management Ideas
            Sandie Turner, ROP
            Carolyn Reese, Gunderson High School

12:00    Lunch--Compliments of Junior's Deli

12:45    Explanation of Hands-on Materials

1:00     Hands-on Experience using the IBM PC

3:00     Closing Remarks
         Questions Answered
```

Exercise 15.2

1. The screen should be clear, and the disk drive where the disk is located should be accessed.

2. Type the following information including the column heading. Use the small letter *o* as a superscript.

3. Use the filename **15exer2**. Save the file and keep the document on the screen.

4. Print one copy using draft or high text quality.

```
         Celsius vs. Fahrenheit

              0°C = 32°F
             10°C = 50°F
             20°C = 68°F
             30°C = 86°F
```

Exercise 15.3

1. The screen should be clear, and the disk drive where the disk is located should be accessed.

2. Type the following letter omitting all underlining. Select a font style and size for the letter.

3. Select a font style and size to use for each underlined item.

4. Use the filename **15exer3**. Save the file and keep the document on the screen.

5. Print one copy using draft or high text quality.

```
(Use current date)



Albert Kalwani
Sparkle Window Washing, Inc.
3400 Central Expressway
Santa Clara, CA 95051

Dear Albert:

In connection with the incorporation and
organizational documents of Sparkle Window Washing,
Inc. (the "Company"), enclosed for your records
please find a copy of the following executed
documents:

    1. Action By Incorporator dated the middle of last
       month;

    2. The Bylaws of the Company. This copy should be
       maintained at the principal executive office of
       the Company. The original Bylaws have been
       placed in the Company's Minute Book;

    3. An original executed Certificate of Secretary
       with respect to the Company's Bylaws;

    4. Restricted Securities Letter; and

    5. The original Stock Certificate evidencing your
       ownership of 2,500 shares of the Company.

If you have questions regarding the enclosed
documents, please contact me.

Yours very truly,



Rose Fisk

Encs.
```

Exercise 15.4

1. The screen should be clear, and the disk drive where the disk is located should be accessed.

2. Center and type the following chemical formulas including the column heading.

3. Use the filename **15exer4**. Save the file and keep the document on the screen.

4. Print one copy using draft or medium text quality.

Sample Formulas

$$H_2SO_4$$
$$CO_2$$
$$NaClO_3$$
$$C_2H_4O_2$$
$$C_2H_5Cl$$

Exercise 15.5

1. The screen should be clear, and the disk drive where the disk is located should be accessed.

2. Type the following letter and use left justification. Select a font style and size for the letter.

3. Correct three spelling errors and two punctuation errors. Use a different font style and size for the corrected words.

4. Use the filename **15exer5**. Save the file and keep the document on the screen.

5. Print one copy using draft or high text quality.

```
(Use current date)



Mrs. Betty Pham
R. W. Associates
2009 Old Oakland Road
San Jose, CA 95131-1415

Dear Mrs. Pham:

Welcome! We are pleased that you have been elected
to become a member of the San Jose Chamber of
Commerce.

I believe you will find that through your
membership your will receive both direct and
```

indirect benefits. Many opportunities are provided
too promote your business, increase your contacts,
and involve you in the decision making process of
issues that affect our community.

As a member, you will receive the Chamber
Newsletter. The newsletter will list upcoming
committee meetings, business mixers, and keep you
up to date with the Chamber's programs and
services.

Watch your mailers, attend the Chamber functions
and let us know if you have suggestions or
questions.

Regards,

Marly Souza
Excutive Vice President

MS/XXX
pham.ltr/dl

Chapter 16

CREATE A LETTERHEAD, FLIER, AND NEWSLETTER USING DESKTOP PUBLISHING

OBJECTIVES

After successfully completing this chapter, you should be able to:

- Create a letterhead.
- Create a flier with a graphic.
- Edit a graphic by moving, scaling, and rotating.
- Change the position of a graphics box.
- Move a graphic down the page.
- Create a newsletter.

CREATE A LETTERHEAD

A letterhead is created by using the desktop publishing capabilities of WordPerfect. Various type styles and sizes can be used as well as the line graphics horizontal and vertical lines.

⇨ Use the Procedure to Create a Letterhead.

Patricia Richter, President   *Telephone: (303) 226-5511*

EXHIBIT 16.1   Letterhead

⇨ Type the letterhead as shown in Exhibit 16.1.

⇨ Use the filename **16pltrhd**. Save the file and keep the document on the screen.

⇨ Print one copy using draft text quality and medium graphics quality. *Optional:* Print one copy using high text quality and medium graphics quality.

Procedure to Create a Letterhead

1. If using a dot matrix printer, set the font for approximately 8.5 or 6.0 cpi (**Ctrl** and **F8; 4**; place cursor on font size; **1**). If using a laser or letter-quality printer, select a font of your choice and a size of 13 or 14 points. (See Chapter 15 for the Procedure to Change Font Style and Size, p. 238.)

2. Center (**Shift** and **F6**) and type each of the first 3 lines in all capital letters.

3. Press the **Enter** key two times.

4. Create a horizontal line.
   a.   Press **Alt** and **F9** for Graphics.
   b.   Press **5** for Line.
   c.   Press **1** for Horizontal (Create Line).
   d.   Press **1** for Horizontal Position.
   e.   Press **1** for Left.
   f.   Press **3** for Length of Line.
   g.   Type **6.5**; press **Enter**.
   h.   Press **4** for Width of Line.
   i.   Type **.02**.
   j.   Press **Enter** twice to return the cursor to the document screen.
   k.   Reveal Codes (**Alt** and **F3**) to view the code **[Hline:Left,Baseline,6.5",0.02",100%]**.
   l.   Press **Alt** and **F3** to exit Reveal Codes.

5. Press the **Enter** key two times.

6. Select an italic font and size of your choice that is smaller than the font selected in step 1. (**Ctrl** and **F8**; **4**; place cursor on chosen font; and select).

7. Type the president's name. Type the telephone number flush right (**Alt** and **F6**); press the **Enter** key once.

8. Create a second horizontal line. Follow step 4, a–l.

9. Press **Shift** and **F7, v** to view the letterhead; press **F7** to exit. If desired, change the font or make any necessary spacing adjustments.

CREATE A FLIER WITH A GRAPHIC

Creating a flier in WordPerfect is similar to creating a flier on a typewriter. However, the text can be boldface, printed in various typestyles and sizes, and graphics can be included easily. (See Exhibit 16.2.)

Graphics can be incorporated in the flier design. WordPerfect has 30 graphics that are included on the Fonts/Graphics disk. All graphics are contained in a box. The box can be printed or omitted.

The graphics can be edited by moving, scaling, and rotating the graphics within the box. In addition, the graphics box can be rearranged on a page so the graphic is to the right or left of text. Text can wrap around the graphic or can be centered in the area beside a graphic. It's magic!

➪ Use the Procedure to Create a Flier with a Graphic.

➪ Type the flier in Exhibit 16.2. Use the spacing shown. Your font size and type will vary depending on your printer.

➪ Use the filename **16flier1**. Save the file and keep the document on the screen.

➪ Print one copy using draft text quality and medium graphics quality.

Procedure to Create a Flier with a Graphic

1. Press **Ctrl** and **F8** to set the font.

2. Press **4** for Base Font.

3. a.   If using a dot matrix printer, select a font of your choice

```
                    FIRST ANNUAL

                       FLY IN

                        AND

                     AIR SHOW




        WHERE:      OAKDALE AIRPORT

        WHEN:       SATURDAY AND SUNDAY
                    JULY 10 & 11

        WHAT:       ACTION IN THE AIR

                        Stearman Biplane
                          Hang Glider
                           Parachute
                           Sailplane
                          Pitts Special
                     Curtiss Wright Speedwing




        GROUND DISPLAYS

                    P-51 Mustand Warbird

                        DC-3

                    North American T-6

                     Piper A-12


        BRING THE FAMILY AND ENJOY THE SHOW!!
```

EXHIBIT 16.2   Flier with graphic

and a size that is **8.5 cpi** or a size closest to 8.5.

    b.   If using a laser or letter-quality printer, select a font of your choice and a size that is 11 or 12 points.

4. Reveal Codes (**Alt** and **F3**). The font code is displayed. Exit Reveal Codes (**Alt** and **F3**).

5. Press **Alt** and **F9** for Graphics.

6. Press **1** for Figure.

7. Press **1** for Create {*Graphics, Figure, Create*}.

8. Press **1** for Filename.

9. **a.** *If using a hard drive,* type **c:\wp51\balloons.wpg**; press **Enter**. If necessary, check with your instructor for the directory name where the graphics are located.

    b.   *If using a floppy disk,* type the letter of the drive where the Fonts/Graphics disk is located. For example, if the Fonts/Graphics disk is located in disk drive B, type **b:balloons.wpg**; press **Enter**.

10. Press **F7** to exit and return the cursor to the document screen; use the filename **16flier1** and save the document.

11. To view the graphic, press **Shift** and **F7**; press **6** for View Document. *Note:* A graphics card must be installed in your computer in order to view graphics on the screen.

12. Press **1** to view the graphic at 100%.

13. Press **F7** to exit and return the cursor to the document screen.

14. Press **Alt** and **F3** to reveal codes. Notice the code **[Fig Box:1; BALLOONS.WPG;]** which indicates the balloon graphic has been placed in the document. Exit reveal codes (**Alt** and **F3**).

15. Center (**Shift** and **F6**) and type the four top lines in all capital letters as shown in Exhibit 16.2. Press the **Enter** key twice after each line, including the last line.

16. Press the **Enter** key 9 times.

17. Type the remainder of the flier. Use a different font and size (if available) for the words "ACTION IN THE AIR." Also, change the font and size (if available) for the words "GROUND DISPLAYS" and the *last line* of the flier. *Re-*

minder: Change the font back again to the original font and size for the lines after "ACTION IN THE AIR" and "GROUND DISPLAYS."

18. Save (**F10**), optional. Press **Shift** and **F7**; press **6** to view the flier with the graphic.

19. Press **1** for 100%. Press the **up, down**, and **right** or **left** cursor movement keys *slowly* to view the document at a "close-up" view.

20. Press **F7** to exit the view screen and return the cursor to the document screen.

⇨ Use the file named **16flier1**.

⇨ Use the Procedure to Edit a Graphic by Moving, Scaling, and Rotating.

⇨ Place the balloon graphic in the box so that no lines of the graphic are touching the box.

⇨ Use the filename **16flier2**. Save the file and keep the document on the screen.

⇨ Print one copy using draft text quality and medium graphics quality.

Procedure to Edit a Graphic by Moving, Scaling, and Rotating

Note: *Place the cursor at the beginning of the document (**Home** twice; **up** arrow key once).*

1. Reveal Codes (**Alt** and **F3**).

2. Place the cursor on the Figure Code **[Fig Box:1;BAL-LOONS.WPG;]**.

3. Press **Alt** and **F9** for Graphics.

4. Press **1** for Figure.

5. Press **2** for Edit {*Graphics, Figure, Edit*}.

6. Press **Enter** to accept the Figure Number.

7. Press **9** for Edit. *Note:* If using a floppy disk system and the message **Can't find WP.DRS** is displayed, replace your file disk with the Fonts/Graphic Disk and select **9** again.

8. *Move the Graphic*
   a.   Press **1** to move the graphic within the box.
   b.   Type **.1** for horizontal inch; press **Enter**.
   c.   Type **−.1** for vertical inch; press **Enter**.

Note: A shortcut to moving a graphic is to press the **up**, **down**, **left**, or **right** arrow keys. Press the **Ins** key to change the percentage that the graphic moves up, down, left, or right, that is, 1, 5, 10, and 25. The percentage is displayed in the lower right corner of the screen.

9. *Scale the Graphic*
   a.   Press **2** for Scale.
   b.   Type **95** for Scale X; press **Enter**. *Note:* The X is the horizontal axis and affects the image width.
   c.   Type **90** for Scale Y; press **Enter**. *Note:* The Y is the vertical axis and affects the height of the image.

Note: A shortcut to scale a graphic is to press the **PgUp** or **PgDn** keys. Press **PgUp** repeatedly until the balloons are almost touching the top of the screen without losing any of the balloons' shape.

10. *Rotate a Figure*
   a.   Press **3** for Rotate.
   b.   Type **30**; press **Enter**; press **n** for no mirror image. Notice the graphic has rotated 30°.
   c.   Press **3** again.
   d.   Type **0** (zero); press **Enter**; press **n**.

Note: A shortcut to rotate a graphic is to press the **−** or **+** key on the numeric keypad.

11. Press **F7** *twice* to exit and return the cursor to the document screen.

12. Save (**F10**), optional. Press **Shift** and **F7**.

13. Press **6** for View Document.

14. Press **3** for Full Page.

15. Press **F7** to exit and return the cursor to the document screen.

⮡ Use the file named **16flier2**.

⮡ Use the Procedure to Change the Position of the Graphics Box and Procedure to Move the Graphic Down the Page.

⮡ Use the filename **16flier3**. Save the file and keep the document on the screen.

⮡ Print one copy using draft text quality and medium graphics quality. (See Exhibit 16.3.)

Procedure to Change the Position of the Graphics Box

1. Reveal Codes (**Alt** and **F3**).

2. Place the cursor on the figure code **[Fig Box:1;BALLOONS.WPG;]**.

3. Press **Alt** and **F9** for Graphics.

4. Press **1** for Figure.

5. Press **2** for Edit {*Graphics, Figure, Edit*}.

6. Press **Enter** to accept Figure number 1.

7. Press **6** for Horizontal Position.

8. Press **1** for Left.

9. Press **F7** to exit and return the cursor to the document screen. *Note:* The figure box lines might not align now.

10. Save (**F10**), optional. Press **Shift** and **F7**; press **6** for View to view the new position of the graphics box.

11. Press **F7** to exit and return the cursor to the document screen.

Procedure to Move the Graphic down the Page

1. Reveal Codes (**Alt** and **F3**).

2. Place the cursor on the figure code **[Fig Box:1;BALLOONS.WPG;]**.

3. Press **Alt** and **F9** for Graphics.

4. Press **1** for Figure.

```
                    FIRST ANNUAL

                      FLY IN
                                            AND

                                         AIR SHOW
```

```
WHERE:      OAKDALE AIRPORT

WHEN:       SATURDAY AND SUNDAY
            JULY 10 & 11

WHAT:       ACTION IN THE AIR

                    Stearman Biplane
                      Hang Glider
                       Parachute
                       Sailplane
                     Pitts Special
               Curtiss Wright Speedwing



            GROUND DISPLAYS

                 P-51 Mustand Warbird

                      DC-3

                 North American T-6

                   Piper A-12


            BRING THE FAMILY AND ENJOY THE SHOW!!
```

EXHIBIT 16.3 Flier with graphic repositioned

5. Press **2** for Edit.

6. Press **Enter** to accept Figure number 1.

7. Press **5** for Vertical Position.

8. Type **.75** for Offset from top of paragraph; press **Enter**.

9. Press **F7** to exit and return the cursor to the document screen.

10. Save (**F10**), optional. Press **Shift** and **F7**; press **6** for View to view the new position of the graphics box. *Note:* The first two lines of text are displayed above the graphic.

11. Press **F7** to exit and return the cursor to the document screen.

CREATE A NEWSLETTER

A typical newsletter includes columns, vertical and horizontal lines, graphics, and typeface variations. (See Exhibit 16.4.)

A newsletter is easily created in WordPerfect by using the desktop publishing capabilities. Vertical and horizontal lines of various widths and lengths can be created. The column and type style features can be used in addition to footers or headers. Once the newsletter has been created, the same design can be used repeatedly to present the same style for each edition of the newsletter.

⇨ Use the Procedure to Create a Newsletter.

⇨ Type the newsletter in Exhibit 16.4.

⇨ Use the filename **16newslt**. Save the file and keep the document on the screen.

⇨ Print one copy using draft text quality and medium graphics quality.

Procedure to Create a Newsletter

1. Set the top margin to .5 inches and the bottom margin to .75 inches (**Shift** and **F8**; **2**; **5**); press **F7** to exit.

2. Create a footer to print the page number (flush right) on every page (**Shift** and **F8**; **2**; **4**; **1**; **2**; **Alt** and **F6**; type **Page**; press the **space bar** once; **Ctrl** and **B**). Press **F7** twice to exit.

Next Meeting

Meetings are held the third Wednesday of every month. Meetings begin promptly at 7:00 p.m. at the Rockridge Community Center.

Rockingham Estates--George Showalter Application for 500 Homes on Masanuttan Ridge

The Rockingham County Board of Supervisors held a Public hearing at 6:00 p.m. last Tuesday, in the Public Works Auditorium, 230 Oakdale Street, Harrisonburg. They took public testimony and continued the hearing the following Thursday at 8:30 p.m. in the Board of Supervisors chamber on 555 Market Street, Harrisonburg.

The Rockingham County Planning Commission approved Rockingham Estates for 300 single family homes and 100 townhouses. The Shenandoah Community Club supported the decision of the Planning Commission.

The Shenandoah Community Club has been working with the George Showalter Company on this project for the past three years. The developer has met all of our initial concerns and has a program for mitigating traffic problems at 10 intersections in the Shenandoah area. The intersection at 29th and "C"

Street is one traffic concern. Other intersections are at Baily and Hansen Streets and Third Street and Fairview Street.

Premier Homes Tract Map 4007-- Lost Creek

The Rockingham County Board of Supervisors in a Public Hearing last Tuesday, denied the petition of Premier Homes to reclassify an approved Planned Development (PD) for 20 Townhomes to a 15 Single Family Homes development.

Shenandoah Fire Protection Measure Vote

The Board of Directors of the Shenandoah Fire Protection District and the Shenandoah Community Club wish to thank you for your vote of confidence by your voting in favor of Measure C. There were 820 yes votes and 38 no votes in the special district election last week.

Welcome New Homeowners and Residents to Shenandoah

We would like to extend a wholehearted warm welcome to all new homeowners and residents to the Shenandoah community. We hope you will enjoy your new home and become actively involved in our community and the Shenandoah Community Club.

Page 1

EXHIBIT 16.4 Newsletter

3. Create a horizontal line.
  a.   Press **Alt** and **F9** for Graphics.
  b.   Press **5** for Line.
  c.   Press **1** for Horizontal.
  d.   Press **1** for Horizontal Position.
  e.   Press **1** for Left.
  f.   Press **3** for Length of Line.
  g.   Type **6.5**; press **Enter**.
  h.   Press **4** for Width of Line.
  i.   Type **.04**; press **Enter** once.
  j.   Press **Enter** three times.
  k.   Reveal Codes (**Alt** and **F3**) to view the codes: **[T/B Mar:0.5″,0.75″] [Footer A:Every page;[Flsh Rt]Page ^B] [HLine:Left,Baseline,6.5″,0.04,″100%]**.
  l.   Press **Alt** and **F3** to exit Reveal Codes.

4. Center (**Shift** and **F6**); type the word *NEWSLETTER* in all capital letters; press the **Enter** key two times.

5. Center and type the words *SHENANDOAH COMMUNITY CLUB INC.* in all capital letters; press the **Enter** key two times.

6. Create a second horizontal line. Repeat step 3, a–l. In step i type .01 for the line width.

7. Type *HARRISONBURG, VA 22801*.

8. Press **Alt** and **F6** for Flush Right.

9. Type *March 19XX*; press **Enter** once.

10. Create a third horizontal line. Repeat step 3, a–l. In step i type .01 for the line width.

11. Save (**F10**), optional. View the newsletter on the screen (**Shift** and **F7**; **6**). Press **F7** to exit.

12. Use left justification and widow/orphan protection, **yes** (**Shift** and **F8**; **1**; **3**; **1**; **9**; **y**; **F7**).

13. Define and turn on newspaper columns (**Alt** and **F7**; **1**; **3**; press **Enter**; **1**).

14. Create a vertical line to print between columns.
  a.   Press **Alt** and **F9** for Graphics.
  b.   Press **5** for Line.
  c.   Press **2** for Vertical.

   d. Press **1** for Horizontal Position.

   e. Press **3** for Between Columns; a message is displayed: **Place line to right of Column:1**; press **Enter**.

   f. Press **2** for Vertical Position.

   g. Press **5** for Set Position.

   h. Press **Enter** to accept the position computed and displayed by WordPerfect.

   i. Press **Enter** once.

15. Create a Figure.

Note: If using a hard disk, the graphics that WordPerfect provides should be on drive C. If using a floppy disk, place the Fonts/ Graphics disk in drive A.

   a. Press **Alt** and **F9** for Graphics.

   b. Press **1** for Figure.

   c. Press **1** for Create {*Graphics, Figure, Create*}.

   d. Press **1** for Filename.

   e. Type the drive letter (where the graphics are located) followed by a colon and the graphic name. For example, type **c:\wp51\news.wpg** or type **a:news.wpg**.

   f. Press **Enter**. (A **Please Wait** message is displayed briefly.)

   g. Press **F7**.

16. Type the text as shown in Exhibit 16.4. Begin typing with the first paragraph heading in the left column. *Note:* The figure box is drawn as text is typed.

17. Before typing the paragraph entitled "Shenandoah Fire Protection Measure Vote," create a figure. Follow step 15, a–e. (In step e use the filename **chkbox-1.wpg**.) After step f follow with step a below.

   a. Press **6** for Horizontal Position.

   b. Press **1** for Left (to position the graphic on the left side of the text in column 2).

   c. Press **F7** to exit.

18. Save (**F10**), optional. View the newsletter (**F7**; **6**).

SUMMARY

- WordPerfect has graphics capabilities that are used to create horizontal and vertical lines as well as to print a variety of type styles and sizes. Using the graphics features, a letterhead, flier, and newsletter can be created easily in Word-Perfect.

● A horizontal line can be created using the graphics function. The line length and width of the line can be varied (**Alt** and **F9**, **5**, **1**, **1**, **1**, **3**, type desired line length in inches, **Enter, 4**, type desired line width, **Enter** twice).

● Thirty graphics are provided on the WordPerfect Fonts/Graphics disk. The graphics are saved with the filename extension **.wpg**. Graphics can be retrieved into a document where desired (**Alt** and **F9**, **1**, **1**, **1**, type the disk drive letter where the graphics are located followed by a colon and type the filename, **Enter**, **F7**).

● A graphic can be edited by moving, scaling, and rotating the graphic within the box (**Alt** and **F9**, **1**, **2**, type figure number, **Enter**, **9**,—**1** to move the graphic, **2** to scale the graphic, or **3** to rotate the graphic—**F7** twice).

● Text can wrap around the graphic boxes. Also, graphic boxes can be repositioned in the document (**Alt** and **F9**, **1**, **2**, type figure number, **Enter**, press **6** for horizontal position or **5** for vertical position, select desired position, **F7**).

● A graphic can be viewed on the monitor if the computer has a graphics card (**Shift** and **F7**, **6**, press **F7** to exit).

SELF-CHECK QUESTIONS

(True / False—Circle One)

T,F 1. A horizontal line can be created by using the **Alt** and **F9** (graphics) function.

T,F 2. Before editing a graphic, the cursor should be placed on the figure code.

T,F 3. A graphic can be edited by moving the graphic within the graphic box.

T,F 4. A graphic cannot be repositioned on a page.

T,F 5. Text will automatically wrap around a graphic.

T,F 6. A graphic can be viewed on the computer screen if a graphics card has been installed in the computer.

T,F 7. Vertical lines cannot be created using the graphics feature.

T,F 8. A graphic can be placed in a document by pressing **Alt** and **F9**, **1**, **1**, **1**, type disk drive and name of graphic, **Enter**, **F7**.

T,F 9. When graphics are placed in a document, font sizes and styles cannot be changed.

T,F 10. Press **Shift** and **F7**, **6** to view a graphic.

ENRICHING LANGUAGE ARTS SKILLS

Spelling/Vocabulary Words

modem a device used to translate computer signals to telephone signals and vice versa.

local area network a system to connect two or more computers in order for the computers to share programs and files.

advice recommendations for solving a problem.

Initials Abbreviated

Place a period and one space after the initials in a person's name.

Example F. A. Turner
S. R. Kerzberg

EXERCISES

Exercise 16.1, Part I

1. The screen should be clear, and the disk drive should be accessed where the file disk is located.

2. Create the following letterhead as shown. (Use the style similar to the one shown in Exhibit 16.1.)

3. Use the filename **16lethd1**. Save the file without clearing the screen.

4. Print one copy of the letterhead using draft text quality and medium graphics quality. *Optional:* Print a second copy using high text quality and medium graphics quality.

```
                    DATA SYSTEMS INCORPORATED
                    2020 LANKERSHIM BLVD.
                    N. HOLLYWOOD, CA 91604


        T. J. Kumar, President
        Telephone: (818) 506-8822
```

Exercise 16.1, Part II

1. Create a letterhead for yourself, friend, or relative.
    a.   If available, use a graphic as part of the letterhead.
    b.   Use different font styles, font sizes, and boldface as desired.

2. Use the filename **16mylthd**. Save the file without clearing the screen.

3. Print one copy using draft or high text quality and medium graphics quality.

Exercise 16.2

1. The screen should be clear, and the disk drive should be accessed where the file disk is located.

2. Create a flier for the information that follows. Create a style of your choice. Create the graphic named **star-5.wpg**. Place the graphic in the top left corner of the page. Type text to the right of the graphic.

3. Use the filename **16exer2**. Save the file without clearing the screen.

4. Print one copy of the flier using draft text quality and medium graphics quality.

```
Engineering Productivity Division
Hewlett Packard


To: All Employees


You are invited to attend the County Fair Days on
Thursday and Friday of next week.

Contact Bill Kurtz for information concerning the
food arrangements and games.

Bring your favorite dish and plan to participate in
the following games:

    Bobbing for apples
    50-yard dash
    Tug of war
```

Exercise 16.3

1. The screen should be clear, and the disk drive should be accessed where the file disk is located.

2. Create a newsletter for the information that follows. Create a newsletter style similar to Exhibit 16.4. Use your choice of fonts and sizes.

3. Use the graphic named **pc-1.wpg**. Place the graphic beside the second paragraph as shown.

4. Use the filename **16news**. Save the file without clearing the screen.

5. Print one copy of the newsletter using draft text quality and medium graphics quality.

NEWSLETTER
VENTURA USERS GROUP NEWS
Rockaway, NY 07866
(Use Current Date)

Next Month's Speaker

Mr. Sawyer from *T. K. Engineering* of Newark will be the featured speaker. He will take the cover off a microcomputer and explain the mysteries within.

 The purpose of this demon- stra- tion is to "get under the hood" with expert guidance. He will explain how to upgrade, install an internal *modem*, add memory, and install a hard disk.

Mr. Sawyer will also provide a guide with suggestions and *advice* on purchasing and upgrading a microcomputer.

Updated Software Classes at Harold College

Starting next month, Harold College will be teaching classes on the new version of desktop publishing software.

Also, a new *local area network* (LAN) class will provide hands-on experience with the 3ComLAN operating system. The network will also be used to provide instruction on the desktop publishing software. A new laser printer has been installed on the network.

Tricks of the Trade

While working on a page that has many details and requires a lot of zooming in and out, instead of using the mouse and menus, the cursor can be moved around much faster by placing the mouse cursor on the location you want to zoom in (reduced view) and press Ctrl and N to obtain the normal view or Ctrl and E to obtain the enlarged view.

Back It Up

Has an entire chapter been lost? Save after any change is made. Or save every five to ten minutes. The keyboard shortcut for saving is Ctrl and S.

Exercise 16.4

1. The screen should be clear, and the disk drive should be accessed where the file disk is located.

2. Create a flier or newsletter of your choice.

3. Use an appropriate graphic(s).

4. Use the filename **16mynews**. Save the file without clearing the screen.

5. Print one copy of the flier or newsletter using draft text quality and medium graphics quality.

Exercise 16.5

1. The screen should be clear, and the disk drive should be accessed where the file disk is located.

2. Use the following information to create a letterhead and letter.
    a. Use your choice of font style and sizes; use of a graphic is optional.
    b. Place approximately one inch between the letterhead and letter date.

3. Correct three spelling errors and three punctuation errors. Print the corrected words or clauses in boldface.

4. Use the filename **16exer5**. Save the file without clearing the screen.

5. Print one copy using draft or high text quality and medium quality graphics.

SHIELDS REALTY
3055 Minuteman Road
Andover, MA 01810-1087

Evelyn Tracy
(617) 685-0085

(Use current date)

Mr. R.E. Arceneau
588 Sandy Street
Burlington, MA 01803

Dear Mr. Arceneau:

Clients like yourself have made my real estate
business what it is today. I have built my business
on referrals and repeat clients.

If you have been thinking about adding an
investment property to you portfolio now is the
time to take advantage of the window of opportunity
that exists in today's marketplace.

Interest rates are affordable, prices are
stabilizing and many sellers are assisting buyers
with closing costs. We have over 8,500 properties
to choose form in Essex County alone.

If you or someone you know are interested in
obtaining addvice for purchasing a home or
investment property, please contact me.

Warm regards,

Evelyn Tracy
Realtor Associate

Chapter 17

CREATE DOCUMENTS USING SPECIAL FUNCTIONS

OBJECTIVES

After successfully completing this chapter, you should be able to:

- Create an organization chart using line draw.

- Create a style for a letter.

- Create a letter using a style.

- Retrieve a style.

- Create a letter using a thesaurus.

- Select synonyms from a thesaurus.

- Create an alphabetic list using sort.

- Create a numeric list using sort.

WordPerfect's special functions are *tools* used to provide professional-looking documents quickly and to provide writing assistance. Some of WordPerfect's functions discussed in this chapter are Line Draw, Sort, Style, and Thesaurus.

An organization chart can be produced using the Line Draw feature. (See Exhibit 17.1.) A sort procedure can be used to alphabetize a list of items or to arrange items in numeric order. A Thesaurus is provided to assist an author in writing with distinctive words in order to provide accurate and well-explained information. A Style can be created to save all format settings for a document.

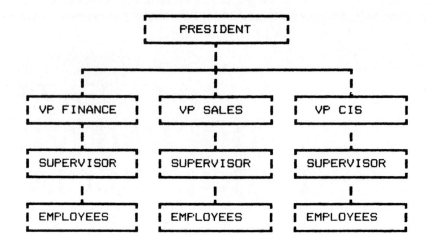

EXHIBIT 17.1   Organization chart using Line Draw

CREATE AN ORGANIZATION CHART USING LINE DRAW

The Line Draw function can be used to draw the boxes and lines for illustrating the organization of a business. Lines of varying widths and double lines are available in the Draw function. The Line menu provides separate keys that are used to select the line types and to move the cursor for drawing or deleting the line.

➪ Use the Procedure to Create an Organization Chart Using Line Draw.

➪ Type the organization chart shown in Exhibit 17.1.

Procedure to Create an Organization Chart Using Line Draw

1. Clear the screen (**F7, n, n**).

2. Press the **Tab** key 4 times to locate the cursor 20 spaces from the left margin.

3. Press **Ctrl** and **F3** for Screen.

4. Press **2** for Line Draw.

5. Press **1** to draw with a single line.

6. Press **Esc**; type 20; press the **right** arrow key once to draw a line.

7. Press the **down** arrow key 2 times.

8. Press **Esc**; type 20; press the **left** arrow key once.

9. Press the **up** arrow key 2 times.

10. Press **6** to move the cursor (without drawing).

11. Press the **down** arrow key 2 times; press **Esc**; type 10; press the **right** arrow key once to place the cursor in the middle of the bottom line.

12. Press **1** to draw with a single line.

13. Press the **down** arrow key 2 times.

14. Press **Esc**; type 17; press the **right** arrow key once.

*Note: If the line is drawn too long, press **5** for Erase; press the **up**, **down**, **left**, or **right** arrow key to erase. Press the **1** key again for Draw.*

15. Press the **down** arrow key 2 times.

16. Press **Esc**; type 7; press the **right** arrow once; press the **down** arrow key 2 times.

17. Press **Esc**; type 7; press the **left** arrow key once; press the **down** arrow key once; press the **up** arrow key once; press **Esc**; type 7; press the **left** arrow key once.

18. Press the **up** arrow key 2 times; press **Esc**; type 7; press the **right** arrow key once.

19. Press **6** for Move; locate the cursor at the bottom of the vertical line that extends from the top rectangle.

20. Press **1** for Draw.

21. Press the **down** arrow key 2 times; press **Esc**; type 7; press the **right** arrow key once.

22. Press the **down** arrow key 2 times; press **Esc**; type 7; press the **left** arrow key once; press the **down** arrow key 1 time; press the **up** arrow key 1 time; press **Esc**; type 7; press the **left** arrow key once.

23. Press the **up** arrow key 2 times; press **Esc**; type 7; press the **right** arrow key once.

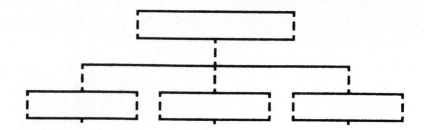

EXHIBIT 17.2 Two levels of boxes drawn

24. Press **6** for Move; press the **up** arrow key 2 times (the cursor should be located on the intersection of the horizontal line that is halfway between the two rows of boxes and the vertical line that connects the two rows of boxes).

25. Press **1** for Draw.

26. Press **Esc**; type 17; press the **left** arrow key once; press the **down** arrow key 2 times.

27. Press **Esc**; type 7; press the **right** arrow key once; press the **down** arrow key 2 times; press **Esc**; type 7; press the **left** arrow key 7 times; press the **down** arrow key 1 time; press the **up** arrow key 1 time; press **Esc**; type 7; press the **left** arrow key once.

28. Press the **up** arrow key 2 times; press **Esc**; type 7; press the **right** arrow key once.

29. *Note:* The first two levels of boxes are drawn with a short vertical line extending from the center of each of the bottom row boxes. See Exhibit 17.2.

30. Press **6** to move the cursor; press the **up** arrow key 1 time; press the **left** arrow key until the cursor is located on the left margin (Pos 1″).

31. Press **F7** to exit the Screen menu.

32. Press **Alt** and **F4** for Block; press the **down** arrow key 4 times to highlight the last row of boxes.

33. Press the **Ctrl** and **F4** for Move; press **1** for Block; press **2** for Copy.

34. *Note:* The cursor is located at the left margin below the bottom vertical lines. Press **Enter** to display the copied row of boxes.

35. With the cursor in its present location, repeat steps 32–34 to copy another level of boxes.

36. Press the **right** and **down** arrow keys to locate the cursor directly under the vertical line and small arrow below the bottom left box.

37. Press **Ctrl** and **F3**; press **2** for Line Draw; press **5** for Erase. Press the **up** arrow key once to erase the vertical line below the box.

38. Press **6** to move the cursor; press the **right** arrow key right (approximately 17 times) and the **down** arrow key 1 time to locate the cursor directly under the vertical line and small arrow below the next box; press **5** for Erase; press the **up** arrow key once.

39. Repeat step 38 to remove the line under the last box in the bottom row.

40. Press **F7** to exit the Screen menu.

41. Press **Ins** to turn on Typeover. *Note:* Insert *must* be on to type information inside the boxes without erasing the boxes.

42. Place the cursor in the top box approximately four spaces from the left edge of the box and one space above the bottom line. (See Exhibit 17.1.)

43. Type the word PRESIDENT in all capital letters.

44. With **Ins** on, use the arrow keys to move the cursor to each box and type the appropriate information. (See Exhibit 17.1.)

45. After all information has been typed in the boxes, locate the cursor at the beginning of the organization chart (press **Home** 3 times; press the **up** arrow key once).

46. Press the **Ins** key once to turn off Typeover.

47. Press the **Enter** key 3 times.

48. Press **Home** 3 times; press the **up** arrow key once to locate the cursor at the beginning of the document.

49. Press **Shift** and **F6** to center; type the title in all capital letters. *Note:* If necessary, press the space bar 2–3 times after the title to center the title over the chart.

Note: On some dot matrix printers the lines may not print solid and/or when using Line Draw, proportionally spaced text may not print correctly.

▷ Use the file named **17pchart**. Save the file and keep the document on the screen.

▷ Print one copy using draft text quality.

CREATE A STYLE FOR A LETTER

A style is a record of format information that affects the arrangement of text and type style and size of a document. The preset style is used to expedite the formatting of an often-used document. For example, an office that originates many average-length letters can create a letter style with 1.5-inch margins and a 2-inch top margin. The style can also include type style and size codes, and a code to place the current date automatically in the letter and text. The style is retrieved for each letter produced.

When a style is created, a name and description are given to the style, and the keystrokes are performed to set the codes for the style. For example, the **Shift** and **F8; 1; 7** are pressed to set the left and right margins.

A style is saved with a document or can be saved as a separate file. Once the style is saved, the style is used when creating a document. For example, when a letter is typed, the first step is to retrieve and use the saved style. The style is retrieved and used with each letter that is produced.

▷ Use the Procedure to Create a Letter Style.

▷ Use the filename **17pstyle**.

▷ Save the file.

Procedure to Create a Letter Style

1. Press **Alt** and **F8** to display the Styles menu on the screen {*Layout, Styles*}. (See Exhibit 17.3.)

2. Press **3** for Create. (See Exhibit 17.4.)

3. Press **1** for Name.

4. Type a name for the style. For example, type **letter frmt**; press **Enter**. *Note:* The name for a style can be 11 or less characters.

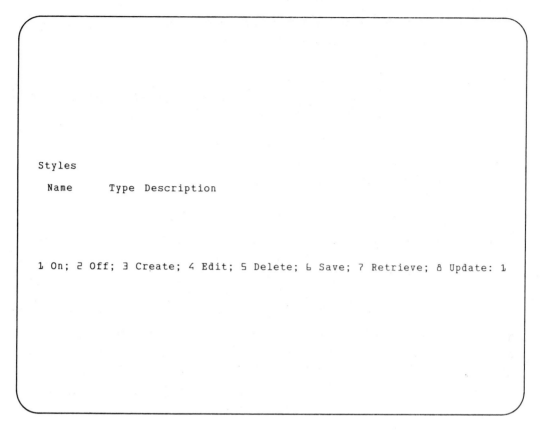

```
    Styles

     Name        Type Description




    1 On; 2 Off; 3 Create; 4 Edit; 5 Delete; 6 Save; 7 Retrieve; 8 Update: 1
```

EXHIBIT 17.3   Styles menu

5. Press **2** for Type; press **2** for Open.

> *Note: The style type can be open or paired. An open style is a style that affects the entire document, such as the letter style. The paired style is used for a format that has a beginning and an end, such as the format for a paragraph that is to be indented from the left and right margins.*

6. Press **3** for Description.

7. Type a description for the style. For example, type **Standard format for an average letter**; press **Enter**.

8. Press **4** for Codes.

Type the Format Instructions

9. Set left and right margins to 1.5 each (**Shift** and **F8**; **1**; **7**); set the top margin to 2 inches; if necessary, use left justification. *Note:* The Margin and Justification codes are displayed on the screen.

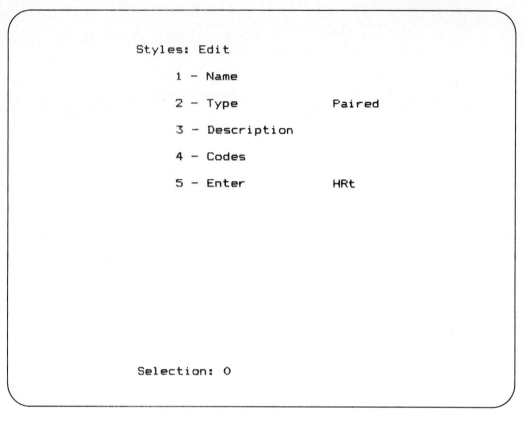

```
        Styles: Edit

            1 - Name

            2 - Type            Paired

            3 - Description

            4 - Codes

            5 - Enter           HRt








        Selection: 0
```

EXHIBIT 17.4   Styles: Edit menu

10. Set the type style and size (**Ctrl** and **F8**; **4**).
  a. If using a dot matrix printer, select a font of **12 cpi**; press **1** for Select.
  b. If using a laser or letter-quality printer, use your choice of style and a **10** point size; press **Enter**.

11. Set the date.
  a. Press **Shift** and **F5** for Date.
  b. Press **2** for Date Code.
  c. Press the **Enter** key five times.

12. Press **F7** to return the cursor to the Styles: Edit menu.

13. Press **F7** once to return the cursor to the Styles menu.

14. Press **6** for Save.

15. Type a name. For example, type **17pstyle**; press **Enter**.

16. Press **F7** to exit and return the cursor to the document screen.

⇨ Use the Procedure to Retrieve the Style.

⇨ Use the style named **17pstyle**.

Procedure to Retrieve the Style

1.	Clear the screen (**F7, n, n**).
2.	Press **Alt** and **F8** for Style {*Layout, Styles*}.
3.	Press **7** for Retrieve; type filename; for example, type **17pstyle; Enter**. If necessary, press **n** to replace style.
4.	Place the cursor on the name and description of the desired style. For example, locate the cursor on **letter frmt, open, Standard format for an average letter**.
5.	Press **1** to turn on the style; the current date displays on the screen.
6.	Press **Alt** and **F3** to reveal codes. Press the **Home** key once; press the **up** arrow key once. *Note:* The entire style code is highlighted. If necessary, the entire style code can be deleted by pressing the **Del** key. Any needed corrections to the style are made through the Edit function in the Style menu.
7.	Exit Reveal Codes (**Alt** and **F3**).
8.	Press **Home** two times; press the **down** arrow key once to return the cursor to the position below the style codes.

⇨ Type the following letter.

⇨ Use the filename **17ltrsty**. Save the file and keep the document on the screen.

⇨ Print one copy using high text quality.

```
Ms. Carla Cole
Corvallis Networks Division
1909 N. E. Circle Blvd.
Corvallis, OR 97330

Dear Ms. Cole:

I wanted to be sure you were among the first to
know about the new Executive Business Class
```

available on Ocean Pacific Air.

Ocean Pacific chose the Asian News Weekly as their
primary advertising medium because it reaches an
elite audience of people in decision-making
positions like yourself--and--because Ocean Pacific
Air values our news environment for their news.

We are proud to be a part of Ocean Pacific's
advertising efforts to introduce the Executive
Business Class and hope that you will follow their
series of advertisements in the coming weeks.

Sincerely,

Gary Ngu
General Business Manager

CREATE A LETTER USING A THESAURUS

As an author is writing a letter or other information, words are
selected to best express his/her meaning. A list of synonyms
(words that have the same meaning) and antonyms (words with
opposite meanings) are saved in the WordPerfect thesaurus file.
The thesaurus can be used during the writing process or after a
document is written.

The cursor is located on the first character of the word to be
looked up in the thesaurus. A selection of words that are possible replacements are displayed on the screen. The author can
choose to replace the word, look up another word, or not select
any synonym.

▷ Use the Procedure to Select Synonyms from a Thesaurus.

▷ Use the practice letter named **17ltrsty**.

▷ Use the filename **17thesar**. Save the file and keep the document on the screen.

▷ Print one copy with draft text quality.

Procedure to Select Synonyms from a Thesaurus

*Note: If necessary, retrieve the letter with the file named **17ltrsty**.*

1. Place the cursor on the first character of the word to be
looked up in the thesaurus. For example, place the cursor
under the *s* in the word *sure*. *Note:* If using a floppy disk

system, replace your file disk with the Thesaurus disk.

2. Press the **Alt** and **F1** for Thesaurus {*Tools, Thesaurus*}.

3. Scan through the words listed on the screen.

4. Press **1** for Replace Word.

5. Press the letter for the word chosen. For example, type **d** to select the word *certain*. The word *certain* will automatically replace the word *sure* in the document.

*Note: If another word on the list is to be looked up, press **3** and type the word. A list of additional word choices is displayed on the screen.*

6. Place the cursor on the first character of the word *Executive*. Repeat steps 2-4. Press **f** to select the word *official*. *Note:* The first letter of the word *official* is automatically capitalized, since the word being replaced had the first character capitalized.

7. Place the cursor on the first character of the word *Ocean*. Repeat steps 2–3. Press **F1** for Cancel, since there is no appropriate word to replace Ocean.

8. Place the cursor on the first character of the word *primary*. Repeat steps 2–3. Press **F1** to cancel.

9. Place the cursor on the first character of the word *proud*. Repeat steps 2–4. Press **j** to select the word *honorable*. Delete *able*. Type the letters **ed**. *Note:* A word can be changed to the desired form.

10. Place the cursor on the first character of the word *advertising*. Repeat steps 2–3. Press **F1** for Cancel.

11. In the last paragraph, change the word *Executive* to *Official*.

Note: If a word is not contained in the thesaurus, a message "word not found" is displayed. Press F1 twice to cancel.

Note: If using a floppy disk system, replace the Thesaurus disk with your file disk.

CREATE ALPHABETIC AND NUMERIC LISTS USING SORT

The Sort function is used to arrange lines, paragraphs, table rows, or merge records in alphabetical or numerical order. An entire document or a portion of a document can be sorted. When

EMPLOYEE DIRECTORY		
NAMES	DEPARTMENT	PHONE EXTENSION
Nguyen, Mai	Sales	5325
Boyd, Charlotte	Sales	5324
Smith, Garland	Accounting	5622
Clarence, Arlene	Sales	5324
Jardine, Larry	Accounting	5622
Underwood, Bob	Marketing	5525
Michaels, Shannon	Sales	5322
Boyd, Frank	Accounting	5623
Nice, Beverly	Accounting	5341
Powell, Mandy	Personnel	5453
Noonan, Tham	Marketing	5525
Phillips, Martin	Personnel	5456
Rodriques, Gina	Personnel	5451
Smith, Terri	Personnel	5452

EXHIBIT 17.5   Employee directory to be alphabetized through Sort

a portion of a document is sorted, the part to be sorted is blocked.

The Sort function can be used to alphabetize a file of names, addresses, phone numbers, etc. (See Exhibit 17.5.) In this textbook the Sort function is used to sort items in a table.

When using the Sort function, each unit of information is considered a field. For example, in Exhibit 17.5 each column is a field, i.e., names is one field, department is one field, etc. Each row of information is one record, e.g., the name of one person, his or her department, and phone extension is one record.

Items can be sorted in ascending or descending order. Ascending order sorts an alphabetic list from a to z and a numeric list from the smallest number to the highest number. Descending order sorts an alphabetic list from z to a and a numerical list from the largest number to the smallest number.

⬦ Create a table with 3 columns and 16 rows. (See Chapter 7 for creating a table.) Type the employee directory shown in Exhibit 17.5. Center the title, column headings, and phone extension column. Decrease column two by six spaces and column three by 3 spaces. Center the table horizontally.

```
┌─────────────────────────────────────────────────────┐
│           EMPLOYEE DIRECTORY                          │
├──────────────┬──────────────┬────────────────────────┤
│    NAMES      │  DEPARTMENT  │    PHONE EXTENSION      │
├──────────────┼──────────────┼────────────────────────┤
│Nguyen, Mai   │Sales         │        5325            │
├──────────────┼──────────────┼────────────────────────┤
│Boyd, Charlotte│Sales        │        5324            │
├──────────────┼──────────────┼────────────────────────┤
│Smith, Garland│Accounting    │        5622            │
└──────────────┴──────────────┴────────────────────────┘
                                   Doc 2 Pg 1 Ln 1" Pos 1"
{   ▲   ▲   ▲   ▲   ▲   ▲   ▲   ▲   ▲   ▲   }   ▲   ▲
────────────────────────────── Sort Table ──────────────────────────────
Key Typ Cell Line Word    Key Typ Cell Line Word    Key Typ Cell Line Word
  1  a   1    1    1         2                          3
  4                          5                          6
  7                          8                          9
Select

Action            Order             Type
Sort              Ascending         Table sort

1 Perform Action; 2 View; 3 Keys; 4 Select; 5 Action; 6 Order; 7 Type: 0
```

EXHIBIT 17.6   Sort Table menu

▷ Use the filename **17psort**. Save the file without clearing the screen.

▷ Print one copy using draft text quality.

▷ Use the Procedure to Alphabetize a Table Column Using Sort

Procedure to Alphabetize a Table Column Using Sort

Note: The cursor should be located in the normal editing screen (press F7 to exit table editor, if necessary).

1. Block the lines to be sorted.
   a. Place the cursor under the first character of the first line to be sorted, for example, place the cursor under the "N" in "Nguyen."
   b. Press **Alt** and **F4** for Block.
   c. Press the **PgDn** key once to highlight all lines to be sorted.

2. Press **Ctrl** and **F9** for Sort {*Tools, Sort*}. The Sort Table menu is displayed. (See Exhibit 17.6.)

3. Press **3** for Keys. The cursor is located under the word *Typ*.

4. Type **a** for Alphanumeric. Notice the cursor moves and locates under the word *Cell*.

5. Press the **right** arrow key once to accept Cell 1 (the first table field).

6. Press the **right** arrow key again to accept Line 1 (first line in the block).

7. Press the **right** arrow key to accept Word 1 (first word in column one).

8. Locate the cursor under Key *Type* 2. Select **a** for alphanumeric, **1** for Cell, **1** for Line, and **2** for Word. By selecting 2 for Word, the second word in column one will be sorted.

9. Press **F7** when the selections are complete.

10. Press **1** to Perform Action. After the **Number of Records** message is briefly displayed, the names are displayed alphabetized. Notice the duplicated last names of Boyd and Smith are alphabetized by both last and first names.

⇨ Use the table editor and remove all lines (**3**, **7**, **1**).

⇨ Insert one blank row above the column headings (place the cursor in row 2, **Ins**, **1**, **Enter**).

⇨ Use the filename **17psorta**. Save the file and keep the document on the screen.

⇨ Print one copy using draft text quality.

⇨ Use the Procedure to Numerically Organize a Table Column using Sort. *Note:* The third column will be sorted and arranged in ascending order—the smallest number to the largest number.

Procedure to Numerically Organize a Table Column Using Sort

1. Block the lines to be sorted. Follow step 1, a–c for the Procedure to Alphabetize a Table Column Using Sort.

2. Press **Ctrl** and **F9** for Sort {*Tools, Sort*}.

3. Press **3** for Keys. The cursor is located under the word *Typ*.

4. Type **n** for Numeric.

5. Select **3** for Cell (column/field), **1** for Line, and **1** for Word.

6. Press **F7** to exit.

7. Press **1** for Perform Action. *Note:* The lines are sorted in numeric order for the right column.

➪ Use the filename **17psortn**. Save the file and keep the document on the screen.

➪ Print one copy using draft text quality.

SUMMARY

- WordPerfect has capabilities to draw lines, sort information, save document styles, and select words from a thesaurus.

- Lines can be drawn to create boxes. The lines can be various widths or can be double lines. (**Ctrl** and **F3**, **2**, select line choice, select the style of line desired, press the **right** or **left** arrow keys to draw, press **6** to move the cursor without drawing, **F7**).

- A style is a preset record of text and/or format information that affects the arrangement of text and type style and size of a document and so on. A style is created, saved, and then retrieved onto the document screen.

- The format information for the style is created by using the keys that are normally pressed to make format selections (**Alt** and **F8**, **3**, **1**, type a name for the style, **2**, select Open or Closed, **3**, type a description for the style, **4**, type the instructions desired for the style, **F7** twice, **6**, type a file name, **Enter**, **F7**).

- When the style is to be used, it is retrieved into the document (**Alt** and **F8**, **7**, type the name of the style, place the cursor on the name and description of the desired style, **1**).

- A thesaurus is a list of synonyms and antonyms that are saved by WordPerfect. A writer can select a word that best expresses his/her meaning (**Alt** and **F1**, scan the list of words, **1** to select or **F1** to cancel).

- The Sort function can be used to arrange information in alphabetical or numerical order. Items can be sorted in ascending (smallest number to highest number) or descending (highest number to smallest number) order (**Alt** and **F4**; highlight lines to be sorted; **Ctrl** and **F9**, **3**; type **a** for alphanumeric or **n** for numeric; select the Cell, Line, and Word; **F7**; **1**).

SELF-CHECK QUESTIONS

(True / False—Circle One)

T,F   1. The Line Draw function can draw horizontal and vertical lines.

T,F   2. To move the cursor in the line draw screen without drawing, press **6**.

T,F   3. A style is a preset record that can be created to remember format, text, and/or font-change information.

T,F   4. A style is created and saved once, and can be used again and again.

T,F   5. A thesaurus is a group of words that includes both synonyms and antonyms.

T,F   6. Words from the thesaurus are obtained by pressing **Ctrl** and **F1**.

T,F   7. Items that are to be sorted are first blocked and highlighted.

T,F   8. WordPerfect can sort alphabetically but cannot sort numerically.

T,F   9. When using Sort, ascending order sorts numbers from the largest to the smallest number.

T,F 10. The **Ctrl** and **F9** keys are pressed to begin the sort procedure.

ENRICHING LANGUAGE ARTS SKILLS

Spelling / Vocabulary Words

accommodations   providing lodging or arranging a convenient situation.

plaintiff   the person who begins a court suit.

defendant   the person against whom a court suit is brought.

Apostrophe Used for Possessive

If a noun is singular and used to show possession, place an apostrophe before the *s*.

Example   The secretary's table was misplaced.

EXERCISES

Exercise 17.1

1.   The screen should be clear, and the disk drive where the disk is located should be accessed.

2.   Type the following organization chart, use line draw to place boxes around the titles.

3.   Use the filename **17exer1**. Save the file and keep the document on the screen.

4.   Print one copy using draft or high text quality.

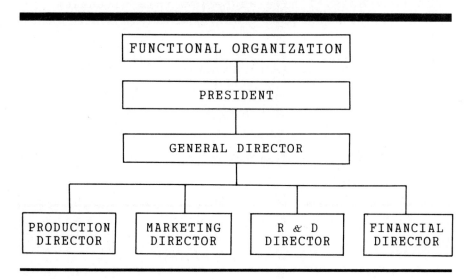

Exercise 17.2

1.   The screen should be clear, and the disk drive where the disk is located should be accessed.

2.   Create a style sheet for a letter. The style should include: 1.25-inch left and right margins, top margin of 2 inches, left justification, a type style and size of your choice, and a date code.

3. Use the created style sheet and type the following letter.

4. Use the filename **17exer2**. Save the file and keep the document on the screen.

5. Print one copy using draft or high text quality.

```
Mr. John Camargo
580 Second Street
Colorado Springs, CO 80907

Dear Mr. Camargo:

Your completion of our comment card during your
recent stay at the Phoenix Executive Hotel was
appreciated.

Our goal is to provide our guests the finest in
service, accommodations, and value so we appreciate
it when a guest takes time to point out plumbing
inconveniences. I have addressed this situation
with our Maintenance Engineer Supervisor.

We enjoyed having you stay with us and look forward
to the opportunity of serving you again, should
business or pleasure bring you back to the Phoenix
area.

Sincerely,


Paula Boatwright
General Manager
```

Exercise 17.3

1. The screen should be clear, and the disk drive where the disk is located should be accessed.

2. Type the following letter. Use the Thesaurus to find synonyms for the underlined words in the letter. Remember, if a word is not found, press **F1** twice.

3. Use the filename **17exer3**. Save the file and keep the document on the screen.

4. Print one copy using draft or high text quality.

(Use current date)

Maxine Parsons
DEBEVEC, SMITH, & HUDSON
1606 Wilshire Blvd., Suite 750
Los Angeles, CA 90017

Dear Ms. Parsons:

Our office has received the identification of expert witnesses from the plaintiff and each co-defendant party in the case of WEAVER v. PIONEER MOTOR COMPANY, et al. In discussion with James Gilley and Maria McCombs it became evident that a large number of expert depositions will be required.

At least two companies have requested that disks be made available for each expert's deposition. We also concluded that it would be in everyone's best interest to have one court reporting firm handle the expert depositions.

I have made arrangements with Diana Germain and Associates to report the expert depositions in this case. They have agreed to furnish a disk to each defendant who orders a copy of the deposition.

By using Germain Associates' services we can effectuate a significant cost savings for all of our clients.

Sincerely yours,

Geoffrey Rook

Exercise 17.4

1. The screen should be clear, and the disk drive where the disk is located should be accessed.

2. a. Create a table with 3 columns and 14 rows.
    b. Join the first row of cells.
    c. Increase column one by 2, increase column two by 2, and decrease column three by 1.
    d. Position the table horizontally centered.
    e. Type the table information.
    f. Center the title and column headings.

3. Use the filename **17exer4**. Save the file and keep the document on the screen.

MANUFACTURING DIVISIONS		
DIVISIONS	LOCATION	PHONE NUMBER
Engineering Operation	Englewood, CO 80111	(303) 773-2345
Andover	Andover, MA 01810	(617) 585-5500
Avondale	Avondale, PA 19311	(215) 366-8900
Instrument Support	Cupertino, CA 95014	(408) 725-6606
Colorado Telecom	Loveland, CO 80537	(303) 655-3355
Information Networks	Boise, ID 83707	(208) 323-6776
Computer Support	Cupertino, CA 95014	(408) 257-9009
Disc Memory	Marysville, WA 98270	(206) 335-0222
Computer Systems	Sunnyvale, CA 94086	(408) 737-8808
Greeley	Greeley, CO 80634	(303) 355-0011
Waltham	Waltham, MA 02254	(617) 890-3388
Software Distribution	Roseville, CA 95678	(916) 788-9911

4. Print one copy using draft text quality.

5. Sort the divisions column in alphabetical order.

6. Remove all lines; insert one blank row above the column headings.

7. Use the filename **17exer4a**. Save the file and keep the document on the screen.

8. Print one copy using draft or high text quality.

9. Sort the location column in numerical order by zip code.

10. Use the filename **17exer4n**. Save the file and keep the document on the screen.

11. Print one copy using draft or high text quality.

Exercise 17.5

1. The screen should be clear, and the disk drive where the disk is located should be accessed.

2. Use memorandum style 1 and type the following memorandum.

3. Correct three spelling errors and four punctuation errors.

4. Use the filename **17exer5**. Save the file and keep the document on the screen.

5. Print one copy using draft or high text quality.

```
                    Memorandum


To:        All General Agents

From:      C. Floy McClung

Date:      (Use current date)

Subject:   Premium Increase


After reviewing the experience on our Agent's Major
Medical Plan it has become apparent an increase is
necessary. The entire industry is suffering from
adverse experience and increased costs.

We invited various excutives from the field to the
home office to discuss this problem, and went over
various scenarios and options. This is not
something that can be accomplished with a "quick
fix" so we are looking into various solutions too
solve this problem in the future.

The premium for a single Agents Major Medical will
be $135 per month, and a family Major Medical
premium will be $360 per month. New premiums will
be effective on the first of next month.

This is a 28% increase and is not a permanent
solution to our problem. We will let you know as
soon as we decide on our future plans for premium
increases.

To expidite the paperwork involved, you will be
sent new forms in two weeks. Please fill out the
new forms immediately and return them to the home
office.
```

Appendix 1

CONTROLLING FILES

Procedure to Exit WordPerfect Temporarily and Return to DOS

WordPerfect can be exited quickly in order to return to DOS and use DOS commands. A disk can be formatted, checked, copied, and so on.

| 1. | Press **Ctrl** and **F1** for Shell {*File, Go to Dos*}. |

| 2. | Press **1** for Go to DOS. |

| 3. | Type **exit** to return to the WordPerfect document screen. |

Procedure to Copy One File to Another Disk

| 1. | Press **F5** for List Files {*File, List Files*}. |

| 2. | Type the disk drive letter followed by a colon for the location of the file disk to copy from or press **Enter** if the desired file is on the accessed drive. |

| 3. | Place the cursor on the filename to highlight the file to be copied. |

| 4. | Press **8** for Copy. |

| 5. | Type the disk drive letter followed by a colon for the location of the disk to be copied to; press **Enter**. |

Procedure to Mark Multiple Files to Be Copied

| 1. | Press **F5** for List Files. |

2. Type the disk drive letter followed by a colon for the location of the file disk to copy from or press **Enter** if the desired file is on the accessed drive.

3. Place the cursor on the first filename to be copied; press **Shift** and the * **(asterisk) to mark**.

4. Repeat step 2 for all files to be copied.

5. Press **8** for Copy; press **y** for yes.

6. Type the drive letter followed by a colon for the location of the disk to be copied to; press **Enter**.

*Note: To unmark a filename before copying, place the cursor on the file and press **Shift** and * .*

Procedure to Rename a File

When a filename is given another name, the original name is erased from the name list and the new name is displayed.

1. Press **F5** for List Files.

2. Type the disk drive letter followed by a colon for the location of the file disk to copy from or press **Enter** if the desired file is on the accessed drive.

3. Place the cursor on the filename to be renamed.

4. Press **3** for Move/Rename.

5. Type a new filename.

6. Press **Enter**. The new name is displayed on the screen.

Procedure to Move a File

When a file is moved, the file is deleted in the original location and transferred to the new location.

1. Press **F5** for List Files.

2. Type the disk drive letter followed by a colon for the location of the file disk to move from or press **Enter** if the desired file is on the accessed drive.

3. Place the cursor on the filename to be moved.

4. Press **3** for Move/Rename.

5. Type the disk drive letter followed by a colon for the location of the file disk where the file is to be moved; press **Enter**. *Note:* To move a file to another directory, type the disk drive letter followed by a colon and a backslash; type the directory name. For example, type **c:\wp51**; press **Enter**.

Procedure to Delete a File

1. Press **F5** for List Files.

2. Type the disk drive letter followed by a colon for the location of the file disk to delete from or press **Enter** if the desired file is on the accessed drive.

3. Place the cursor on the filename to be deleted.

4. Press **2** for Delete.

5. Press **y** for yes; the file is removed from the disk.

Procedure to Search for a File Using a Word or Phrase

1. Press **F5** for List Files.

2. Type the disk drive letter followed by a colon for the location of the file disk to be searched or press **Enter** if the desired file is on the accessed drive.

3. Press **9** for Find; Name Search.

4. Press **4** for Entire Doc.

5. Type the word or words being searched.

6. Press **Enter**.

7. A message is displayed: **Searching file # of #**. The program searches each file and indicates the number of the file being searched out of the number of files on the disk.

8. The filenames that contain the word or words being searched are displayed on the screen.

Note: Before retrieving a document, print screen a list of the filenames. After a document is retrieved, the list of filenames returns to the directory listing of all files.

Procedure to Lock a File by Using a Password

A file can be locked so that the correct password must be entered to retrieve or print the file.

| 1. | With the document on the screen, press **Ctrl** and **F5** for Text In/Out. |

| 2. | Press **2** for Password. |

| 3. | Press **1** for Add/Change {*File, Password, Add/Change*}. |

| 4. | Type the password (up to 24 characters); press **Enter**. The password does not appear on the screen. |

| 5. | Reenter the password; press **Enter**. |

| 6. | Save the file (**F10**). |

Procedure to Retrieve a Locked File

| 1. | Press **F5** for List Files. |

| 2. | Type the disk drive letter followed by a colon for the location of the file disk or press **Enter** if the desired file is on the accessed drive. |

| 3. | Place the cursor on the filename to be retrieved. |

| 4. | Press **1** for Retrieve. A prompt is displayed: **Enter Password (a:\filename):**. |

| 5. | Type the password; press **Enter**. *Note:* If the password is incorrectly typed, a message **File is locked** is displayed on the screen; the cursor returns automatically to the document screen. |

Procedure to Unlock a Document

| 1. | Retrieve the document. |

| 2. | Press **Ctrl** and **F5** for Text In/Out. |

| 3. | Press **2** for Password. |

4. Press **2** for Remove.

5. Save the document (**F10**). When the file is retrieved, the document is no longer locked.

Procedure to Save a Document as DOS Text (ASCII)

1. With a document on the screen, press **Ctrl** and **F5**.

2. Press **1** for DOS Text.

3. Press **1** for Save {*File, Text out, DOS text*}.

4. Type the name of the document to be saved as DOS text.

5. Press **Enter**.

> *Note: The document can be retrieved into WordPerfect through the normal retrieve process. The document will be converted automatically while being retrieved.*

Procedure to Convert Other Software Files to WordPerfect

Note: The following document files can be converted to WordPerfect: Wordstar 3.3, Multimate 3.22, WordPerfect 4.2, Navy DIF (Data Interchange Format), and Revised Form Text (IBM word processing format).

1. Access the disk drive where the file to be converted is located and write down the name of the file that is to be converted.

2. Press **Ctrl** and **F1** for Shell {*File, Go to DOS*}.

3. Press **1** to Go to DOS.

4. Type the drive letter where the **convert.exe** file is located followed by a colon; type **convert**. For example, type **c:\wp51\convert**; press **Enter**. If using a floppy disk system, remove the WordPerfect program disk from drive A and replace with the Conversion disk.

5. The document conversion utility screen is displayed briefly.

6. The prompt **Name of Input File?** is displayed on the screen.

Name of Input File a:exhib1.2
Name of Output File? a:translate

0 EXIT
1 WordPerfect to another format
2 Revisable-Form-Text (IBM DCA Format) to WordPerfect
3 Final-Form-Text (IBM DCA Format) to WordPerfect
4 Navy DIF Standard to WordPerfect
5 WordStar 3.3 to WordPerfect
6 MultiMate Advantage II to WordPerfect
7 Seven-Bit Transfer Format To WordPerfect
8 WordPerfect 4.2 to WordPerfect 5.1
9 Mail Merge to WordPerfect Secondary Merge
A Spreadsheet DIF to WordPerfect Secondary Merge
B Word 4.0 to WordPerfect
C DisplayWrite to WordPerfect

Enter number of Conversion desired

EXHIBIT A.1   Software names that can be converted to Word-Perfect files

7. Type the disk drive letter followed by a colon for the location of the input file; type the filename. For example, type **a:letter.ws**; press **Enter**.

8. The prompt **Name of Output File?** is displayed on the screen.

9. Type the drive letter followed by a colon and filename. For example, type **c:letter.ws**. *Note:* The same filename or a new filename can be typed.

10. A list of software names that can be converted to WordPerfect is displayed on the screen. (See Exhibit A.1.)

11. Type the number or letter desired from the software list. For example, type **4** to **select** WordStar 3.3 to WordPerfect. (See Exhibit A.2.)

12. A message is displayed: **letter.ws Converted to c:letter.ws**.

13. *Type* **exit**; press **Enter** to return the cursor to the WordPerfect document screen. The file can now be retrieved into WordPerfect.

Name of Input File a:exhib1.2
Name of Output File? a:exhibit

0 EXIT
1 WordPerfect to another format
2 Revisable-Form-Text (IBM DCA Format) to WordPerfect
3 Final-Form-Text (IBM DCA Format) to WordPerfect
4 Navy DIF Standard to WordPerfect
5 WordStar 3.3 to WordPerfect
6 MultiMate Advantage II to WordPerfect
7 Seven-Bit Transfer Format To WordPerfect
8 WordPerfect 4.2 to WordPerfect 5.1
9 Mail Merge to WordPerfect Secondary Merge
A Spreadsheet DIF to WordPerfect Secondary Merge
B Word 4.0 to WordPerfect
C DisplayWrite to WordPerfect

Enter number of Conversion desired 5
a:exhib1.2 Converted to b:exhibit

Enter 'EXIT' to return to WordPerfect
A:\>

EXHIBIT A.2 Screen used to select file conversion

Note: Once a file has been converted to WordPerfect, the format settings such as tabs, returns, margins, and so on may need to be set.

Procedure to Convert WordPerfect to Other Software Files

1. Follow steps 1-6 for Procedure to Convert Other Software Files to WordPerfect.

2. Type the disk drive letter followed by a colon for the location of the input file; type the filename. For example, type **a:appendix**; press **Enter**.

3. Type the disk drive letter followed by a colon for the location of the output file; type the filename. For example, type **b:sample.app**.

4. Press **1** to select **WordPerfect to another format**.

Name of Input File b:1chap.51
Name of Output File? b:sample.51

0 EXIT
1 Revisable-Form-Text (IBM DCA Format)
2 Final-Form-Text (IBM DCA Format)
3 Navy DIF Standard
4 WordStar 3.3
5 MultiMate Advantage II
6 Seven-Bit Transfer Format
7 ASCII Text File
8 WordPerfect Secondary Merge to Spreadsheet DIF

Enter number of output file format desired

EXHIBIT A.3   WordPerfect files can be converted to these forms/files

5. The list of forms that WordPerfect can be converted to is displayed on the screen. (See Exhibit A.3.)

6. Press the number for the desired file format. For example, press **4** for MultiMate Advantage II.

7. A message is displayed that conversion has been accomplished.

8. *Type* **exit** to return the cursor to the WordPerfect document screen.

Procedure to Use Two Documents

1. The cursor should be located on the screen with a status line that reads **Doc 1 Pg __ __ Ln __ __ __ Pos __ __ __**.

2. Press **Shift** and **F3** for Switch {*Edit, Switch Document*}.

3. The second screen has a status line that reads **Doc 2 Pg __ __ Ln __ __ Pos __ __**.

Note: One document can be retrieved into document 1 and a second document can be retrieved into document 2, thus making it easy to copy a paragraph(s) from one document to another.

Appendix 2

PULL-DOWN MENUS

WordPerfect 5.1 has a menu bar that can be displayed on the top of the editing screen. The menu bar can be selected by using keys from the keyboard or by using the mouse. The menu bar is displayed by pressing the **Alt** and = keys.

The mouse is used to place the cursor on a menu item and click (press the left mouse button) to select the menu item. If the keyboard keys are used, the **Alt** and = keys are pressed to locate the cursor in the menu bar. The arrow keys are used to move from menu to menu. When a menu item is highlighted, press the **Enter** key to select it.

The menu bar can be selected to always display on the screen. Use the **Shift** and **F1** for set; select **2** for display, select **4** for menu options. Press **8** and **y** for yes to always display the menu bar. Press **F7** to exit and return the cursor to the editing screen.

There are nine pull-down menus, i.e. File, Edit, Search, Layout, Mark, Tools, Font, Graphics, and Help (see Exhibits A2.1 through A2.9).

```
File Edit Search Layout Mark Tools Font Graphics Help        (Press F3 for Help)
┌─────────────────────────┐
│ Retrieve    Shft-F10     │
│ Save        F10          │
│ Text In     Ctrl-F5  ▶   │
│ Text Out    Ctrl-F5  ▶   │
│ Password    Ctrl-F5  ▶   │
│                          │
│ List Files F5            │
│ Summary                  │
│                          │
│ Print       Shft-F7      │
│                          │
│ Setup       Shft-F1 ▶    │
│                          │
│ Go to DOS   Ctrl-F1      │
│ Exit        F7           │
└─────────────────────────┘




                                              Doc 1 Pg 1 Ln 1" Pos 1"
```

EXHIBIT A2.1   File menu


```
File Edit Search Layout Mark Tools Font Graphics Help        (Press F3 for Help)
    ┌─────────────────────────────┐
    │ [Move (Cut)    Ctrl-Del ]    │
    │ [Copy          Ctrl-Ins ]    │
    │  Paste                       │
    │ [Append                  ]   │
    │                              │
    │  Delete        Del           │
    │  Undelete      F1            │
    │                              │
    │  Block         Alt-F4        │
    │  Select                 ▶    │
    │  Comment       Ctrl-F5  ▶    │
    │ [Convert Case  Shft-F3  ]    │
    │ [Protect Block Shft-F8  ]    │
    │                              │
    │  Switch Document Shft-F3     │
    │  Window        Ctrl-F3       │
    │                              │
    │  Reveal Codes  Alt-F3        │
    └─────────────────────────────┘




                                              Doc 1 Pg 1 Ln 1" Pos 1"
```

EXHIBIT A2.2   Edit menu

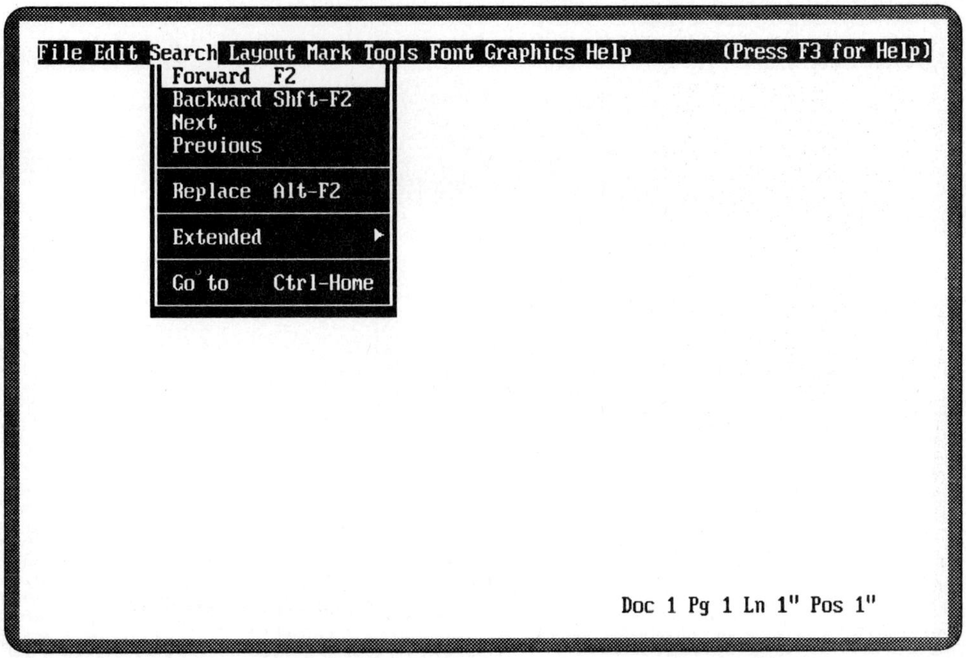

File Edit Search Layout Mark Tools Font Graphics Help   (Press F3 for Help)

Forward   F2
Backward Shft-F2
Next
Previous

Replace   Alt-F2

Extended   ▶

Go to   Ctrl-Home

Doc 1 Pg 1 Ln 1" Pos 1"

EXHIBIT A2.3   Search menu

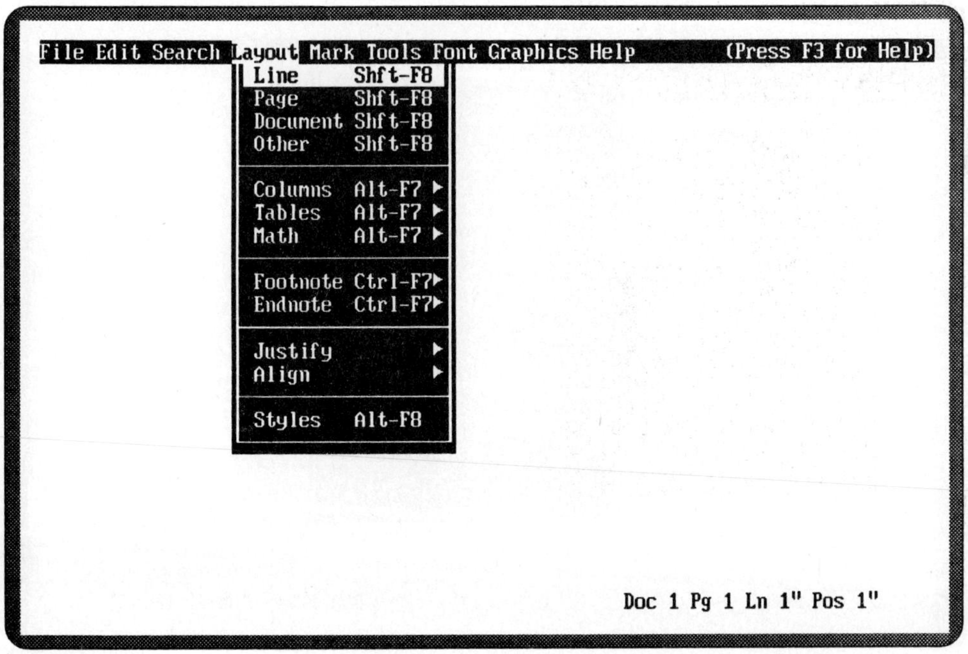

File Edit Search Layout Mark Tools Font Graphics Help   (Press F3 for Help)

Line   Shft-F8
Page   Shft-F8
Document Shft-F8
Other   Shft-F8

Columns   Alt-F7 ▶
Tables   Alt-F7 ▶
Math   Alt-F7 ▶

Footnote Ctrl-F7▶
Endnote   Ctrl-F7▶

Justify   ▶
Align   ▶

Styles   Alt-F8

Doc 1 Pg 1 Ln 1" Pos 1"

EXHIBIT A2.4   Layout menu

```
 File Edit Search Layout Mark Tools Font Graphics Help      (Press F3 for Help)
                       Index          Alt-F5
                      [Table of Contents        ]
                      [List                      ]
                       Cross-Reference Alt-F5▶
                       Table of Authorities   ▶

                       Define          Alt-F5▶

                       Generate

                       Master Documents        ▶
                       Subdocument     Alt-F5

                       Document Compare        ▶




                                              Doc 1 Pg 1 Ln 1" Pos 1"
```

EXHIBIT A2.5 Mark menu

```
 File Edit Search Layout Mark Tools Font Graphics Help      (Press F3 for Help)
                       Spell           Ctrl-F2
                       Thesaurus       Alt-F1

                       Macro                   ▶

                       Date Text       Shft-F5
                       Date Code       Shft-F5
                       Date Format     Shft-F5

                       Outline         Shft-F5▶
                       Paragraph Number Shft-F5
                       Define          Shft-F5

                       Merge Codes     Shft-F9▶
                       Merge           Ctrl-F9

                       Sort            Ctrl-F9

                       Line Draw       Ctrl-F3



                                              Doc 1 Pg 1 Ln 1" Pos 1"
```

EXHIBIT A2.6 Tools menu

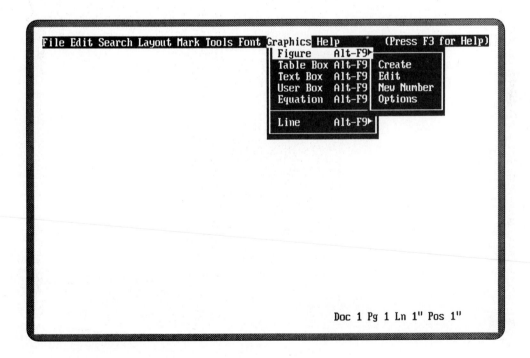

EXHIBIT A2.7 Font menu

```
File Edit Search Layout Mark Tools Font Graphics Help        (Press F3 for Help)
                                     Base Font   Ctrl-F8

                                     Normal      Ctrl-F8
                                     Appearance  Ctrl-F8▶
                                     Superscript
                                     Subscript
                                     Fine
                                     Small
                                     Large
                                     Very Large
                                     Extra Large

                                     Print Color Ctrl-F8

                                     Characters  Ctrl-V




                                                   Doc 1 Pg 1 Ln 1" Pos 1"
```

EXHIBIT A2.7 Font menu

```
File Edit Search Layout Mark Tools Font Graphics Help        (Press F3 for Help)
                                        Figure    Alt-F9▶
                                        Table Box Alt-F9   Create
                                        Text Box  Alt-F9   Edit
                                        User Box  Alt-F9   New Number
                                        Equation  Alt-F9   Options

                                        Line      Alt-F9▶




                                                   Doc 1 Pg 1 Ln 1" Pos 1"
```

EXHIBIT A2.8 Graphics menu

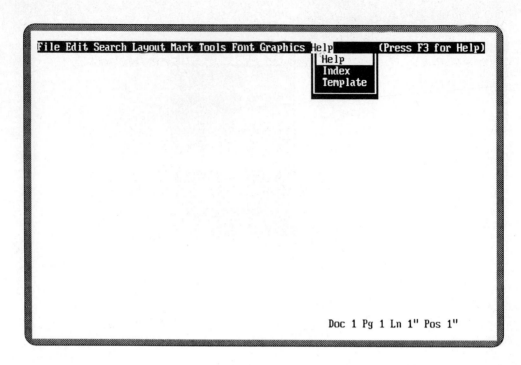

EXHIBIT A2.9 Help menu

ANSWERS TO SELF-CHECK QUESTIONS

Chapter 1
1. T
2. F
3. F
4. F
5. T
6. T
7. T
8. T
9. F
10. F

Chapter 2
1. T
2. F
3. F
4. T
5. T
6. T
7. F
8. F
9. F
10. T

Chapter 3
1. T
2. T
3. T
4. F
5. F
6. T
7. T
8. T
9. F
10. T

Chapter 4
1. F
2. T
3. T
4. T
5. F
6. T
7. T
8. T
9. F
10. T

Chapter 5
1. T
2. F
3. T
4. F
5. T
6. F
7. T
8. T
9. T
10. F

Chapter 6
1. T
2. T
3. F
4. T
5. F
6. T
7. T
8. F
9. T
10. F

Chapter 7
1. T
2. F
3. T
4. F
5. F
6. T
7. F
8. F
9. T
10. T

Chapter 8
1. T
2. F
3. F
4. T
5. T
6. T
7. F
8. F
9. T
10. T

Chapter 9
1. T
2. T
3. T
4. F
5. T
6. T
7. T
8. F
9. F
10. T

Chapter 10
1. T
2. F
3. T
4. T
5. T
6. F
7. F
8. T
9. T
10. T

Chapter 11
1. T
2. T
3. F
4. F
5. T
6. T
7. T
8. T
9. T
10. T

Chapter 12
1. T
2. F
3. T
4. T
5. T
6. F
7. T

8. F
9. T
10. T

Chapter 13
1. T
2. T
3. F
4. T
5. T
6. T
7. F
8. T
9. T
10. T

Chapter 14
1. T
2. F
3. T
4. T
5. T
6. T
7. T
8. F
9. T
10. T

Chapter 15
1. T
2. F
3. T

4. T
5. T
6. T
7. F
8. F
9. T
10. T

Chapter 16
1. T
2. T
3. T
4. F
5. T
6. T
7. F
8. T
9. F
10. T

Chapter 17
1. T
2. T
3. T
4. T
5. T
6. F
7. T
8. F
9. F
10. T

INDEX

SUMMARY OF FUNCTIONS AND INSTRUCTIONS

Functions	Instructions	Page
Access a disk drive	F5	3
Boldface	F6	87
Center horizontally	Shift + F6	4
Center page vertically	Shift + F8, 2, 1	119
Clear screen	F7, n, n	10
Compose	Ctrl + 2	91
Copy text	Alt + F4, Ctrl + F4, 1, 2	70
Date code (for merges)	Shift + F9, 6, highlight {DATE}, Enter	152
Delete a code (hard return)	Alt + F3, Del	21
Delete space	Del	20
Delete tab/return	Alt + F3, Del	21
Delete table column	Alt + F7, place cursor in column, Del, 2, Enter	124
Delete text	Alt + F4, Del, y	21
Delete word	Ctrl + backspace	22
Display the directory	Press F5 twice	25
Double underline	Alt + F4, Ctrl + F8, 2, 3	122
Field (merge) codes	Shift + F9, F, type number, Enter	152
Fonts	Ctrl + F8, 4	238
Footer	Shift + F8, 2, 4, 1, 2	206
Footnote	Ctrl + F7, 1, 1	209
Graphic retrieval	Alt + F9, 1, 1, 1	255
Graphics box repositioned	Alt + F9, 1, 2, Enter, 5 or 6	258
Hard page	Ctrl + Enter	200
Hard return	Enter	4
Hard space	Home, Space bar	90
Header	Shift + F8, 2, 3, 1, 2	203
Horizontal line	Alt + F9, 5, 1, 1	252
Hyphenation	Shift + F1, 3, 7, 3 or 1, F7; Shift + F8, 1, 1, y, F7	75
Indent	F4	76
Insert text	Ins (defaulted on)	22
Justification	Shift + F8, 1, 3	55
Line draw	Ctrl + F3, 2, 1	272
Line spacing	Shift + F8, 1, 6	38
Load the program	B>a:wp	2
	C:>cd wp51, Enter, wp, Enter	2
Lower-/uppercase	Alt + F4, Shift + F3	91
Macro activate/use	Alt + F10	240
Macro define/describe	Ctrl + F10, name macro, describe macro, type contents, Ctrl + F10, F7, n, n	240
Margins (left/right)	Shift + F8, 1, 7	52
Margins (top/bottom)	Shift + F8, 2, 5	54
Merge	Ctrl + F9, 1	154
Move	Alt + F4, Ctrl + F4, 1, 1	68
Move cursor	Arrow keys	4
Move graphic	Alt + F9, 1, 2, type figure number, Enter, 9, 1	257
Newspaper columns	Alt + F7, 1, 3, Enter, 1	135
Outline	Shift + F5, 4, 1	220